I0806623

"A complete history of the team… Not just an exciting read, but an important one."

—Bob Harlan, Packers president and CEO (1989–2008)

"Thomas Nelson expertly weaves the unique story of the Green Bay Packers through the experiences of the people who led, played for, and followed this hallowed franchise from the beginning. *The Green and Gold Standard* is a new and fun take on the history of the people's team."

—Wayne Larrivee, play-by-play announcer,
Packers Radio Network

"Tom Nelson approached this book like a football staff preparing for a championship game. No detail was overlooked, and the result was a testimony to the people who made a small-town team into the envy of professional sports."

—Bill Jartz, Lambeau Field public address announcer;
anchor, WBAY-TV (1998–2025)

"Thomas Nelson absolutely 'Carries the G' with this unique perspective on the history of the Green and Gold. A must-have for any Green Bay Packers fan."

—Aaron Nagler, cofounder of Cheesehead TV

"I saw it firsthand for almost a decade: the way a community, a city, a region, a state, a vast Packer Nation wrap themselves around a football team, unlike anywhere else in professional sports. In a town of barely 100,000 people, the Packers not only survive, but thrive. It is one of the greatest stories in sports."

—Andrew Brandt, Packers vice president (1999–2008)
and author of *Smarter About Sports: My Life Navigating Athletes, Agents, Media, and the Business of the NFL*

"I grew up in Wisconsin. The Packers weren't just a team—they were a civic religion, a shared identity, proof that where you come from still matters. The Packers shouldn't work: smallest market, no billionaire owner, a model the NFL tried to stamp out. And yet—more titles than anyone. That's the point. Nelson makes a clear, compelling case that Green Bay's success isn't a fluke. It's a blueprint: community over ego, shared ownership over concentrated power, roots over flash. As a Wisconsin native—and lifelong fan—this one hit home. It reminded me why the Packers matter, and why they always will."

—Jim VandeHei, cofounder and CEO, Axios;
cofounder and former CEO, Politico

"A true history of the Packers, full of the kinds of trivia and facts that our uncle, Lee Remmel, used to tell wherever he went. Tom faithfully captures the spirit of the team in all its eras and skillfully weaves together connected institutions like the *Press-Gazette* and the history and more about Green Bay and the state of Wisconsin. Lee would be proud."

—Rosemary Bieker, TQ Berg, Ellen Batchelor,
and other nieces and nephews of Lee Remmel, vice president
and team historian (1974–2007) and book dedicatee

"Tom Nelson brings the same energy, curiosity, and deep commitment to community that I've seen firsthand over the years to *The Green and Gold Standard*. From the opening story of a young fan discovering the Packers through a janitor's season tickets, Tom makes clear that this is a book about people as much as football. He captures the essential aspect of the franchise, that its success has always rested on ordinary individuals who believed in it and sustained it together as a community. It is no small accomplishment to take on a project of this scope while serving the public, and Tom writes with both rigor and heart."

—Sachin Shivaram, Green Bay Packers board member

"Tom Nelson captures the history and excitement of the Green Bay Packers franchise."

—Peggy Kostelnik, wife of Ron Kostelnik,
Packers Hall of Fame inductee (DT, 1961–68)

"Tom Nelson, a unique political leader, gets regular folks in small Wisconsin cities and towns. That's why he gets the Packers. *The Green and Gold Standard* should be required reading for all political writers covering Wisconsin."

—Bill Kaplan, columnist,
Wisconsin State Journal (1995–2009)

"I loved this well-written, well-researched book. It's a perfect anthology for any Packers fan, of course. It's also a great resource for anyone curious about how a small city like Green Bay rose to global prominence and became a defining member of the NFL."

—Laura Kostelnik Biskupic, coauthor of *Lambeau Ladies—*
Stories of the Boundary-Breaking Women Behind Lombardi's Packers
and cohost of the *Lambeau Ladies* podcast.

The Green and Gold Standard

A People's History of the Green Bay Packers

THOMAS M. NELSON

TRIUMPH BOOKS

Copyright © 2026 by Thomas M. Nelson

No part of this publication may be reproduced, stored in a retrieval system, or transmitted in any form by any means, electronic, mechanical, photocopying, or otherwise, without the prior written permission of the publisher, Triumph Books LLC, 814 North Franklin Street, Chicago, Illinois 60610.

Library of Congress Cataloging-in-Publication Data available upon request.

This book is available in quantity at special discounts for your group or organization. For further information, contact:

Triumph Books LLC
814 North Franklin Street
Chicago, Illinois 60610
(312) 337-0747
www.triumphbooks.com

Printed in U.S.A.
ISBN: 978-1-63727-837-6
Design by Nord Compo

To Steve "Janssen" Vander Loop and Lee Remmel,
the greatest Packers fans ever

Contents

Foreword

You may be thinking, *Another Packers book?* Hold on. This one is different.

There have been fine pieces on important eras, remarkable players, and memorable seasons and games. But something's been missing, and it's something pretty obvious: a complete history of the team, from 1919 to now. One book in one sitting. That's what makes *The Green and Gold Standard* not just an exciting read but an important one.

As you begin this adventure, I'd like to point out a few things that stuck with me.

One, the author's personal touch. For Tom, the Packers mean more than just a good sports story. They hold a special meaning for Tom and his family. That comes out in the first page when he introduces us to a classic Wisconsin Packers fan, Steve the janitor, and regales the reader with a rendering of his first game, the 1983 Monday night showdown against Washington (thanks to Steve's season tickets). I'm certain every fan can relate to their own special memory, be it a big game, tailgating party, or sharing a bike with a player at minicamp.

Second, it's a complete history. From Curly Lambeau's first snap under center at Hagemeister Park on September 14, 1919, to the brilliant Micah Parsons trade of 2025—and all points in between. It's all here in one book including stories you probably never heard. I learned a thing or two as well.

Third, people. Behind the big games, spectacular finishes, and championship seasons are the people who make it all possible, from the players and coaches on the field to the PR staff in the press box, and folks behind the scenes on game day. I think of the giants at the beginning (Curly Lambeau, George Calhoun, and Andrew Turnbull), pioneers of the formative years (Paul Hornung, Vince Lombardi, Bart Starr), saviors in the comeback era (Ron Wolf, Reggie White, Ted Thompson), and unsung heroes (Jack Vainisi, Jerry Parins, and Lee Remmel), the latter of whom this book is dedicated to in part. Each one stands on the shoulders of someone who came before them. Lambeau–Lombardi; Wolf–Thompson; White–Parsons. People. Without good people you're doomed to failure. Maybe that's why we have the best winning record of any team in the NFL for the last four decades!

Couple of years after I took a job at Marquette in the sports information department, I was at a Packers game at County Stadium with my wife, Madeline, when I told her, "You know, I would really like to become good enough in this field that maybe someday I could become the public relations director of the Packers." Well, I got that wish—and then some. The Packers have been good to me, and I've tried to pay it back by building a winning tradition and, along the way, giving a few other Bob Harlans a chance to live out their dreams. I'm proud of that legacy and story. This book will make sure it'll be told for years to come. I hope you enjoy Tom's book as much as I did. Go Pack Go!

Bob Harlan
Green Bay, Wisconsin
October 2025

After joining the Green Bay Packers in 1971 as assistant general manager, Bob Harlan served as president and CEO from 1989 until his retirement in January 2008. He was the team's chairman emeritus until his death in March 2026 at 89.

Introduction

"Watch out. Or I'll sweep you up, too."

Steve Vander Loop was the janitor at Janssen Elementary School in Combined Locks, Wisconsin, a mill town of some 2,500 in the early 1980s. My dad was a mission pastor trying to start up a congregation at the time, and Vander Loop came in on weekends to open the school for my dad's church services.

In addition to being a tireless worker and a good soul, Vander Loop swung his industrial-length broom with a swiftness and confidence that Paul Hornung, the Hall of Fame halfback/kicker and hero of the famed Green Bay Packers sweep play, would've appreciated. Nothing got in Vander Loop's way—not even a derring-do seven-year-old chancing fate by running back and forth over the broom's bristled arms.

Vander Loop was a lifelong Packers fan and season ticket holder. Which meant that he was at the home games on Sundays while my dad and I faithfully watched the Green and Gold on TV following a full morning of church, coffee hour, and Sunday school. This was a downside to my otherwise halcyon childhood: our hectic Sunday morning schedules meant we couldn't go to Packers games because nearly all of them had noon kickoff times. (I also couldn't have sleepovers on Saturday nights because of the early wake-up calls for church.)

This was an era well before Thursday or Sunday night NFL matchups. It was also when poor-to-mediocre teams—including the Packers of the 1970s and '80s—rarely received a coveted slot on *Monday Night Football.* And if it did land in primetime, Green Bay would be overmatched against a big-name team.

I was in second grade at the time, and I stood out. Not because I was a Lutheran in a sea of Catholics or wore double-nosed eyeglasses, but because I took a keen interest in world politics. On October 23, 1983, the Doomsday Clock ticked one minute closer to midnight when terrorists bombed a Marines barracks in Lebanon. Forty-eight hours later, the United States invaded Granada to eradicate a supposed communist enclave of intrepid Cuban construction workers who were holding US medical students captive. Nuclear war was not out of the question, either: a month earlier, on September 1, the Soviet Union shot down an American commercial airliner near the Korean peninsula. Only a couple of levelheaded Soviet military staff and an American general prevented a nuclear holocaust.[1]

It was against this backdrop that my dad accepted Vander Loop's offer for the three of us to go to a *Monday Night Football* game, the Packers' second of the 1983 season that October, against the Super Bowl–champion Washington Redskins. We sat in the second row in the southeast corner of an end zone. The crowd was boisterous (and drunk), the atmosphere electric, and I was staying up late on a school night. It was a long game—or so it seemed. A steep incline from our section to the playing field made it difficult to follow the relentless action, especially since there would be an astounding 95 points scored, more than 1,000 total offensive yards, five lead changes in the fourth quarter alone, and just two punts.[2]

As the final seconds ticked off the scoreboard, Redskins kicker Mark Moseley lined up behind placeholder and quarterback Joe Theismann, who could barely squat after throwing for nearly 400 yards and two touchdowns in three hours. His Packers counterpart, field general Lynn Dickey, was remarkably efficient that night, keeping his offense on the field for only 20 minutes, which meant the Packers defense and

Theismann's squad had to grind it out for 40 long, torturous minutes. Everyone on the Redskins looked exhausted, including Moseley, the NFL's most accurate kicker the previous season. Packers Nation collectively held their breath in Lambeau Field and around the world as Moseley shanked the kick wide right, the ball landing with a splat just a few sections away from us in the concrete tunnel that led into the bowels of the stadium.[3]

I had just witnessed, as the *Milwaukee Journal* described it, "one of the most exciting victories in the Packers 65-year history." My bragging rights began the next morning and hold to this day.[4]

It was also the night I became a Packers fan.

When my dad later explained to me what a season ticket holder was, my brain exploded. *Every game? How much does that cost?* (Was it more or less than $100, the number that separates "average" from "rich" according to a seven-year-old?) *Steve must really like the Packers. I want to be a janitor when I grow up!*

Steve certainly wasn't rich, but he held the keys to something quite valuable and important. How could a janitor—not a mill owner or a lawyer or doctor—afford to spend money on all these football games? What was it about the sport, and this team in particular, that drove our God-fearing neighbors—and some congregants—to skip church to watch grown men throw around a ball made of a pigskin in freezing temperatures while sitting stuck to metal bleachers? What exactly was so special about these "Green Bay Packers"? I could be forgiven for my ignorance. This was a day and age when people were willing to obliterate the planet many times over just because of disagreements. Neither adults nor the world in general made a lot of sense to this seven-year-old. Could you blame me?

Few cities the size of Green Bay, Wisconsin (population 107,395), can claim worldwide fame and a global fan diaspora for their pro sports team. From Times Square to Tokyo, Prague to Paris, you can spot Packers fans—affectionately known as "cheeseheads"—wearing the team's signature "G" on a hat or hoodie or FAVRE, RODGERS, or LOVE on the back of a jersey. For those unable to make the pilgrimage to Lambeau Field, where the team has sold out every game since 1960, there are more than 1,500 Packers bars, restaurants, and fan clubs dotting the globe.[5]

In the galaxy of sport, there's virtually no end to Cinderella stories. Maybe it's a worst-to-first baseball season that ended in a World Series title. Or a scrappy college basketball program that busted everyone's brackets on the way to the Final Four. The Packers themselves are no strangers to come-from-behind seasons, with improbable championship runs among their 13 titles (including both the pre– and present Super Bowl eras). But what separates them from every other team in the National Football League is that the franchise itself is a Cinderella story.

The Packers are one of the oldest teams in the NFL, and they reside in the league's smallest city, yet they have won more league titles than any other franchise. And after 106 years, they still have the same owner: the fans. There are underdogs, there are Cinderellas, and then there are the Packers.

The Packers are the only professional sports team in the country owned by their fans—not a multi-millionaire or a billionaire. More than 500,000 shareholders hold stock in the franchise, which has operated as a non-profit corporation since 1923.[6] Packers fans from all 50 US states claim ownership bragging rights—even if the stock holds no monetary value. Packers shares are non-transferable and do not pay dividends; all profits are re-invested into the franchise. The team cannot be sold, though if a shareholder dies, their stock can be passed on to a lineal descendant, like any asset. How many football fans without the last name Kraft, Mara, Rooney, or Jones can say they own a piece of a football team?

The Packers organization is the exception to all other sports franchise structures not because it doesn't work, but precisely because it does. It's such a successful model that the league banned it altogether and (reluctantly) grandfathered in Green Bay. How could it not? The NFL is a $20-billion-a-year industry. Why leave money on the table when the line of millionaires and billionaires waiting to buy their own pro sports team is almost as long as the waiting list for Packers season tickets?

NFL fans across the US extol—even revere—the Green Bay Packers because they are the antithesis of a greedy owner who can buy, sell, and, worse yet, move a franchise with impunity. A YouGov survey consistently ranks the Packers as one of the most popular teams in the league. Even the opposing teams' fans like them! So why do legions of other football fans over the decades and across the globe tolerate a system where they have little say and zero control over their treasured pursuit?[7]

There must be a better way. And there is: the Packers way.

The Green Bay Packers are the fulfillment of the American promise, the actualization of the American dream. This is the story of how a tiny city and its football team in America's heartland defied the odds by conquering the world's largest, richest, most powerful sports league.[8] A feat they accomplished by winning 13 championship titles while maintaining their small-town character and values, leaving 31 other privately owned teams in the dust.

The Packers are about people of diverse backgrounds, experiences, faiths, and political views rallying around a single goal and common cause—and winning, repeatedly and improbably. Which is not to say easily. In fact, achieving the team's historic success has been a herculean effort; getting everyone to agree on a radical economic order that rejects the status quo and defies the country's age-old cultural and political traditions built around capitalism is no small feat. How many teams, let alone a single group or organization, can say they've done the same? Especially in northeast Wisconsin, the very bull's-eye of a political battleground state.

Packers Nation knows it is doing something right, and they're proud of it. Packers fans wear their team ownership distinction with pride, be they Democratic or Republican, liberal or conservative, young or old, white or black. Save for the family, few institutions have achieved a level of social stability and strength as the Packers have in Green Bay. The proof is easy enough to find: the city and region consistently rank at the top of quality-of-life indices. In 2023, *U.S. News & World Report* rated Green Bay as the best place to live in the entire country![9]

But for most Packers fans, supporting the team is not about political stability, social cohesion, or economic equity—it's about fun. In Green Bay, football is life. On game day, family, friends, and neighbors gather before TVs in bars, basements, garages, and living rooms, flanked by potluck spreads on card tables, packed coolers, and crowded liquor carts. Cheeseheads come together to cheer on the team, to celebrate victory, or to comfort each other in loss. "Packers don't necessarily have the best fans, they have the most emotionally attached fans," one team public relations officer told me. (Joyfully, baby deliveries tick up nine months after bye weekends in the NFL schedule. Sadly, domestic violence calls go up after losses.)

Non-Packers football fans have always puzzled me. How connected can you possibly be to a pro sports team that you do not own or have a personal stake in, such as a high school or college program? Green Bay and the Packers are the storybook tale of the two hometown sweethearts who fall in love and never leave each other's side—an increasing rarity these days. Expansion teams like the Carolina Panthers or Jacksonville Jaguars seem like fleeting romances by comparison. And relocated teams such as the Indianapolis (Baltimore) Colts, Arizona (Chicago, St. Louis) Cardinals, or Las Vegas (Oakland, Los Angeles, Oakland) Raiders resemble a crummy boyfriend who unceremoniously dumps you at prom in front of your entire class. Truth be told, I kind of feel sorry for those fans; they'll never experience a true sports romance.

Green Bay and the Packers have overcome countless ups and downs, endured endless trials and tribulations, and ultimately flourished in a marriage stretched to its breaking point. This has meant surviving three bankruptcies, overcoming multiple scandals, living hand to mouth on high school fields in city parks in the early years, beating back attempts by the NFL to move the team to a larger city, and boxing out greedy would-be owners (including two former coaches) with a one-of-a-kind stock corporation that eliminates hostile takeover threats.

Along the way, the team has reached dizzying heights and logged remarkable accomplishments: passing the first stadium referendum in the NFL, developing the modern-day scouting system, pioneering the forward pass, leading the incipient player's union, having the Super Bowl trophy named after a former coach, earning three consecutive league MVP awards by a Hall of Fame quarterback, and, above all, winning—Green Bay has claimed more titles than any other team in the league. No other pro football team can objectively match the Green and Gold's rich, fascinating, and compelling history.

The Packers are the great American story. This is the first time it is being told in full.

Chapter 1

Beginnings

On Thanksgiving Day, November 30, 1922, a reported "twelve-hour rain" nearly ended pro football in Green Bay. Or so the *Duluth Herald* reportedly described the backdrop to the matchup between its hometown Kelleys and the host Green Bay Packers. The reporter may have exaggerated a bit—it rained only five hours—but that was more than enough for him to describe the field as it were, a veritable mud puddle. Despite such dramatic exposition, the weather was not the biggest of the Packers' problems that day.[1]

For nearly four full seasons, the team from Green Bay hosted some of the biggest names in the nascent National Football League at Hagemeister Park on the city's east side, posting winning records every year. Cofounder, coach, and offensive virtuoso Earl "Curly" Lambeau called the bucolic Hagemeister home, but it was more outdoor flophouse than stadium. The team didn't own the field and was forced to share it with another football squad and a couple baseball teams, plus the neighborhood kids and families who ranged throughout the park's wide-open green spaces. (Practices were held elsewhere during the week.)

The playing field itself was little more than a small rectangular plat along the park's south side near Walnut Street. That day in 1922, the rain was likely sweeping the sod and sediment from the gridiron into the nearby East River. The spectators in attendance could surely hear the low groan of the river's streaming current over the torrential downpour. On drier days, the playing surface resembled a sandlot field. To unprotected quarterbacks and well-covered ends, it likely felt more like a parking lot. Nevertheless, what Hagemeister lacked in basic amenities it made up for in location. The park was a logical choice for the team's home games because it served as a social and recreational center for the city. Just north of the field was an oval track for horse races—the site of the city's first local football game in 1895. Next to the track was a clubhouse complete with a dance hall and bowling alley. Farther north still was an armory. If Lambeau feared a low turnout for his games—a financial death sentence to his young team—he had built-in audiences nearby to cheer on his players or perhaps better amusement options for the fans who did show. Then again, this was Green Bay—it didn't take much to rally a football crowd.[2]

The city had endured its share of travails over the centuries. Despite being on the small side—it was just the eighth-largest city in the state[3]—Green Bay was the oldest city in Wisconsin and one of the earliest established in the United States interior. It had weathered natural disasters, overcome bloody Euro-Native battles, and survived city-wide fires. A rainstorm was something Green Bay could handle with relative ease. Or could it?

It was ironic that Thanksgiving in 1922 fell on game day; the Packers had little to be grateful for. The team had taken plenty of hits to the pocketbook, but this one was setting up to be a knockout blow. Lambeau's fledgling Packers were living hand to mouth. Curly himself could command an offense like a gridiron maestro, pick top talent among a gaggle of has-beens with uncanny precision, and motivate average Joes to play like superstars. But he couldn't seem to make ends meet for the team. And while fiscal problems were not unusual among other clubs—football was a new sport, and the NFL a new league—the Packers had a few more strikes against them than most.

For starters, they were a small town on the edge of the league's geography, over 100 miles away from their nearest competitor.[4] If they felt alone and disconnected it was because they were; even their train station was a terminus.

They also had nowhere near the economic resources of their big-city competitors. Most of those towns (Chicago and later New York, Detroit, Washington, DC, Philadelphia, and Pittsburgh) were home to other professional sports teams on whom an NFL franchise could lean for expertise, financing, and talent. In fact, several NFL owners had stakes in other pro teams in their cities. So, most of Lambeau's counterparts operated in local economies that dwarfed that of tiny Green Bay. Those other teams played largely in the nation's industrial base, which was pumping on all cylinders and expanding spectacularly in the 1920s. (The city of Akron, Ohio—home to the first champions under the American Professional Football League, precursor to the NFL—tripled in size between 1910 and 1920.[5])

Perhaps most crucially, the Packers had to settle for a poor excuse of a "stadium." Hagemeister Park could accommodate just 3,500 fans, the lowest capacity in the league.[6] It was little more than a patch of grass in a city park. Because ticket sales were the only source of revenue, turnout had to be maximized, or prices set at a premium—an unlikely possibility in a small, blue-collar economy. In other words, no matter how many wins the Packers racked up or how large a fan base they grew, the team could only make so much money playing in Hagemeister Park.

For now, they just had to get through Thanksgiving Day in 1922.

About a mile west of Hagemeister, wind and rain pummeled the downtown *Green Bay Press-Gazette* storefront. Outside the newspaper's Cherry Street office, a battered, rolled-up awning knocked around while Model T's and trucks destined for the city's paper mills, pickle factories, and pre-Prohibition breweries splashed mud against the sidewalk.[7] The cacophony of noises from the weather and its accomplices played like a soundtrack to the morning's proceedings. Team captain Lambeau and fellow cofounder and *Press-Gazette* editor George Whitney Calhoun were at a crossroads.

Lambeau and Calhoun were the twin pillars of the Packers organization—and could not have been more different. Lambeau, with his rich, black, tussled hair and Hollywood looks, was a ladies' man who could pull in adoring amours like a tractor beam. A revered local-boy-done-good, he was an early prodigy of Knute Rockne, the great Notre Dame player and coach. Calhoun seemed a proverbial spouse who ignores their partner's wandering eyes in his tendency to overlook his other half's intrinsic flaws—particularly Lambeau's penchant to stretch the truth. According to Packers historian Cliff Christl, citing former team historian and Packers Hall of Fame member Lee Remmel, "[Calhoun] knew he lied to him repeatedly."[8] In Calhoun's defense, he may have seen some of his former self in Lambeau the athlete. During his glory years, Calhoun was a three-sport jock exceling in baseball, football, and hockey, activities he later gave up when his rheumatoid arthritis acted up, a condition compounded by a career-ending football injury he suffered while playing for the University of Buffalo. A tackle and follow-on cheap shot were so bad it paralyzed Calhoun temporarily and physically impaired him permanently, according to the *Buffalo Evening News*.[9]

Rather, Calhoun was the archetypal gruff newsroom editor, "straight out of central casting," said former *Press-Gazette* reporter Jeff Ash. "He's the guy that you've seen in every movie from the '30s, the '40s."[10] Calhoun's understudy and future Packers board member John Torinus remembered his boss as someone who spoke "in streams of profanity" and "chewed and ate cigars instead of smoking them." Calhoun's softer side came out by way of his Boston terrier, Patsy, who followed him everywhere from the office to his favorite haunts, where the dog would sit atop the barstool next to him.[11]

Despite their glaring personal differences, Calhoun and Curly were a match made in pigskin heaven. Calhoun was the PR man who tirelessly promoted the Packers at every opportunity: in his daily columns, in ample pre- and post-game stories, or by working his state and even national networks of newsmen.[12] Calhoun was like a distant beacon in far-off Green Bay pulsing signals to the rest of the sports universe. He built fan bases locally and name recognition nationally. Lambeau, for his part, was the able athlete with the moxie of a door-to-door salesman and imagination of an entrepreneur willing to say and do whatever was necessary to keep pro football alive in Green Bay.[13]

On Thanksgiving in 1922, however, the dream team of Lambeau and Calhoun were humbled. Resigned to giving in to a wrathful Mother Nature, every peal of thunder reminded them how their dreams were washing away figuratively while their playing field did so literally. Curly had scheduled an exhibition game that day against the Duluth Kelleys, a semi-pro team and not yet a member of the NFL, to shore up November's lackluster ticket sales. But would they be forced to cancel the game?

Heavy showers had also depressed turnout at a game against the Columbus Panhandles earlier that month. A meager performance at the ticket booth didn't cover the customary visiting team fee, and Lambeau had no choice but to pay up. The Panhandles' manager, Joe Carr, doubled as the NFL's president, and the game marked Carr's first trip to Green Bay. Lambeau was resolved to make his first impression a strong one.

Paying Carr his team's fee proved painful, a loss equal to $1,500 in ticket sales. Adding insult to financial injury, the rainfall was officially three one-hundredths of an inch shy of triggering the team's weather insurance policy.[14] Going into the game, the Packers were $3,400 in debt. But there was a silver lining: what Curly suffered financially was balanced in part by Carr's lasting impression of the town. "Seeing is believing, and I take my hat off to Green Bay," he said. "I've heard a lot about Green Bay as a football community and to my estimation it has more than lived up to all the nice things which have been said about it."[15]

That morning, a blanket of heavy, putrid-smelling cigar smoke had hung in the *Press-Gazette* newsroom, accentuating the day's dreariness. A small-town newsroom, with its ink-stained desks, toppled coffee cups, and old yellowed newspapers, offered a less-than-ideal place to contemplate the future of what would become America's preeminent pro football team. Had they been any of the other much larger franchises (Green Bay was by far the smallest NFL city, even in 1922), underwritten by powerful businessmen, the occasion would surely have taken place in a corporate board room or sequestered table at a swanky restaurant.

Not the Packers. Lambeau and Calhoun's environs matched their near-hopeless predicament perfectly; the very nature of the club was improbable and scrappy, an outlier in a league dominated by big city teams. Now, they were at a precipice. As Calhoun recounted decades later, "They were about ready to call the contest and forget about football for good."[16]

Then Andrew Turnbull, the *Press-Gazette's* general manager and Calhoun's boss, walked in and broke up the pity party. The no-nonsense executive with beady, piercing eyes, squinting with the complete confidence of a manager seasoned in impossible deadlines and crises, insisted that if the Packers didn't play, they could kiss pro football in Green Bay goodbye. "Their credibility would be shot," said Tom Pigeon, a longtime Lambeau Field tour guide and docent whose family has been going to Packers games since day one.[17]

Turnbull knew what his NFL counterparts in Milwaukee did not earlier that month. The Milwaukee Badgers had called off two home games due to inclement weather. The first cancellation, on November 5, 1922, stranded about a thousand fans braving the elements in the stands. Green Bay was battling the same storm, but the Packers played on that day. The Badgers were roundly "criticized and ridiculed" for the cancellation, according to one newspaper, which then further taunted, "They must be squeamish chaps who play pro football out Milwaukee way." The club would fold four years later.[18]

Despite the Packers balancing on a dangerous fiscal cliff, Turnbull would have none of the doom and gloom overtaking the room. Green Bay would always be a football town, he declared. Besides, a respectable 1,300 fans were expected to show at the 2 PM kickoff, and they deserved a game. It would be an insult for the Packers to allow pro football to die in Green Bay in such a shameful way. To clinch the deal to play, Turnbull pledged to cover any losses the team might incur and guarantee the Kelleys were paid their travel fee. Crucially, Turnbull also promised Lambeau and Calhoun that he would fashion a long-term solution to shore up the team's finances. It was settled: Curly and the others prepared for the afternoon match.[19]

On the field, Lambeau and favorites Eddie Glick and "Cub" Buck struggled to stay upright as they slopped around the mud-soaked sod, which sank deeper and grew thicker as the afternoon dragged on. Glick wowed the crowd with "snappy dashes down the field," according to the *Press-Gazette* coverage. Buck had an especially good day, kicking the point-after following the only touchdown of the game.[20]

As the afternoon wore on and the players wore down, the wind picked up and the weather became even more unforgiving. With 45 mph gusts pummeling the crowd, the fans had few options for shelter. The armory was closed on Sundays, so waiting out the storm there wasn't an option; only the spectators' Model T's, with their flimsy, collapsable leather roofs, offered cover. Downfield, the trees along the East River were making their last stand as the rushing waters tore apart their roots along the banks.

On the field, Lambeau and his squad fought just as hard as they did on sunny days. (The Packers would adopt a slogan in the game's wake: "The team that plays rain or shine!"[21]) Fittingly, the captain scored the lone touchdown, giving the local boys the lead in the third quarter, one they would not relinquish. Curly's Packers pulled it off, downing Duluth 10–0.[22]

Lambeau and the team had done their part to save football in Green Bay. Now it was time for Turnbull to make good on his word.

Where exactly French explorer Jean Nicolet landed on the shores of Green Bay in 1634 has been lost to history. We do know, however, that he did so with guns literally blazing. The moment of his arrival is memorialized in a mural in the Brown County Courthouse in Green Bay: Nicolet, clad in Chinese garb because he thought he was on the way to the Far East, his arms extended, pistols in hand—known as "thunderbirds" to the Indigenous peoples—firing off a round, scaring the life out of the locals, the Menominee and Ho-Chunk (formerly known as Winnebago).[23]

The story may have been fudged based on new evidence, yet the rendering seemed typical for the times; the French would use whatever means necessary to pound the First Peoples into submission and get their hands on the goods they so desperately sought from the region's bounty of beaver pelts and fox hides.

The eponymous city at the southern tip of Green Bay (the body of water that is an arm of Lake Michigan) would become a focal point of the French fur trade, which attempted to quench the insatiable thirst of Europe's aristocrats and bourgeoisie for animal-hide coats, hats, and other apparel.[24] The trade and follow-up missionary work of French Jesuits would commence shortly after Nicolet's landing. It would endure for nearly two centuries until the beaver population was depleted and other goods and commodities were needed to feed the voracious appetite of European consumers. The Jesuits were also resoundingly successful: by the beginning of the twentieth century, two of every three citizens in Green Bay were Catholic.

The first permanent European settlement in Green Bay was established in 1764 for the French by Charles Michael de Langlade.[25] Then, in 1783, shortly after the Revolutionary War ended, the British took over the region and constructed Fort Edward Augustus, which would serve as a bulwark for the area against unwanted fur trade competitors and visitors. European immigrants began to arrive in masse in the mid-19th century. Belgians and Norwegians made up much of the first wave. Many were skilled craftsmen who built the city's housing, places of worship, and economic base of foundries, smelters, and pulp and paper mills, the latter of which remain an economic mainstay. Shingle-making dominated the local economy in the mid- and late 19th century. In 1866, 25 *billion* one-foot shingles entered or left the port of Green Bay. The trade was pioneered and perfected by the Belgian Walloons, who constituted the largest white-ethnic population along the Bay Settlement in northeast Brown County and neighboring Kewaunee County.[26]

The Walloons hailed from the southern region of Belgium and spoke a French dialect. That they drove the growing economy in northeast Wisconsin was no surprise—their kith, kin, and antecedents were skilled artisans and laborers in the Old World. The Walloons emigrated to the United States because of a push (continent-wide crop failures) and a pull (cheap farmland to the tune of $1.25 an acre in Wisconsin).[27] The legacy of the Walloons is alive and well today. The state boasts a strong workforce in the building trades, ranking seventh in the commercial and industrial construction economy among the fifty US states.[28] In 2023, there were more than 110,000 construction and extraction (i.e., mining) jobs in Wisconsin.[29]

One Walloon in particular left an indelible mark on Green Bay: Curly Lambeau, a third-generation Walloon-American who followed in the footsteps of his forebearers, building not physical structures but a mighty pro football club. Improbable as it may have seemed back in the 1910s, Green Bay's largest building would one day bear his name.

For Curly, life was football and football was life. Unsurprisingly, he made the varsity squad at East High School when he was just a freshman in the autumn of 1913.[30] By the following year, he had earned his reputation as an expert in the passing game, dominating the backfield as both a quarterback and half-back.[31]

By 1915, the *Press-Gazette* crowned Lambeau "one of the best high school athletes in the city."[32] And not just for football; Curly was a track star, as well, competing in the hurdles, discus, and shot put, in which he took honors at local meets.[33] His senior year would mark a football win as enduring as any that would come on the professional gridiron. The occasion was the city's annual East-West game, which pitted crosstown high school rivals at Hagemeister Field.

On November 30, 1916—exactly six years prior to the fateful Thanksgiving matchup with the Duluth Kelleys—the largest crowd ever to attend an East High game witnessed Curly and the Hilltoppers end their school's seven-year losing streak by way of a 7–6 win. Curly naturally scored the lone touchdown for East, writing a new chapter in the East-West rivalry, one that helped solidify the town's deep interest in football.[34]

Passing up college in 1917, Curly stayed home and fed his gridiron appetite by playing the amateur football circuit, taking snaps for the

South Side (Green Bay) Skidoos and Green Bay All-Stars.[35] Back in high school, Lambeau had considered playing for the University of Notre Dame, one of the country's emerging top college football programs, but the cost was too high. He also didn't see eye to eye with Fighting Irish Coach Jesse Harper, who seemed indifferent to the prospect of East High's standout star playing for him. "If you are willing to work, I will be very glad to try to help you," said Harper. "If you are not willing to work and in addition looking for an offer, I assure you, you will have to consider some other institution."[36]

But Curly's luck turned in 1918 when Harper stepped down and assistant coach Knute Rockne took the helm. That September, Rockne announced freshmen would be eligible to play varsity, and Lambeau jumped at the opportunity. Less than two years removed from the East-West game, where his star shone bright above Green Bay and his future seemed boundless, Lambeau found himself in the Notre Dame backfield alongside George Gipp (aka "The Gipper") and a team led by one of the greatest college football coaches of all time.[37]

Lambeau didn't just fill a slot on Coach Rockne's roster. Rather, Curly and the Gipper proved invaluable to Rockne, who soon "discovered that he couldn't get anywhere without Gipp and Lambeau," according to the *Indianapolis Sunday Star*.[38]

But football wasn't Lambeau's only true love at the time.

It is said distance makes the heart grow fonder. So it was for Curly Lambeau in South Bend, Indiana, in the fall of 1918, when he penned love letters to his hometown honey, Marguerite Van Kessel of Green Bay. "I suppose you noticed the wonderful moon Sunday night. I did, and it made me very lonesome," he wrote on October 21, 1918. "I would give a great deal to spend an hour with you on such a night."[39]

Lambeau had tumbled head over heels in love.

Marguerite, long sought after by many of Curly's contemporaries, was quite a catch, too. He seemed to have landed the big one. This despite competition on the home front where, according to friends, she had been dating other men. Competitive to the core, Lambeau never backed down from a challenge on or off the field.

When his old employer, the Indian Packing Company, came calling with a coveted front-office job in early 1919, about $3,000 a year plus stock ($67,000 current dollars)—the job market was flooded with returning doughboys—Curly could see not just hearts, but dollars.[40] If he was looking for a sign to return home, this was it. "If I could land a big job with a large salary I would hop right to it," Curly had written Marguerite earlier in the year.[41]

Love wasn't the only bug he was battling. After the 1918 season, Lambeau had come down with what seemed at first a sore tooth but was soon diagnosed as tonsillitis. It then became infected, which led to a painful surgery; post-op complications made matters worse. Meanwhile, Curly's college expenses and medical bills piled up.

The decision was soon made: Curly would leave Notre Dame and return home permanently. His college football days were over, and a new chapter had begun. Curly arrived home in the spring. And by late summer, Marguerite and Curly had traded nuptials. The two married on August 16, 1919.[42]

Before their big day, however, another milestone in Lambeau's life and Green Bay's history would take place. The city's pro team, the soon-to-be-named "Packers"—a nod to Lambeau's Indian Packing Company boss, who underwrote the team's initial expenses—were established on August 11. A week later, Curly and Marguerite traveled through Wisconsin for their honeymoon, taking in the sights and stopping in towns with semi-pro football teams. Opening Day of the inaugural season was just a couple weeks away, and Curly had to lock in the matchups. In those days, games were announced throughout the offseason on a rolling basis in place of an established schedule. Since the Packers were only a week old, Curly had to field opponents for the coming season in a truncated time frame. In between meals and rest, he also placed phone calls to out-of-state clubs to fill out the fall schedule.[43]

As would define Lambeau's existence and, to an extent, that of Green Bay for decades to come: life was football and football was life.

Chapter 2

Pigskin Pioneers

The morning of September 14, 1919, broke with clear blue skies and pleasant temperatures—one of the last comfortable weekends before the onset of a punishingly cold winter in Green Bay. A record crowd of 1,500 football fans took advantage of the weather to flock to Hagemeister Park for the first game of the Packers inaugural season. The leaves around the park were burnished with autumn colors, creating a majestic backdrop of magentas and yellows for Earl "Curly" Lambeau as he took the first snap under center for the Packers.

Slicing through the soft defensive line of the visiting Menominee North End Athletic Club, Lambeau systematically led his team downfield. On the last down of the drive, he pitched the pigskin to teammate "Dutch" Dwyer, who punched through the Menominee defense on a "straight line plunge" and scored the first of what would be eight touchdowns. The beating on the visitors from Michigan was definitive 53–0. Curly notched a near-perfect passer rating. "Captain Lambeau was the main figure, and his forward passes went true almost every time," wrote George Calhoun of the *Green Bay Press-Gazette*, who was pulling his usual double duty as team official and game-day reporter.[1]

Indeed, the Packers' passing offense made all the difference and soon proved the secret to the team's success. "[For] most of the coaches the running game is your basic offense," said team running back Clarke Hinkle (1932–41), "[but] Lambeau was the first and only coach that made the forward pass his basic offense."[2] (Honors for calling the very first pass play as a coach goes to another Wisconsinite, Eddie Cochems of Sturgeon Bay, who headed up the St. Louis University football squad in 1906.[3])

The decision to feature the forward pass went well beyond ingenuity and imagination. It was far more difficult to employ a passing offense: early footballs were fat, oblong, and prone to deflate. "The rules were stacked somewhat against the pass," explained Packers historian and author Eric Goska. Compared to today's rules, early passing regulations were hugely punitive. For example, a quarterback could only pass from five yards behind the line scrimmage, and if he threw to a receiver in the end zone and it fell incomplete, it was an automatic turnover.[4] Unless you had a true gunslinger at quarterback and a brick wall for an offensive line, or were otherwise supremely confident you could complete a touchdown pass, it was best to stick with the tried-and-true running play. The Packers had and were all of those things.

Passes were also a crowd favorite, so it didn't hurt to feature them as a way to add some color to the games. "Throw a forward!" the fans would beg, and Lambeau would invariably oblige.[5] The Packers employed the novel play for strategic reasons beyond the game: they were struggling to make ends meet and needed to goose the crowd. Calhoun, who took the place of the ticket-taker, would circulate his hat at halftime. If the team put on a good show in the first half, collections would tick up.[6] Lambeau put it bluntly: "I don't think we ever would have gotten into the National Football League without passing."[7]

Lambeau's success in pioneering the forward pass was perhaps even more remarkable because of who was on his 1919 squad, which featured a mixture of former rivals from the Green Bay East and West high schools.[8] The two programs diverged strongly along lines of not just geography or allegiances, but offensive strategies. West embraced the traditional run offense while East, coached by Lambeau from 1919 to 1921, was unmistakably pass oriented. Nevertheless, Lambeau, the renowned East Alum and team captain, was able to rally the entire squad to great effect. Their success was in no small part because of Lambeau's leadership, along with team pride among the players and the city's enduring love for football.[9]

The early 1920s was an ideal time to develop the game. The sport was at a low ebb and had only one direction to go—and it would be a long time before it truly captured the country's interest. Fifteen years hence in 1934, "[m]uch of America continued to view pro football as little more than a lark, a cousin of professional wrestling," said John Eisenberg, author of *The League,* which explains the evolution of professional football from the perspective of, and pioneering work by, five founding families (although Eisenberg inexplicably excludes Lambeau). "[M]any did not even know a professional football league existed."[10]

The Packers' first season was one for the history books, amassing a state-best 10–1 record and outscoring their opponents 565 to 12.[11] Had it not been for a hometown ref who threw the game to the Beloit Fairies at the end of the year, the Packers would've recorded a perfect season, shutting out every opponent they faced in their inaugural season.

During the offseason, the halfback-cum-thespian dazzled theatrical audiences just as he did purveyors of the pigskin. Which made sense. In high school, Lambeau starred in a couple of school plays. He was naturally charismatic and supremely talented—add in his movie-star looks and he was born for the stage, be it an auditorium or the gridiron. Between his first and second pro seasons, Lambeau starred in the city's annual Elks club minstrel show. He sang in a quartet, too, and in summer managed Green Bay's semi-pro baseball team. This, on top of captaining the Packers and coaching his alma mater Green Bay East, which he'd do until 1921.[12]

Despite or perhaps because of Calhoun's pass-the-hat model, the Packers barely broke even in 1919. The following season, the team hired its first business manager, Neil Murphy, whose initial job was to figure out how to get the squad's on-field performance to equal its box office performance and turn a profit. The solution wasn't novel, but the manner in which it was employed was—and fit perfectly with Curly's quick wit and penchant for creativity, qualities shared throughout the Packers team and organization. In his ode to Mark Twain, Murphy played his Tom Sawyer to Green Bay's St. Petersburg, Missouri, and lured the fans to erect a fence around the field's perimeter. "Murphy gets the fans out to build this fence so he can charge them to walk through it on Sundays to watch the games," explained Packers team historian Cliff Christl, a longtime *Green Bay Press-Gazette* and *Milwaukee Journal Sentinel* reporter. "Ingenious!"[13] The move would help turn the team's financial fortunes, bringing the Packers a $6,000 profit for the season along with a 9–1–1 record.[14]

But tossing around a football once a week in the fall wasn't enough to pay the players' bills. They held jobs between game days. Some worked with Curly at the recently rechristened Acme Packing Company in January 1921 or hauled rolls of paper from the area's pulp mills. One player, Martin Zoll, worked the pro wrestling circuit.[15] Side jobs also helped the players work out and improve their overall body conditioning. Meatpacking—pulling beef slabs off tender hooks and tossing them into trucks eight hours a day—could easily double as football practice, particularly for linemen. In this sense, Green Bay's many industries doubled as an effective training ground for an elite football team. The local mills and foundries offered plenty of exercise for their worker-athletes, as did dairy farming, which could be punishing work. Harvesting crops while tending to cow herds year-round made Midwestern boys into men and men into gridiron heroes.

The Pack had some real donnybrooks over the years, but few games matched the tumult and action of the showdown between Green Bay and the visiting Minneapolis Marines on October 23, 1921. "The word was that if the Packers didn't win that game," explained Christl, "they would have been booted out of the league."[16] The team had joined the American Professional Football Association (APFA, a precursor to the NFL) that August.[17] Membership bestowed a seal of approval for serious professional clubs, but it also raised expectations—the Packers had to perform at its highest level.

The Minneapolis club drew first blood with a pair of field goals in the opening quarter. The game then went scoreless until the last six minutes of the fourth quarter. Like the great late-game marches that define the modern NFL, Lambeau and his squad set the standard that their progenies would repeat time and again. Think: Denver Broncos quarterback John Elway's "The Drive" in the 1986 AFC Championship Game, the Pittsburgh Steelers' "Immaculate Reception" 1972 playoff win, or Packers quarterback Brett Favre's 69-, 79-, 80-, and even 99-yard marches in the final minutes of games.[18]

Faced with fourth-and-4, "a plunge over the tackle" put the Packers within 10 yards of the end zone. Green Bay would not disappoint. On the next play, fullback Art Schmaehl punched it in across the goal line. Lambeau kicked the winning point after touchdown to seal the victory: Green Bay 7, Minneapolis 6.

Calhoun declared the matchup "the greatest game of football ever seen on a Green Bay gridiron." Little did he know this would be just the first of many "greatest games ever," with each new wonder one-upping the previous contest. Calhoun spared no detail in his assessment: "Cushions went flying in the air while soaring hats were as thick as Green Bay flies on a July night. Staid gray-haired businessmen jumped around like school kids…"[19]

"That was the start of Packer football on a much more major level than we had played in 1919 and 1920," said Tom Pigeon in the team documentary *Legacy*.[20] The Minneapolis takedown would not be the only memorable game of the 1921 season. The team's reward for pulling off an upset against the much larger and favored Minneapolis squad was a trip to the Windy City to play both the Cardinals and Staleys[21] in back-to-back matchups.

Packers fever had swept the city; no one was immune. If anything, the football bug made the faithful feel stronger and more empowered. November 27, 1921, would go down as another milestone for Green Bay: the first Packers–Staleys matchup, essentially the birth of one of the league's greatest and most enduring rivalries.

Green Bay fans must have sensed something great in the making. Clad in black-and-red-checkered flannel and donning trapper hats, the Green Bay Lumberjack Band caught a Chicago & North Western train to the Windy City and drank throughout the 200-mile journey south. Whiskey and brandy flasks were tossed around like hot potatoes against an anthem of tooting horns, thumping drums, tweeting piccolos, and strumming banjos. When they arrived in downtown Chicago, they made quite an entrance. According to Christl, "They got off the train in the Loop, started playing their instruments, [and] they marched through several hotel lobbies, including the Packers."[22]

As "On, Wisconsin!" belted out of trombones and tubas, it became too much for Chicago in the Roaring '20s. Before long, the 20-piece band was socked with fines and arrested, a kerfuffle that was eventually "smoothed over" according to one witness. Local sportswriters embraced the visiting fanatics. "Never in my experience have I witnessed a better display of spirit," wrote Ed Smith, the dean of Chicago sportswriters. "I was often told that Green Bay was one of the best sporting towns in the northwest. I believe it now and one thing is sure hereafter, whenever a Green Bay team comes to Chicago, they will be given a warm welcome."

What the fans carried in spirit and song, however, the team could not make up in touchdowns and field goals. The Packers fell to the Staleys 20–0.[23] But the small town's outsize presence in the nation's second largest city—home to corporate giants like Sears, Roebuck and Co. and Pullman, site of the World's Fair and America's railroad hub—sent an unmistakable message. Even the little guy, strong in spirit and mighty in resolve, can compete against the big-city teams. For Lambeau, the dynamic was not a source of insecurity but rather a well-spring of motivation, one that would propel the Packers–Bears rivalry through the decades. For those Green Bay players and fans who may have thought twice, watershed matchups with big cities in 1921 fed a virtuous cycle. Every match fought and won boosted confidence and built enough momentum to outlast the other smalltown squads that fell off the map one by one, leaving Green Bay alone in the company of the nation's largest metropolises.

While the on-the-field rivalry played out, a contentious and complicated relationship between Lambeau and Bears owner George S. Halas boiled behind the scenes and would personify their clubs' enmity. In his autobiography, Halas mentioned his Green Bay counterpart just a few times despite the importance of the two teams' rivalry but then stuck it to him when he did: "And if Curly Lambeau had trouble seeing the play from his specially allocated bench in a far corner [at Wrigley Field], so much the better for my Bears," wrote Halas, referring to the deliberate placement of the Packers sideline bench to disadvantage them.[24] "They made it a point never to shake hands after a game," said longtime Packers historian Lee Remmel.[25]

In the lead-up to the games, both men worked themselves up to a froth, but particularly Lambeau. "Before the game, he was wild. During the game, he was wild," said one player. "He'd call for someone to go into the ballgame who was no longer on the football team. He'd lose his cool." Another player recalled, "And how he would rant and rave. During a game nobody would want to talk to him. You'd stay as far away as you could on the bench."[26]

Still, neither were blinded by hatred or contempt of the other to the point where they missed an opportunity to help their franchises. "[Halas] was [a friend] when it benefited his bottom line," according to Christl.[27]

On December 4, 1921, Lambeau had to do what was necessary to beat Wisconsin rival Racine Legion for the state championship. It was only an exhibition game at Milwaukee's Borchert Field, but statewide bragging rights were at stake. So Lambeau did what many clubs were doing at the time and stacked his lineup with top-flight college talent: Notre Dame's Hunk Anderson, Arthur Garvey, and Fred Larson. At the time, high-caliber college players were considered pros—even more so than regulars on NFL rosters.[28]

But Curly's efforts were for naught. The match ended in a 3–3 draw, and Packers fans left disappointed. Then things got worse. When Notre Dame learned of the scheme, the athletic director stripped Anderson, Garvey, and Larson of their letters and banned them from college play. Both Racine, Wisconsin, and South Bend, Indiana, dailies carried the story and two days later, on December 15, a *Chicago Daily Tribune* columnist called for the Packers "to be banished" for fielding college players.[29]

At the end of the month, during a league owner's meeting in Canton, Ohio, Curly's colleagues voted unanimously to drop the Packers from the American Professional Football Association, the precursor to the NFL. Adding insult to injury, the team's franchise holder, J. Emmett Clair of the Acme Packing Company, now a Chicago-based entity, recommended that the team be dissolved.[30]

Lambeau was devastated. Despite the ban against it, playing college talent was rampant. In fact, it was rumored that Racine recruited eight Marquette University players for the state championship game. The argument for doing so was akin to the baseball doping scandals of the 1980s and '90s: How do you win or even remain competitive when everyone else is doing it? Christl downplays the controversy. "Whatever clandestine activities were taking place," he said, "it probably wasn't anything unusual."[31]

Still, nothing sells newspapers quite like controversy. According to longtime *Press-Gazette* reporter Tony Walter, "many Green Bay people" believed Halas ginned up the story by tipping off his hometown paper.[32] Which made sense: Why would a Chicago paper cover an out-of-state match that didn't feature a Chicago team? Let alone a game that readers probably didn't care about? Was there a shortage of newsworthy events, sports or otherwise, from the nation's second-largest city?

Halas and the Bears had a clear incentive to rat out Curly and the Packers. In the event the Packers were removed from the league, the Packers would not be able to draft the Notre Dame all-stars—which Curly aimed to do—and Halas would thus be free to sign the players he so desperately coveted. Indeed, the trifecta would star on the team's squad in the coming season; the Bears would finish second in the league. Even more damning, Halas took credit for Lambeau's ejection from the league and delighted in his competitor's misfortune.[33] He even entered the motion to kick out the Packers at the league meeting, writing in his autobiography, "We revoked the Green Bay franchise and demanded an apology from Curly."[34]

In addition to Christl, who said "there's no evidence" of Halas' involvement in initiating and leading the Packers expulsion from the league, Chris Willis, author of *The Man Who Built the National Football League,* rejected the Halas conspiracy theory. "[It] sounds a little too far-fetched that Halas would cause all the trouble of punishing the small-town franchise just to sign a guard," he wrote.[35]

Consider as well that a permanent ban on the Packers meant the Bears would then lose their top rival and meal ticket. Green Bay football fans traveled well—sometimes more than 1,000 of them would make the trip from the Dairy State—and the game drew Halas' largest crowd of the season. Halas further insisted that Lambeau's squad come to town *at least* twice a year instead of the customary once.[36]

During that same offseason, Halas was amid a fight with his business partner over ownership of the team. His focus was likely on that predicament—there was simply too much at stake for him to engage in any off-field shenanigans regardless of the reward. If the situation blew up in his face, it could sacrifice the financial stability of his team, particularly when his hold on his team was on the line.[37]

For Curly's part, not all was lost. Before the December owners' meeting concluded, Lambeau applied for a new NFL franchise. Carr promised a decision at the June owners' meeting. In the meantime, Lambeau worked the phones, lobbying the league as furiously as he played football and spurring a grassroots movement in Green Bay to bring football back to town.

He also waged an internal battle. Former franchise holder J. Emmett Clair made a play to regain the club himself and then move the Packers to Chicago. (Apparently, two pro teams were not enough to sate Chicago's appetite for football.) Through it all, Curly never lost hope, nor did his partner Calhoun, who wrote, "We have a hunch that the alleged scandal will blow over without any fireworks."[38]

He was right. On June 24, 1922, Carr and team owners granted Green Bay a new franchise. Lambeau was ecstatic, though characteristically unhumbled. "One thing is sure," he said. "The football magnates all over the country take their hats off to Green Bay as a football town."[39] Curly wasn't the only one to rejoice. The owners also sided with Halas, granting him ownership of the newly christened Chicago Bears (fka Chicago Staleys).[40]

It was telling that Curly used the word "magnates" when describing his reprieve. Lambeau knew exactly what he was up against in the NFL—and where he stood in the pecking order of other team owners: at the bottom, because he wasn't one. He was a small-town meatpacker and college dropout. Lambeau knew he probably wouldn't have been invited into the Halas or Carr social circles had he lived in their cities. Everything Curly accomplished came from dogged effort and unflinching resolve. Anything less meant not keeping up with their toughest competitors in the largest cities. Indeed, that spirit went a long way toward explaining why Green Bay, population 31,643 in 1920, was still around at the end of the decade while their NFL counterparts in Buffalo (506,705), Akron (208,435), and Columbus (237,031) would all be gone.[41]

A week after the rain game against the Duluth Kelleys in 1922, *Press-Gazette* general manager Andrew Turnbull and local attorney John Kittell gathered about 150 businessmen at Green Bay's downtown Elks Club. All agreed that their city was and ever shall be a football town, but they couldn't figure out how to avoid the unforced errors and bad luck, including the college player controversy in 1921 and the biblical rainstorms that killed box office sales in 1922.

Another gathering came a couple of days later at the Beaumont Hotel. The square brick behemoth on the corner of Washington and

Main streets claimed half the block. Outside it was the coldest day of the coming winter, the Fox River in front of the hotel chilled the air to sub-zero temps. But inside, the air was electric, the enthusiasm nearly combustible because of Turnbull's unorthodox idea: a stock sale. Instead of a single wealthy owner, the Packers would be owned by the people of Green Bay.

Fourteen businessmen ponied up $1,300 that night, with 33 others pledging to raise funds from family, friends, and neighbors.[42] In the time it would take their great-great grandchildren to create a fantasy football league, Turnbull and Kittell laid the long-term groundwork to save the real thing in Green Bay.

Just as the *Press-Gazette* served as the team's publicity arm in the early days, it played a central role in the Packers' maiden stock sale. The paper printed stock coupons that readers could clip and return for $5 apiece at the main office. "There's no Packers without the *Press-Gazette*," said former reporter Jeff Ash.[43] The sale was a success. While the team racked up a 7–2–1 record for the season, 200 stockholders purchased 1,109 shares for a total of $5,585, more than enough to get the team back up and running.[44]

The sale and the spirit that drove it began a tradition that would define the team and their relationship with the city they called home: "Whatever It Takes to Keep the Packers Alive, Do It."[45]

Unfortunately, the stock sale wasn't a panacea to the team's every problem. That summer, the Packers ran into another hurdle. Hagemeister Park, home for their first three seasons, was plowed under to make way for the new East High School. Curly may have cheated death by surviving the college player scandal, but now he needed a new home. Fortunately, a semi-pro team also called Green Bay home and was building a new field across the East River. They were called the "Lynchmen"—the name was abhorrent even in its time—and they too once played in Hagemeister Park on the same gridiron as the Packers. The two squads would once again share a field, this time at the newly christened Bellevue Park for the 1923 season.[46]

The Packers posted winning seasons for the balance of the decade. The stretch of excellence firmly established Green Bay as a football town, and its team, as one of the NFL's premier clubs. The success came quickly—the Packers outgrew Bellevue Park by the end of the 1923 season. Fortunately, kismet took the form of an open field next to new East High School, an ideal location for a bigger and better stadium.

But new stadiums weren't cheap. City Stadium, the team's future home, would cost $16,000, about three times what the 1923 stock sale raised. Lambeau had gone all in with the previous stock sale, and it had taken him nine months to raise the funds. Now he had to do the same thing, but for three times as much.

In 1924, Green Bay Mayor Wenzel Wiesner spearheaded a fund-raising drive to construct the stadium. Generosity was contagious—one citizen supposedly covered half the cost—while others chipped in what they could afford. The team broke ground in August 1924. Wiesner's contributions, financial and otherwise, proved decisive. "How he did it I don't know, but he scraped up the money somewhere," wrote Calhoun. "If the mayor had turned us down…We might have had to quit."[47]

Between 1922 and 1927, 12 NFL teams closed shop. Meanwhile, the Packers racked up winning season after winning season. Attendance records at City Stadium fell time and again, as bleachers were added, repeatedly increasing capacity.

Packers fever gripped the city. Even the little ones caught the bug. "You don't pay to see the Packers when you're a kid," recalled fan John Lafor. "You went under, over, or through the fence." Like Formica ants pouring into a mound, kids of all ages would scale the sides of the towering fence that encircled City Stadium. Atop the last row, spectators—maybe a parent, neighbor, or older brother—would lean over the backside and pull the kids in over the edge.

For parents more mindful of the rules, the team cordoned off standing room space in the north end zone, known as the "knothole," for the younger fans to watch games unobstructed. The namesake was a nod to the holes in wood fences that kids peered through to watch play. The same spirit is alive today at the Packers annual family night scrimmages before preseasons. Thankfully, tickets are a fraction of the regular season price, so kids no longer have to run under turnstiles or come through the service entry to watch the team play.[48]

If there is one thing that set Lambeau apart from the competition, it was his knack for finding great players. It's how he logged just three losing seasons in his 31 years as Packers head coach. It's why he won twice as many matches as he lost and why only four other NFL coaches in history can claim more victories. His preternatural gift was never more obvious than it was in summer 1929, when he nabbed three future Hall of Famers in five weeks: Cal Hubbard, Johnny "Blood" McNally, and Mike Michalske.

"To this day, it is probably the biggest offseason signing coup in the history of pro football," said Christl. Blood, Hubbard, and Michalske would form the nucleus that transformed the Packers from a winning club into a championship team. The trio's arrival also represented a changing of the guard. Curly would play his final game in the 1929 season, though he would remain at the coaching helm for two more decades.[49]

To say the Packers showcased an embarrassment of riches in talent would be an understatement. While the 1972 Miami Dolphins claim the only undefeated NFL season in the playoff era, the Packers could claim a close second in 1929, when they compiled a near-perfect 12–0–1 record capped by a big win in the Big Apple against the Giants that basically sealed the team's first championship title.[50] (At the time there were no playoffs, and league titles were simply awarded to the squad with the best record.) The crowning victory happened in New York City, the perfect juxtaposition for tiny but mighty Green Bay. It was a storybook ending to the Packers' first full decade in pro football, all of it culminating under the glow of the country's leading newspapers and sportswriters.

"Green Bay Blasts Giants' Title Hopes!" ran the headline in the *New York Times*.[51]

"And what a machine the Packers have become," gushed columnist Frank G. Menke, "one that is the super team of professional football history, and one which the old and the young, the expert and near expert, point to with enthusiastic gesture and declare the greatest football team of all time!"[52]

Millions read Menke's syndicated columns.

A homecoming fit for royalty greeted the team on Sunday December 9, 1929, as they returned to Green Bay. Nearly one-third of the city poured into the train depot to greet the newly crowned NFL champions. "People were packed in an almost immovable mass around the station," wrote one historian. "They were overflowing into the yards and perching on top of roofs, box cars, in every available window—some even climbed telephone poles."

In the wake of the stock market crash of 1929, the fans had collected more than $5,000 for a "Championship Fund." "Green Bay may be the 241st city in size in the United States," declared Mayor John Diener, "but it is the first city in football." Turnbull presented each player with a pocketwatch and $220 inside a leather wallet drawn from the fund. It was a value considerably higher than what the Giants received when they won their championship in 1927. "New York presented each player with a ten-dollar gold piece as evidence of their enormous appreciation," said Packers player Johnny Blood. "That makes you people worth at least twenty-two times as much as the fans in the big city."[53]

Chapter 3

An Unlucky Fall

While the United States was descending deeper into the economic and political morass of the Great Depression, the Green Bay Packers were reaching new heights. Lambeau and his 1929 championship squad had humbled the league's preeminent team before a national audience. The Packers had a bona fide box-office hit; now it was time for the sequel. Would Curly, Calhoun, Turnbull, and the others in the Packers brain trust defy convention and meet, if not exceed, the flash, boom, and bang of the original?

Before the next installment of football glory, adoring Packers fans turned out in droves on Valentine's Day in 1930 at Green Bay's brand-new Fox Theatre to take in a highlight reel of the previous year's Giants game and celebrate the opening of the latest addition to the city's thriving downtown.[1] The Packers players seemed to permeate every facet of life in Green Bay: nurturing the illicit liquor trade in the Prohibition era, participating in community theater, worshiping side by side with fans in church, playing the pro wrestling circuit, and now opening a major cultural center.

On the horizon loomed another Packers championship that was theirs to lose. The team's roster remained relatively intact from the 1929 season; most importantly, the McNally–Hubbard–Michalske nucleus stayed unbroken and continued anchoring the team's explosive offense. Replacing the now-retired Curly Lambeau under center, Joseph "Red"

Dunn proved a perfect complement to the triumvirate. More a competent field general than a flamethrowing gunslinger, Dunn is a lesser-known star in NFL lore who nonetheless shares third place with Terry Bradshaw and Joe Montana for most wins in Super Bowls or NFL championships (four). (Tom Brady holds the top distinction with seven). Nicknamed for his brilliant red hair and equally colorful personality, Dunn piled up more than 4,600 passing yards and 29 touchdown passes, an impressive figure in a pre-statistical era with few league passing offenses. No wonder Lambeau named him his favorite quarterback.[2]

The 1930 season went much like the previous one. For Dunn, it was even better, as he threw 11 of his career 29 touchdowns in 1930 alone. Dunn and the team marched into the final game of the year against the Portsmouth Spartans at an impressive 10–3. The Packers only needed a tie to repeat their championship run of 1929. Each team notched a touchdown in the first half, and both missed their point-after attempt, knotting the score at 6–6. Despite a scoreless second half, the contest was far from a bore. A classic war of attrition kept fans engaged all the way to end. When defensive lineman[3] Bernie Darling ran down the Spartan quarterback and sacked him a yard and a half shy of a first down on the fourth play from scrimmage, he put to bed all the taunts and fights he had suffered throughout his childhood. "This closed the book on Portsmouth," the *Press-Gazette* reported. All thanks to Bernie "Boob" Darling.[4]

Tying Portsmouth 6–6 was an anticlimactic end to the season to be sure, but at 10–3–1, the Pack were four-one-thousandths of a percent better than the Giants, enough to nab their second consecutive title.[5]

Packers fans were euphoric. A front-page *Press-Gazette* headline the day after the big win said it all: "City to Burn Red Fire For 'Grid' Heroes."

"The lid is off tonight as the Green Bay Packers…return to their hometown—the smallest city in the 'pro' league," the hometown paper reported. "Expect thousands to throng station." The football heroes pulled into a festively decorated Chicago & North Western station, with red flares along the train tracks and a convoy of motorcycle police awaiting them.[6]

Opposite the Packers' celebratory newspaper announcement was a national wire story that made Green Bay seem as if it were on a different planet.[7] It had been 14 months since the stock market crash, and economic recovery was still a long way off. President Herbert Hoover's tactics to ameliorate the Depression prior to Franklin D. Roosevelt and his New Deal legislation, namely bank mergers on Wall Street, were falling through, while bankers and politicians couldn't manage to shore up investor insecurity. What seemed like the rest of the country's problem was coming closer to Green Bay's door.

These Green Bay readers were likely better off than most others across the country who were seeing the same story, and not just because an NFL championship was making Wisconsin folks forget their troubles. As the Packers topped the NFL in the early years of the Great Depression, so too did the town persevere within the country-wide economic calamity. The secret to the town's success lay in its strong and diverse economy.

Known as the tissue capital of the world, Green Bay's pulp and paper industry not only held its own but expanded during the Depression. Neighboring Fox River Valley, whose citizens shared Green Bay's love affair with the Packers and trekked up the road to City Stadium on game days, dominated the print paper and packaging sectors. In the Fox River Valley, companies continued to pay healthy dividends to stockholders and ensure steady paychecks for employees. Sears, Roebuck & Co., for example, relied on the mill in Combined Locks to supply newsprint for the department store giant's ubiquitous coffee-table catalogs.[8]

On top of pulp and paper sat an ever-expanding rail economy. Wisconsin's net miles of rail grew at a steady pace of about 10 percent decade over decade between 1910 and 1930, connecting the Northwoods forestry and lumber economies with the rest of the state and parts of the Midwest. By 1937, the Green Bay and Western line was one of the most expansive among the Wisconsin lines.[9]

The state's agriculture sector, however, was pounded hard in the early 1930s and took longer to rebound than urban economies. A severe drought in 1930 only compounded political-economic problems.[10] Making matters worse, the US Congress adopted the so-called "Eau

Claire Rule" (aka the Federal Milk Marketing Order), which pegged milk prices to the distance a farming region sat from the western Wisconsin city. The law spurred milk production elsewhere and capsized rural incomes. The law would remain in effect until 1997.[11]

Farming woes in general affected Green Bay because, like all Wisconsin urban centers, the city was built around agriculture and, in their case, cheese-making and meatpacking. Nevertheless, despite these crucial rural-urban linkages, the city economy—and the hometown football team—hummed right along. While bread lines and soup kitchens animated the Great Depression experience for residents of big cities like George Halas' Chicago, Tim Mara's New York, and Joe Carr's Columbus, Ohio, in Green Bay they were nearly nonexistent.[12]

Prohibition, meanwhile, was essentially a non-factor in Green Bay—all thanks to telephone switchboard operators. Presiding over the communication nerve center for the city, eavesdropping switchboard operators would be the first to hear tips going out to regional FBI offices. Before the G-men got to town, drinking establishments could manage to hide the hooch or drain the evidence.

The city's thriving black market for booze was so expansive it also kept the mafia out of town. Homebrew distilleries were pumping out 1,000 gallons of booze per day. "Green Bay didn't need anybody to provide illegal liquor because it was here," said Brown County Library historian Mary Jane Herber. And as Green Bay's reputation for illicit indulgences grew, so too did the thirsty, visiting away crowds who bolstered attendance at City Stadium. "Football fans when they came to town there were speakeasies all over the place that they could go to and celebrate and drink all weekend," said Packers historian Cliff Christl.[13]

No NFL team had ever won three titles in a row. None. And neither had any team from the NFL's much older brother, Major League Baseball. The New York Yankees came close in 1929 after winning back-to-back titles in '27 and '28, marking a career capstone for arguably sport's greatest athlete, Babe Ruth. To utter "Yankees" and "Packers" in the same sentence would have been absurd at the time; for history to later align the two in comparison would be unthinkable. But today it is accepted wisdom.[14]

On September 20, 1931, in their second game of the season, the Packers hosted the football Brooklyn Dodgers,[15] who were considered stiff competition. A well-rounded defense and an offense that featured "[t]onnage in the forward wall and speed in the backfield" made the Big Apple squad title contenders. A player-by-player, position-by-position analysis by the newspaper painted a grim picture for Lambeau's team. It was yet another example of tiny Green Bay going up against big names and big city teams with deep pockets.

Before the showdown with Brooklyn, George Halas, Curly Lambeau's eternal thorn-in-the-side adversary, had announced he would be in attendance in Green Bay. The following week's Packers game was against the Bears. And while scouting opponents wasn't unusual, scouts announcing themselves in advance certainly was. (Halas even called the team to get comped tickets—they obliged. Papa Bear's chutzpah was unbounded.)

Playing in unseasonal 80-degree temperatures, Green Bay pounded Brooklyn 32–6 as the powerful Packers defense made mincemeat of their opponent's backfield and cut up their otherwise feared "forward wall." The home team scored four touchdowns, including a pick-six in the third quarter to seal the win. The Dodgers offense finally came alive in the fourth quarter, adding a perfunctory touchdown to the scoreboard with minutes remaining. Brooklyn left town with just 10 rushing yards and its tail between its legs. It was a long ride home to Chicago for Halas, too, who had plenty of time to ponder his team's prospects for the following week.[16]

Halas and the Dodgers weren't the only ones who had a bad day.

Life was never easy for Packers fan Willard J. Bent. The 49-year-old maladious Green Bay resident couldn't keep a job, couldn't stay healthy, and couldn't satisfy a disappointed family. How many times had he heard it: *Why can't you be just a little more like your brother?* Gordon Bent, tall, athletic and handsome, was a successful and respected businessman who had given jerseys and equipment in kind to the 1919 Packers squad.[17]

When Willard managed to score a ticket for the big game against Brooklyn, he found himself in a choice seat on the top row of the northwest bleachers. Like any excited fan dialed into the action, Bent leapt to his feet after a big play. When he came back down, he slipped and fell, tumbling eight feet to the hardened earth below. The fall created quite a spectacle. A call for a doctor went out over the public address system and an ambulance was summoned. At nearby St. Mary's Hospital, Bent was diagnosed with serious injuries, including the fracture of his second lumbar vertebrae.[18]

The ordeal didn't tamp down enthusiasm for the upcoming Bears game. "Never has there been so much pregame interest over a Packer-Bear argument," opined the *Press-Gazette*. The Packers didn't seem too concerned about the Bent accident and proceeded to prep the stadium by adding park benches, cordoning off standing room for 1,000 fans, and installing turnstiles.[19] In the much-anticipated game, the only score came from Packers end Lavvie Dilweg after pouncing on a fumble late in the first half. After grinding down the Bears defensive line with handoffs alternating between Dilweg and fullback Herdis McCrary, the former punched it into the end zone with a two-yard run. Packers 7–0. Green Bay was all too willing to rub it in to old man Halas.[20]

The Packers would finish the season 12–2–0 and earn their third championship title in a row—a feat that wouldn't be repeated until future Packers coach Vince Lombardi's squads hit the trifecta in 1965, 1966, and 1967. No NFL team has matched this incredible feat since. Dominant clubs of their time like the Kansas City Chiefs (2020s), Dallas Cowboys (1990s), Pittsburgh Steelers (1970s), or New England Patriots (2000s, 2010s) would come close but always fall short.

Fanfare for this feat would die down in the offseason—and then come to crashing halt on August 10, 1932, when Bent decided to sue the Packers after all. The team was insured and at first appeared nonplussed; but then again, the Packers hadn't had much luck with insurance companies paying previous claims. Perhaps most absurdly, the team once missed a crucial rain insurance payout for its November 5, 1922, game because the rainfall measured three one-hundredths of an inch shy of triggering the policy claim.

And while the Packers had persevered admirably through the depths of the Great Depression, their string of good fortune was about to run out. The team's insurer, Southern Surety Company of New York—one of thousands of businesses that folded amidst the crushing national economic catastrophe—had been liquidated earlier in the year. By summer nothing was left of the company.[21] The Packers were staring down a $20,000 lawsuit and without insurance, they were totally exposed.

Enter Lavvie Dilweg, the Packers' all-pro end.

During the offseason, the star end's teammates umpired and played for semi-pro baseball teams, sold insurance, ranched in Texas, and farmed in Alabama; pro football was still a less than lucrative business, and players had to supplement seasonal incomes. Dilweg earned his keep as a licensed attorney and had saddled up with team lawyer Gerald F. Clifford at the latter's law practice. Dilweg's haunting face and mesmerizing glare betrayed a brilliant analytical mind that enabled him to read secondary defenses to run routes to perfection; it also helped him win tough cases and unravel complex litigation schemes.[22]

On January 14, 1933, the *Press-Gazette* announced that Dilweg would represent the Packers in court against Bent.[23] Nothing less than the fate of pro football in Green Bay rested in Dilweg's reliable hands. A not guilty verdict would free the team of a massive liability payment; a guilty verdict would bankrupt the asset-poor team, leaving Curly and his Packers few options but to close up shop. Perhaps this conundrum proved the exception to the rule: A wealthy owner could have cut a personal check and settle with Bent? Maybe. It would have been more likely that a private owner would have unloaded the team as a liability. Indeed, no fewer than eight franchises had folded, while Green Bay was the only small-town that made it through the Depression.[24]

But the Packers front office was no stranger to escaping tough predicaments. Lambeau had sweet-talked his way back into the league after getting kicked out in 1921, and Andrew Turnbull rallied Green Bay denizens to put the Packers on solid financial ground after the 1922 season. Could Dilweg do in court what his forebearers accomplished in their most existential moments?

Fans may have considered the five-time all-pro as the perfect end on the gridiron, but Dilweg came up short in court despite his many abilities. Then again, Dilweg was set up to fail from the start because the facts of the case fit Wisconsin's newly adopted contributory negligence law to a T. Had Bent tumbled off the bleachers in 1930, he may not have even filed suit in the first place. The new law, which was adopted on June 15, 1931, had relaxed the burden of proof for plaintiffs seeking awards.[25]

On February 28, 1933, the hometown jury found in favor of Bent and awarded him $5,544.10 ($138,148 in today's dollars).[26]

To date, the account of Bent's bleacher accident has been one-sided. Bent revealed little detail at the time, but his grandson Matthew Bent takes exception to the story as it's been told until now. Matthew argues that the lawsuit was not some scheme to make a quick buck. Nor was it the culmination of earlier ailments, as Dilweg argued in court; rather, it was a serious and legitimate accident.

In the end, Lavvie lost his case, Bent got a reprieve from his medical bills, and the Packers were officially bankrupt.

The calamity of Bent's fall notwithstanding, the 1932 season and 1933 postseason was hardly doom and gloom. Quite the opposite. For most of the team, it was all sun, surf, and sand. It was common for NFL teams at the time to "barnstorm" in the offseason, just as their predecessors did in the early years of the NFL. The classic example of early barnstorming was the Chicago Bears tour orchestrated by renowned sports promoter C.C. Pyle, who in 1925 took his client Harold "Red" Grange and the Bears on a whirlwind tour of the country playing pickup games with local teams in St. Louis, Philadelphia, New York, Washington, New Orleans, and Tampa. In total, they played eight games on a tour of the South and the West Coast. Pyle's venture would become a huge deal in the annals of pro sports helping propel the sport to eventually become "America's game." Together, Pyle and Grange earned more than $500,000 in promotions ($9 million today). In the wake of the Bears' barnstorming success, the Packers saw two tempting reasons to play on after the season had concluded: more money and bolstered league image.[27]

On December 10, 1932, following a punishing seven-game road trip on the East Coast, the Packers' first leg of a West Coast barnstorming tour began in Hawaii. As was typical of these exhibition games, opposing teams were composed of local players. Together, the two Hawaii matches attracted 30,000 fans, the second game garnering the biggest crowd for any football game in island history (about 17,000). Throw in the hometown Packers' faithful—games were relayed back home via wireless (island to mainland) and telegraph (California to Wisconsin) with the play-by-play read over a local radio station—and the total audience rivaled those of regular season games.[28]

Projected gate sales were $16,000, yet the two games hauled in $23,358 (more than $500,000 today). The tour's second leg included matchups in San Francisco and Los Angeles that also generated big crowds, with about 43,000 over the two contests. On February 7, 1933, the Packers returned home tanned, refreshed, and relaxed—and with plenty of pocket money to last through the offseason.[29]

The trip's lasting impact, however, came not from the games or the money, but from the expanding fissures between Curly and the guys. Star halfback "Blood" McNally, who organized the trip, didn't want the old man tagging along in the first place, and players were getting fed up with Lambeau's off-the-field antics. "He was kind of crude and a schemer and a womanizer. He was a real cheat. I don't know how the hell he kept his job as long as he did," according to placekicker and back Ward Cuff. "A lot of the players didn't like Lambeau and there was pretty good reason for it. He was taking their money, trying to date their wives. I'll tell you he was bad…just a miserable guy."[30]

Lambeau's "insatiable appetite for power, women, and riches," as Christl put it, was a truly combustible combination that could sink any enterprise.[31] McNally would ultimately relent and make room for the coach while agreeing to his demand of a guaranteed $1,000 for his troubles. As cracks deepened in Lambeau's relationship with the players, his marriage was falling apart. On the voyage to Hawaii, Curly met and fell in love with a former Miss California, Billie John Copeland. "Two of the players got in a fight over her, and Curly stepped in to break up the fight and walked off with the girl," recalled a friend of Lambeau's wife.[32] Curly had found true love. Again.

When Curly returned home to Green Bay in February, he asked Marguerite for a divorce. If he expected a quick resolution, he was mistaken. Marguerite was tough and would fight Curly hard in court to keep her home, her son, and above all her dignity, a remarkable effort given Curly's national recognition.

How did Lambeau keep his cool while his beloved squad teetered on a legal precipice? "The darkest day in Packers history," said team broadcaster Kevin Harlan, referring to August 15, 1933, when the team filed for receivership.[33] And yet Curly came across as unfazed, according to extensive news coverage at the time. Was he simply putting on a public face? Did Lambeau not fully appreciate the implications of the lawsuit? Or was he compartmentalizing and staying focused on what mattered for the team on the field?

On the 15th, team president Leland "Lee" Joannes petitioned Judge Henry Graas to appoint a receiver to get the team out of its legal and financial mess.[34] Receivership law is similar to bankruptcy, but instead of the court ensuring continued operations of a business and affording a smooth transition to long-term sustainability, power is handed over to a single individual, the "receiver," who can do whatever they please. That could mean selling the business to an entity that would strip it of assets and leave it for dead. If bankruptcy is a critical care unit, then receivership is hospice.

The outlook was not entirely bleak, however.

Joannes, whose gentle smile softened Graas' authoritative presence, knew the judge was a Packers stockholder and shared his love for football. Given the apparent conflict of interest, would Graas' extracurricular interest translate into the appointment of a friendly receiver? Someone interested in making the most of a bad situation?

Local accountant Frank Jonet, who had worked with the Packers and knew his way around the team's books, certainly fit the bill. Like Graas, Jonet loved the Packers and, as the newly appointed receiver, resolved to push and pull every lever of power at his disposal to save the team. Square-jawed and tall, the 50-year-old resembled another contemporary, Woodrow Wilson, and was similarly respected, according to Jonet's grandson on the occasion of his grandfather's induction into the Packers Hall of Fame in 2011. "[Jonet] was probably one of the most influential members of the executive committee the team has ever had," said Christl.[35]

The hometown judge agreed with Joannes and his petition, granting the latter's request to "conserve all assets of the corporation, and handle all its money, until such time as a final determination of the case should be made by the Supreme court." (The case was still on appeal at the time.) More important, Joannes got the court to enjoin any creditor from "bringing legal action to collect their claims." The terms of the receivership order gave Jonet the time and space to do his thing while Curly did his.[36]

Receivership was likely not far from the players' minds as the Packers mailed in their first losing season in team history, going a measly 5–7–1 in 1933, which included an unprecedented three losses to the Bears, a particularly painful experience for Curly. In Chicago, the site of two of the matches, Halas would stalk the sidelines opposite Lambeau, rubbing it in after every first down, every touchdown. At one point, "Halas danced up and down the sidelines, accompanied by a chorus of boos by the Packers' faithful," according to author Glenn Swain.[37] Green Bay fans shared their coach's deep contempt for Halas.

The disappointing 1933 campaign was even more a letdown because the team came into the season with high hopes and expectations of a return to glory with "one of the best Packers squads," as the *Press-Gazette* declared on the eve of kickoff Sunday. In the same story, the writer brought hopeful readers back to Earth by reminding them where the team stood in the NFL universe—a supernova in its final stages or a protostar just beginning its life cycle with so much more to come? "The wonder continues to grow throughout the country, that this comparatively little city, can continue year after year to put on the field the greatest or nearly the greatest football team in the world."[38]

And then there were the Bears. Halas lived to beat and belittle the Packers whenever he could—especially when the Packers were down and Chicago, on top.

As Papa Halas claimed his second NFL title at the end of the 1933 season, the Windy City's press corps were having their way with dejected Green Bay fans. "The Packers," crowed the *Chicago Tribune*, "will move to Milwaukee next fall and if the change is not made then it certainly will be made in 1935."[39] The charge wasn't unfounded. Milwaukee had petitioned the league for an expansion team in 1930–31, and the Packers had whetted the city's appetite by playing NFL-requested exhibition games in Milwaukee.[40]

The Packers turned things around slightly in the 1934 season, when they finished third in the Western Division at 7–6. More importantly, they were digging their way out of the deep financial hole of the Bent lawsuit. In December, Joannes and four contemporaries—known as the "Hungry Five" for their eager appetite for financial gain—formulated and executed a plan to bail out the Packers from their worst financial and legal crisis to date. Along with Joannes, the quintet included Andrew Turnbull, prominent physician Dr. W.W. Kelley, team attorney and vice president Gerald Clifford, and Lambeau. Others who played a pivotal role in resolving the crisis included receiver Jonet and executive committee member Charles Mathys.[41]

If one member of the group didn't need money, it was Joannes, who had spotted the squad $6,000 to tide them over until the receivership was resolved. Joannes' intentions from the beginning were pure and sought no financial gain—simply put, it would have been a terrible investment. More importantly, he had taken complete responsibility for the team's financial and legal liabilities by taking title of the franchise with the crushing verdict in the Bent case still unknown.[42]

On December 14, Joannes hosted a "Big Talk" with 25 business and civic leaders including the Hungry Five and members of the team executive committee. Just 12 years after the most recent and first financial crisis, the team seemed right back where it started: deep in debt with limited options. Still, it must have felt different; back in 1922, they were in the aging and cramped *Press-Gazette* storefront office on Cherry Street. Now, they were at the outsized Joannes Bros. wholesale grocery buildings that occupied half of a city block on Washington Street.[43] The December 14 meeting turned out to be as successful as Joannes had been in other business ventures. He secured unanimous support and $10,000 in pledges to set the team on sound financial footing.

The *Press-Gazette* naturally beat the fundraising drum with campaign updates, advertisements, and organizational meeting announcements, just as George Calhoun had done in the early years when he filled the newspaper's pages with columns, pre- and post-game reports, and plenty of pigskin gossip. Successive publishers would do the same as the team continued needing a helping hand navigating future financial challenges.

It worked for Calhoun in 1922, and it worked for the Hungry Five in 1935.

Joannes and the Packers returned to the courthouse on January 29. Two years earlier they were facing certain death in Judge Graas' courtroom; today they were celebrating a joyous occasion in the same room where the team's fate seemed forever sealed. They were a few pen strokes away from approving the terms of incorporation and locking in pro football in Green Bay for generations.[44]

The only question: How long until the next crisis?

Chapter 4

Going Hollywood

Marguerite Lambeau's love for Curly would endure for 15 years, their marriage passing one stress test after another. Between extended scouting trips, end-of-season barnstorming, meetings, and practices, he was all but married to his job. Even their honeymoon doubled as a work trip.

And then there were the women.

"He had a lady in every place that the Green Bay Packers played football," said one daughter-in-law of Lambeau's third wife.[1]

"Women used to call him all the time," recalled a friend of Marguerite's. "She was amazed at how the women would call him and ask to meet for a drink or something. Even people she knew real [sic] well."[2]

Lambeau's three month road trip with the Packers in late 1932 and early 1933, which included a barnstorming tour of the West Coast, would mark the beginning of the end of their marriage. Curly's ongoing affair with the former Miss California Billie John Copeland, whom he met on the team's voyage to Hawaii, filled local and national gossip columns and proved the final straw for Marguerite. This was much different than the errant phone call here and there or a secret paramour in a distant NFL city. Marguerite had tolerated those dalliances—but not this one.

On May 18, 1934, she sued for divorce, citing "cruel and inhuman treatment."[3] Marguerite resolved to do right by herself and her son. "I have given you the best years of my life," she wrote her husband, whose limited calls and letters to her had strained their marriage further. "[I] have [had] faith, respect, and confidence in you for fifteen years and have a faith like that broken…my life was spent trying to please you in every way"[4] Her letter revealed a strong woman who wasn't afraid to stand up to such a famous and powerful man.

On May 22, 1934, Brown County Circuit Court judge Henry Graas—who had sided against Curly and the Packers in the Willard J. Bent lawsuit a year earlier—dispensed with the Lambeaus' marriage and granted Marguerite a divorce. Graas also slapped Lambeau with a $5,000 judgment ($115,000 in current dollars), gave Marguerite title to their home, and awarded her full custody of their son.[5]

Marguerite refused to remain just "Curly's wife" and would live a full life, raising a son as a single parent while supporting herself financially as a national buyer for the Wisconsin-based department store chain H.C. Prange. Marguerite traveled the country extensively to scout and acquire the most recent fashions, and her eye for style ensured Green Bay's families were as presentable as those of well-to-do scions on the East Coast. Where Curly connected Green Bay to the sports world, Marguerite connected it to the fashion world. She worked until age 65, and enjoyed a long and well-deserved retirement, outliving her former husband by 36 years.[6]

Billie John Copeland[7] wasn't the reason Curly Lambeau got the rap of "going Hollywood" or why he earned the sobriquet "The Earl of Hollywood." Rather, she was a byproduct of Curly trying to reinvent himself as the coach fast became a national name in a sport gaining country-wide traction. He helmed one of the oldest teams, one that hailed from the league's smallest town that had thrived when dozens of other small-town clubs dissolved like specks of dirt in a Great Plains dust storm. In the throes of the Great Depression, Americans desperately needed a hero: a Great American like a Davy Crocket, an intrepid soul who conquered new frontiers, or even a Charles Lindbergh, an ambitious, egocentric figure seeking new heights and fame. Lambeau understood the phenomenon well and saw himself at the center. This ol' country boy from Green Bay, Wisconsin, could become more than just that.

Lambeau bought a home in celebrity-rich Malibu and made friends with the who's who of Hollywood. Not surprisingly, Curly's newfound notoriety made him popular among his new California cohorts. "He lived the life of luxury, driving big, fancy cars and always carrying a large wad of bills in his pocket," said Packers team historian Cliff Christl.[8]

Nevertheless, football always came first, as Marguerite knew all too well. Curly devoted time on the West Coast picking over talent in a region with an increasingly rich reservoir of college talent. He'd go beyond the available pool of talent and lure underclassmen into the draft. Nothing got between Lambeau and a promising gridiron star. If a good player was ineligible, he'd convince them to quit school and go pro. If he was told not to scout a practice session, he did so anyway. Once he climbed a wall to watch Bear Bryant's secret practice, ripping his pants on the way down. (It was worth it, he insisted.)[9]

San Francisco was the site of the big East–West Shrine Game, where college's hottest prospects clashed under the bright blue California skies before coaches, scouts, players, owners, and fans. On New Year's Day 1935, futures would be made or dreams shattered.[10] (Indeed, this was the same annual college all-star game where, years later in 1991, future Packers general manager Ron Wolf became convinced that Brett Favre would be "the best player in the draft.")[11] Here, Lambeau had scouted many future Packers stars, notably the great multi-position talent Don Hutson—the target of his earlier Alabama recon mission—who would utterly transform not only the franchise but the sport itself.[12] There's a reason Ron Wolf named the team's state of the art practice complex in Hutson's honor in 1994. He is arguably the greatest of all time to don a Packers uniform.[13]

Before there was Paul Hornung or Brett Favre there was Don Hutson: a rare talent who defined his era. It isn't a stretch to put Hutson in the pantheon of the greats like Michael Jordan, Wayne Gretzky, and Ted

Williams. The records and stats speak for themselves. When he retired from the game in 1945 after just 11 spectacular seasons,[14] he was professional football's leading scorer, leading receiver, and second leading interceptor (with 30 picks as a defensive back). He won two MVPs, earned eight All-Pro selections, and even kicked his team's short-range field goals and extra points.[15] His reputation would only grow as his long-established records remained intact, and the NFL record book has an entire page dedicated to him.[16] As of late, Hutson holds 10 unbroken records, including most seasons leading the league in scoring; most seasons leading in touchdowns; and most seasons leading in receptions. He once scored 29 points in a *single quarter.*[17]

"He held 19 NFL records, some still standing," said Lambeau Field tour guide Tom Pigeon. "I don't see them being broken. He was a man, really, ahead of his time."[18]

In his looks, Hutson could pass for Lambeau's taller, younger brother (or, more generously, actor Paul Newman). His tussled hair with chiseled cheek bones framed a serious face; he was all business. Deep into his playing career, after years of braving punishing Wisconsin winters while defying secondary defenders, Hutson's boyish looks had matured into those of a timeless elder statesman, a countenance he would keep for the rest of his days.

Despite playing his entire career single-platoon (i.e., both offense and defense) as a wide receiver, safety, and kicker, he never missed a game due to injury. (Players would play both sides of the pigskin until 1949.[19]) No matter how hard he got knocked down, Hutson always got up, always returned to the game. He was like the Secretariat of football, a physical specimen unlike any other in his genus.

Hutson's innovative style of play redefined his position as the "first modern receiver" who "changed the way football was played," according to ESPN's *Sports Century.*[20] What we accept as normal today was anything but in the 1930s and '40s. Before Hutson there was no such thing as triple or even double coverage, and opponents soon learned it was the only way they could stop him, if at all. He was one of the first to use planned routes and invented basic plays like the slant. Where other players caught a ball by trapping it against their chests, Hutson used his hands away from his body, which enabled him to snag under- or over-thrown passes.[21]

Hutson's signature play was a football version of the basketball alley-oop. Speeding toward the goalposts, which were then set at the goal line, Hutson would spin himself around a post with one arm, catching the ball in the other for a touchdown. So notorious was this play, an apocryphal story developed that the goalposts were moved to the back of the end zone to stop Hutson.[22] (They were moved for safety purposes in 1974, 29 years after Hutson retired.)

His play was pure art. "Hutson would glide downfield, leaning forward as if to steady himself close to the ground," Lambeau said. "Then, as suddenly as you gulp or blink an eye, he'd feint one way and go the other, reach up like a dancer, gracefully squeeze the ball, and leave the scene of the accident, the accident being the defensive backs who tangled their feet up and fell trying to cover him."[23]

Perhaps unsurprisingly, under quarterback Arnie Herber the Packers became the first team to throw for more than 1,000 yards in 1936, Hutson's second year, an impressive number since the run offense still dominated teams' playbooks.[24] Together, Hutson and the Packers would win three titles.

In addition to the player himself, Hutson was the finest example of Lambeau's personnel genius. First, Curly had the foresight to sign Hutson despite his size—he was on the skinny side for ends. Second, a few years into Hutson's career, when Lambeau saw his gifted receiver getting beat up on the defensive line, he drafted a player specifically to protect him on defense. By slotting Larry Craig (class of 1939) on end, Lambeau could move Hutson to a less physical secondary position, ensuring he didn't get clocked by a mismatched offensive line on every down. Curly's strategic move made all the difference: "Don lasted 11 years, but I don't think he would have survived more than a couple if the Packers had not latched on to Larry Craig," said teammate Cecil Isbell.[25]

As long as Lambeau and the Packers kept winning, the team executive board continued to put up with the controversial coach's greed, bullheadedness, spendthrift habits, double standards (he frowned on players carousing),[26] and salacious gossip. Victims of his neglect and misdeeds—like ex-wives or barkeeps with unpaid tabs—kept their opinions to themselves, while jealous husbands and boyfriends controlled their justified rage.[27] But even as the Earl of Hollywood ruffled feathers in Wisconsin, the wins kept rolling in.

In 1936, Lambeau found himself back in championship contention, the closest that the club had come to winning a title since the three-peat in 1931. The Packers that regular season had enjoyed one of the best records of all time, going 10–1–1.[28] It was also one of the league's most exciting seasons to date, as it was also the Packers' first-ever head-to-head title match.[29] Before 1933, championships were based rather anticlimactically on season records alone.

The NFL Championship Game was held on December 13, 1936, in New York City, marking one of the few times the league used a neutral location for its championship matches. Here Green Bay matched up with the Eastern division champions, the Boston Redskins (today's Washington Commanders). The pregame pomp and circumstance which included a robust number of national interviews presaged modern day Super Bowl media feasts. The game was billed as a clash of "offense against defense," with the Packers dominating with their air attack, thanks to Hutson and deep thrower Arnie Herber at quarterback and the Redskins boasting one of the league's top defenses, besting Green Bay in nearly every defensive statistical category including best overall.[30]

The media framed the game as the big guy–vs.–little guy matchup. Redskins owner George Marshall accommodated his team at the exclusive Westchester Country Club north of the city while Lambeau searched out public parks for practice fields. Marshall boasted that his team would beat the Packers, though the laundry magnate was probably doing all he could to hide the real news brewing: He had all but decided to move the team out of Beantown.[31] Indeed, Marshall would relocate the Redskins to Washington, DC, after the season, becoming one of the first owners to move an NFL team, a trend that would only hasten and ultimately define the unseemly side of sports economics today.

Packers proved Marshall wrong by downing the Redskins 21–6 before a world audience. Hutson and the rest of the Packers offense put on a clinic. Within three minutes after kickoff, Hutson snagged a deep route pass from Herber and punched it into the end zone for a 48-yard touchdown. The big play set the game's pace as the Green Bay offense ran circles around Boston's ineffective defense. Boston's offense fared no better, gaining just 144 total yards, 76 fewer than the Packers. Meanwhile, Green Bay's special teams were at the top of their game, blocking a pair of punts, including one deep in Boston territory to set up a touchdown.[32]

Packers partisans were thrilled with their team's performance: "Packers Again Reign as Champions" screamed the *Press-Gazette*'s banner headline.

America's top sportswriters were effusive. "For just one half it was a thrilling and spectacular affair. Then it was a rout," observed the dean of the nation's sports press corps, Arthur Daley of the *New York Times*.[33]

"The Green Bay Packers, a name synonymous with powerful football for 15 years, rule the professional gridiron for the fourth time" wrote Ken Smith of the *New York Daily Mirror*.[34]

Coming up from Milwaukee on the team train to Green Bay the following afternoon, the Packers made an unscheduled layover in Plymouth, Wisconsin, a small town halfway between the two cities. Packers fever was now a statewide contagion. The Plymouth city band's pounding drums, crashing cymbals, and bellowing tubas beckoned the NFL champs to stop. It seemed like the entire town of 3,880 souls came out to the train depot to greet the team as Hutson, Lambeau, and the rest of the squad basked in the glory. Then it was off to Green Bay for another homecoming and banquet. (So confident in their team's ability to win the game that tickets had been sold out for a week.) Packers legend Lavvie Dilweg was slated to emcee, and players from the 1929 squad would be featured.[35]

The Pack maintained strong showings on the field in 1937 and 1938, going 7–4 and 8–3. More significantly, in the latter season, NFL owners voted unanimously to grant Green Bay another operational exemption (in addition to its non-profit corporate status) and extend the team's "territory" to Milwaukee. The reason: to end all talk of moving the team to Wisconsin's largest city once and for all.[36] The owners were emphatic, including league pillar Tim Mara and rival George Halas.[37]

The owners seemed spellbound by the Packers' small-town, little-guy mystique. The team gave the league a wholly unique character. With about half the country still residing outside metropolitan areas, Green Bay seemed a logical bridge to small market regions that constituted the other half of the nation's populace. The city and its team's very existence epitomized the can-do, defy-all-odds American ethos that birthed the great nation back in 1776.

The *Press-Gazette* described the phenomenon well: "[T]here is an indefinable thing about [the Packers] that could never be transferred. It is a thing of spirit one might compare it without blasphemy to the soul… Great institutions are not constructed in a day or a year. It took 20 years to bring the Packers to their present proud position of power…It was accomplished with the aid of faith and loyalty about [the people of Green Bay]…"[38] Well before Vince Lombardi coined the adage, "God, Family, and the Green Bay Packers," Green Bay's faithful had interweaved their religion and football passion like the double helix of a DNA strand. For Green Bay, Lombardi's trinity was truly three-in-one.

Back on the field, replacing Hutson on defensive end with Larry Craig had proven decisive in the Packers' return to the NFL title game in 1939. After a 9–2 finish for the season, they marched into Milwaukee for a title match against the New York Giants. City Stadium's low capacity meant lower ticket sales and smaller checks for the players. Then as now, it came down to the bottom line, and with higher ticket sales in the offing at a larger venue, the Packers board reluctantly accepted.

New York news reporter Bill Corum did Packers fans a favor by calling on the NFL to remove the Packers from the league because Green Bay would never be a "big league city."[39] The *Press-Gazette* ran the story ahead of the game to good effect amping up the team and fanbase alike. Green Bay may have been one percent the size of New

York City (it still is), but the Big Apple's pigskin club was no match for the outsized Packers, who shut out the Giants 27–0, the largest margin in NFL championship history to that point.[40] The Packers dominated like few other title matches. "The Packers were complete masters, both on the ground and in the air," reported the *Milwaukee Sentinel*. It was truly a team effort on offense. Green Bay opponents—especially perennial rivals like New York—had long since caught on to Hutson and applied double- or triple-coverage. Arnie Herber made the most of the Giants' strategy, utilizing his star receiver as a "decoy" by feinting passes to him while hitting end Milt Gantenbein and halfback Joe Laws. Meanwhile, on offense, New York "hardly got started," according to the *Milwaukee Journal*. Indeed, one Packers defender, Charley Brock, logged two of the Packers' six total interceptions.[41]

Fans were well practiced in welcoming home championship teams with a rousing celebration. This year was no exception. The city outdid the 1936 festivities, doubling the size of the victory banquet. Hutson, who was showered with the longest applause, sounded nonplussed: "[J] ust another of the happy things which happen to one who lives in Green Bay," the drily humorous star told the crowd.[42]

Board member W.W. Kelly was one of many who took to the rostrum to fete the team. He did not hold back his praise for the coach, either. "What we are in football, we owe to Curly Lambeau," he said.

The city had much to celebrate. Truly, Green Bay was in rare company, as an enthusiastic governor declared: "There is no better known city in America than Green Bay."[43] With their fifth championship in eleven seasons, the Packers now held more titles than any other NFL team. Among American pro sports leagues, only the New York Yankees of Major League Baseball owned more championships. It was an accomplishment that was unthinkable not two decades earlier. What more was there to achieve?

Curly Lambeau must have wondered that himself. He may have gotten an answer sooner than expected. In January, a Hollywood studio dangled the possibility of a Packers feature film in front of him. The coach was retained as a technical advisor, and the studio had secured funding for the project. All that remained was a green light. For someone who harbored Hollywood-sized ambition, it was surely a dream come true.

It had to be too good to be true—and so it was. The project eventually fell through—if it even existed in the first place. (Curly, no stranger to fibs and fabrications, likely fed false information to the Green Bay press.)[44]

Despite his filmmaking gambit not panning out, Lambeau hadn't given up on California. He saw the future of pro football on the western horizon. Hollywood was dominating American culture, and the national economy was shifting west. The Hoover Dam and the air conditioner made development in the American southwest possible on a massive scale. Oil strikes in Oklahoma and Texas were reimagining the entire regional economy, generating massive wealth and millions of jobs. New Deal programs were funding hospitals and school construction, expanding housing stock and rebuilding roads and bridges. FDR's arsenal of democracy was revving up, and with it a nascent billion-dollar military-defense industry would feed the free world's war machine while lifting whole economies in every state of the union, finally bringing the Great Depression to an end. Soon the country's dominating economic powerhouses like Pittsburgh, Cleveland, and Indianapolis would be joined by Phoenix, Denver, and Houston.

Collegiate and pro football rosters emptied out during World War II, just as they had for colleges in the 1917 and 1918 seasons.[45] (Indeed, Lambeau got his big break by assuming Notre Dame roster positions from upperclassmen on duty overseas in 1918.) The Packers lost 35 starters, including offensive lineman Howard "Smiley" Johnson, who earned two Silver Stars before being killed in action at Iwo Jima, the lone Packer to perish in World War II.[46] Fortunately for the team, Don Hutson wasn't conscripted for military service and stuck around to lead the club as both a star receiver and assistant coach.[47] The team peaked in 1944 when it finished 8–2 for the season. The Green and Gold again took down the Giants 14–7 for their sixth title.

Amidst the distractions and disruptions of the war, a paltry 1,500 Packer backers met the team at the Chicago & North Western depot upon their return from the championship game in New York.[48]

The fans' minds were elsewhere, and the country was exhausted. Indeed, the *Press-Gazette* gave cursory reference to the championship game and the team's subsequent homecoming. No fewer than five articles on the war ran on the front page alone on December 18, 1944. Anxiety could be felt just by reading the day's headlines: "Americans Battle to Stem Great German Counterattack"; "...Nazis Score Hourly Gains in All-Out Push"; "Japs Return to West Coast."[49]

For the nation, 1945 marked the end of World War II. For the Packers, the Hutson era enjoyed much stability. Since the future Hall of Famer first laced up as a Green Bay Packer, Curly's squad knew only winning, placing first in the western division five times while taking home three NFL titles over his 11 seasons. Hutson had smashed record books to bits and pieces, claiming 19 league records—some of which stand to this day. Recognized league-wide for his on-field exploits, Hutson was named to eight All-Pro teams and awarded league MVP twice.[50] He would be missed. If Curly and the team hadn't recognized it at the moment, they would soon enough.

About 20 miles northeast of Green Bay sat a white elephant atop the Niagara escarpment. In 1946 the team purchased the Rockwood Lodge for practice and team meetings, which overlooked the bay and its namesake city, at Lambeau's insistence. It would be the Earl of Hollywood's home away from home (both Green Bay and Hollywood) as well as a respite from the watchful eye of the Packers executive committee. The bigwigs were getting tired of their coach's antics and untoward behavior, not to mention his increasing unwillingness to pay team bills, and were above all frustrated by recent lackluster performance on the field in the seasons following the 1944 championship.

The lodge matched its surroundings well. The cut-stone-and-timber structure was shaped like a cross for its original owners, the Catholic Norbertine order of De Pere, also known as the Premonstratensians. The front door, which looked like a castle drawbridge in miniature, opened into a lobby that on one end featured a European-style hearth and fireplace and a grand staircase on the other. The location for the monastery made sense. Just miles away sat a Catholic shrine that marked the appearance of the Virgin Mary in the 19th century. Today, the shrine is the only Vatican-recognized Marian apparition in the United States. How appropriate that a team revered like a religion and whose players worshiped as biblical figures seek refuge in a Holy Land of sorts.

Lambeau was now on to his third marriage, having dispensed with his second wife in 1940.[51] Five years later, in the fall of 1945, Lambeau married Grace Garland, a thrice-divorced Hollywood socialite who counted a successful businessman and movie director as ex-husbands. It seemed a good match for Curly.

Lambeau's Rockwood Lodge soon began to weigh heavily on the team's bottom line—it was a money pit. Within two years, its operating expenses matched its sale price. Grace's expensive taste didn't help. She made the lodge her canvas. "I have an interior decorating job on my hands," she pronounced after laying eyes on the veritable man cave. Mrs. Lambeau held grand designs, dressing its ornate features with finest accoutrements and styles.[52] According to former board member John Torinus, the board's finance committee once threatened to resign over a bill from Marshall Field's in Chicago.[53] The team paid it, though reluctantly.

If anyone had a birthright to buy the Packers it was Curly Lambeau—or so he thought. Tension with the board continued unabated. With his newfound wealth from his most recent bride, he was now financially equipped to make a move and purchase the franchise. The team had been without a star since Hutson left and the Packers had lost their sparkle. Between 1946 and 1949, Green Bay posted an overall losing record, 17–29–1. It was not their finest hour.

Following the 1949 season, Lambeau attempted to cobble together $200,000 ($2.7 million today) among four quiet investors who each pledged $50,000 a pop, according to Torinus. Other investors could have been local businessman Victor McCormick and J. Emmett Clair, former co-owner of Acme Packing Company and sponsor of the 1919 squad.[54]

Lambeau had figured out how to take a small-town pickup football team and turn it into a national powerhouse that would claim more championship titles than any other team, and that included the big-boy franchises in New York, Chicago, and Philadelphia. His drafting acumen attracted dozens of talented players to a cold, distant outpost in the American interior, many of whom would become Hall of Famers. Surely, he could find a way to buy his baby, the team he founded, nurtured, and knew better than anyone else?

While he no doubt desired personal gain from the attempted takeover, he prudently crafted his public persona by arguing the move was in the best interest of the club. “It isn’t what I want. I am not demanding a thing,” Lambeau said to a skeptical press corps when he unveiled his plans.

A for-profit model would modernize the franchise, so he argued, and put it on even footing with its competitors, which were not publicly owned. “Professional football is a battle of managements,” he said. “In the old days, the battles for success in the league were fought on the field. Today, there is an added battle—management. Therefore, we must operate efficiently.”

Lambeau likewise carefully crafted the terms of a sale and its constituent bylaws. The current board would remain intact; profit-sharing stock paying dividends, rather than reinvesting profit, would be issued; and ownership would be limited to state residents. The latter clause seemed to have disqualified Lambeau because he had listed California as his official address on his recent marriage certificate.

The pivotal question turned on whether Lambeau would be granted “complete authority over the operations of the corporation.” In other words, would he take on coaching and general manager responsibilities free of board interference?

It was unmistakable that Lambeau was making a play to buy the team. While his proposal seemed innocuous, two pieces stood out. First, Lambeau made clear in his remarks the stock would pay dividends (i.e. “profit-sharing”). Second, by omission, there was no mention of limits on controlling ownership shares. That is, one individual or group of investors could purchase a majority of the team. Who else but Lambeau, the longtime coach and cofounder, would be better positioned to take over the club?[55]

Packers board members knew Lambeau all too well. Something was amiss. It would not end well for the team's founder and, after 30 years, only coach. "What he underestimated was the tenacity of his enemies," according to Packers historian Cliff Christl.[56] The board was unmoved by Lambeau's plea and made quick work of dismissing the idea.

The year ended with a $45,000 loss. The good news: the team had company. The Giants had hemorrhaged $250,000 over the prior two seasons; Detroit lost $218,000. The Los Angeles Dons of the All-America Football Conference (AAFC) took the cake with a staggering $1.425 million shortfall. So much for Hollywood thespians and denizens knowing how to run a football team.[57]

On January 24, 1950, Lambeau's home away from home burned to the ground. Rockwood Lodge caught fire, evidently due to faulty wiring in the attic. Even though the team stood to gain handsomely from the devastation, arson was soon ruled out. Skepticism remains to this day, however, which is understandable given the team had taken out a robust insurance policy and keeping the practice facility/quarters meant enduring an estimated $90,000 shortfall.[58]

While conspiracies evolved over the years, nothing came to pass. No wrongdoing was unearthed; no action taken against the franchise or any other party. Concrete facts made arson unlikely. Chiefly, the fire took place in broad daylight with the caretaker's family, including four young children, inside. The Packers were desperate for money, but not that desperate—there is no evidence to suggest anyone associated with the team contemplated a ruse that involved young children getting hurt. Moreover, faulty wiring was eventually discovered (it was a money pit, after all), and most of the damage was due not to the original fire but the wind/accelerant that destroyed the entire complex. The team's policy paid out a cool $75,000, more than enough to cover the year's shortfall. Once again, the Packers lucked out.[59]

Chapter 5

A New Home

Despite dollar signs billowing above the smoldering wreckage of the Rockwood Lodge in the late afternoon of January 24, 1950, the team's robust fire insurance wasn't enough to bail it out from its most recent financial calamity. Yet, for once, a Packers existential crisis may not have been Curly Lambeau's problem.

The cofounder and coach had dedicated his life to the club—indeed, it was he who signed the founding papers three decades earlier. Longtime guard/back Buckets Goldenberg (1933–45) couldn't distinguish between the man and the institution: "He was the Packers." So intertwined were the fates of the team and its coach that one seemingly could not exist without the other. "I don't see how the Packers can last without him," Goldenberg said.[1] Despite the ongoing frustration and tension between Lambeau and the executive board, the team offered him a two-year contract extension on November 29, 1949, that included head coaching and general manager duties and the title of vice president—everything a coach could want. But was it enough for Curly?[2]

One week after Lambeau's return to Green Bay on January 31, 1950, the once unthinkable happened.[3] Curly Lambeau and the Green Bay Packers parted company. That same day, Lambeau was on the 4 PM train bound for Chicago, where he'd helm the Cardinals for two seasons at a cool $30,000 per year ($400,000 in current dollars).[4] By way of comparison, Lambeau's successor would be paid half that amount, about $12,000 to $15,000 according to contemporary accounts.[5]

As Curly's train chugged out of the Chicago & North Western depot—the same station that welcomed him home after six NFL championships—Lambeau was no doubt upset with the denouement of this six-act play. Yet it couldn't have been enough to wash away the nostalgia for all those late-night arrivals on the Milwaukee special—Johnny Blood running around the train-car tops whooping it up; headlights flashing and car horns blaring amid thousands of delirious fans; fire engine sirens rallying the faithful like klaxons from the trenches of World War I, celebrating war's end.

But now, all of it gone.

No trophies were held high above the victors, no fanfare. Just the 51-year-old Lambeau with his third wife, Grace Garland, suitcases of silk ties, slacks, and pressed Hollywood suits, and memories from a bygone era. His once jet-black tussled hair, perfectly coiffed like a head of broccoli, had thinned out with gray swatches on either side. Flabs of wrinkles squared his face and eyelids drooped ever so slightly. News of the day could have buried the farewell in the *Press-Gazette*'s back pages; President Harry Truman had just announced the development of the hydrogen bomb, an existential threat of another level.[6]

Meanwhile, the Packers board was stuck with the Lambeaus' home makeover bills, an ash-laden practice field up the road, an aging roster, and plummeting fortunes both on and off the field. None of those headaches compared to their most pressing need: a new coach, just the second in franchise history.

Among other historical signposts, the year 1950 marked the midpoint of what *LIFE* magazine publisher Henry Luce termed the "American Century." His February 1941 essay of the same title was a call to service and not just a descriptor of the country's achievements and milestones.

Luce was careful to distinguish between what we now know as "soft" versus "hard" power. American power wasn't just the latter, military might, but rather the former, an "indefinable, unmistakable sign of leadership." That included influential cultural phenomena, everything from Hollywood films to the uniquely American artform of jazz, as well as the country's slang and consumer goods; "trivial ways," Luce admits, but still essential to our nationhood.

The Packers were the American Century writ small. Football is a uniquely American sport; Lambeau was its spirited frontiersman and pioneer, and Green Bay remains the quintessential American city. Indeed, Green Bay would feel the chill of the Cold War.

US Senator Joe McCarthy of neighboring Outagamie County led the Red Scare charge in the early 1950s with his wide and deep accusations of communist infiltrators hiding in the federal government, the press, and high society. His crusade peaked with the so-called Army-McCarthy hearings in 1954 when, after accusing the military of communist sympathies, the US Army's attorney castigated the senator for having "no sense of decency."[7] By targeting a revered and respected institution that had finally just reached a stalemate in the Korean War, McCarthy's popularity would dry up overnight. He plunged into obscurity and suffered an early death due to alcoholism in 1957. At the senator's height of power and influence, official Washington cowered at the power he lorded over the American political psyche.[8] In this sense, Wisconsin—northeast Wisconsin in particular—was at the tip of the spear in the Cold War's domestic front.

The Packers had survived the Great Depression and made it through World War II, nabbing six league titles between 1929 and 1945. The Cold War brought its own challenges politically, economically, and otherwise, and yet the Packers would continue to thrive.[9] In the early 1950s, the Packers continued to field competitive squads, secure sound business practices, and maintain an engaged and inseparable fanbase. When they strayed on any facet, they promptly corrected and returned the club to solid ground.

On Monday, February 6, 1950, less than a week after the Lambeaus left town, team shareholders gathered in the courthouse's assembly room for yet another milestone event. Attendees of this standing-room-only meeting voted unanimously to expand the team's stock holding thirtyfold from 300 to 10,000 shares. Like the previous stock issue in 1935, shares did not pay out dividends, though they came with voting rights. For the team, it was a tried-and-true fundraising mechanism to resolidify the club's financial footing and to keep the community invested in the team.

This third stock issue expanded the team's shareholder reach to include the rest of the state and Upper Michigan, making the franchise a truly "statewide institution"—a movement that would only grow over time. Shares were $25 a pop and limited to 200 per person to avoid any one individual (like, say, a Curly Lambeau figure) from gaining control of the corporation. In addition, the board of directors was expanded from 15 to 25 members.[10]

When the drive commenced on April 11, 1950, it was met with great fanfare. Packer backers would not be disappointed. With the Lumberjack band pounding bass drums, strumming banjos, and tooting trombones at the downtown Columbus Club auditorium, 1,500 of the Green Bay faithful rose to their feet clapping in unison and singing along with fan favorites like "Go! You Packers Go!" Team President Emil Fischer read a telegram from league Commissioner Bert Bell: "[T]he National Football League would not be the National Football League without the Green Bay Packers. May I wish you success on behalf of every club in the league in your stock drive."[11] About a dozen speakers rallied the capacity crowd.

Fischer added to the delirium telling the assembled faithful that the team was no longer in dire straits thanks to the rich insurance payout. Proceeds would go toward "future [team] investments" and not debt. Fischer, a Plymouth, Wisconsin, native who made his money in the cheese industry, had taken the helm in 1947 following Lee Joannes' 17-year tenure. His riches and demeanor gave him entree into the country's high society, where he took in the Churchill Downs as guests of the derby's chairman and hobnobbed with the rich and famous. He served as team president for six years (1947–53).[12]

If the other speakers were to be believed, though, the team and its facilities needed much more than some fixing up and a couple fresh paint jobs. Most were clear-eyed and understood the Packers faced yet another financial reckoning this time a garden variety of problems: unpaid bills, poor on-field performance and heavy liabilities like the ash-laden white elephant and practice facility in Door County. Compounding these financial problems was the loss of the team's longtime leader and founder, Curly Lambeau. In a word, they were rudderless. When the issue was first approved, Lambeau's contract was up and his future uncertain. At best, it was only a matter of time before the 51-year-old coach hung it up. He'd been grinding it out on the field, on the sideline, and in the front office for 31 years.

Perhaps Fischer was putting a good spin on things. He didn't amass his riches by making ill-advised moves and scaring off investors. Talking down team prospects could dampen fan and investor interest. According to Connie Mraz, wife of the team's director of ticket sales, "[I]f we didn't sell the stock, we'd lose the Packers."[13]

Thirty platoons of about ten citizens fanned across the city. Folks young and old swarmed Green Bay's neighborhoods, rattling tin cups and signing up new shareholders. Nothing was left to chance. No block missed, no door un-knocked. This town of millwrights, meatpackers, and cheesemakers were never afraid of work, and the drive in spring of 1950 was no exception. Meanwhile, Packer backers around the state and the Upper Peninsula of Michigan commenced drives, too.

Just the previous fall, the team raised almost $50,000 in 11 days. Fischer and Murphy were resolved to bury that record by setting an ambitious $200,000 ($2.7 million today) to be raised in two weeks. Half of the proceeds would come from Green Bay, the other half from Milwaukee, outstate Wisconsin, and the Upper Peninsula.

The campaign slogan—"Back the Drive with 25!"[14]—was plastered on a highway-sized billboard planted on the courthouse lawn. On the billboard sat a Packers figurine that slid along a scale at the bottom that measured $0 to $200,000, not unlike today's ubiquitous fundraising thermometers. The figurine moved one notch for every $20,000 raised. In two weeks, the self-imposed deadline, he sat on the 40-yard line, having raised $80,250. Two weeks later, on May 11, 1950, the city met their goal: $104,137.50. The rest of Packer Nation was a bust, however. Just 121 shares were sold in neighboring Appleton. The Upper Peninsula bought a paltry 38 shares; Lakeshore Packer backers claimed a few more for a total of 45. Packer mania had been catching on, but fans outside Green Bay weren't willing to put up the funds to sustain the franchise—yet. For now, the money raised would be enough to keep the team going.[15]

"Where in the whole world can anybody sell over $100,000 in stock—without offering profit?" Commissioner Bell rejoiced upon hearing the news. The former Philadelphia Eagles owner always had, and always would have, a special place in his heart for the Packers. "[T]he greatest, biggest little town in the country can compete in major league professional football!" roared the *Press-Gazette* under the headline "Workers Boom Rousing Victory."[16]

Unfortunately, the team could not match the front office's performance on the field. The team would post just one winning season in the 1950s, and even then they missed the postseason. They solved the team's money problems, a pivotal accomplishment and no easy feat, but sound finances meant nothing if the team couldn't win. Stockholders weren't in it for money.

The Old Testament had its minor prophets; Green Bay, its minor coaches. As Micah, Amos, and Haggai offered important contributions to the Hebrew bible, each foundational to the Christian faith, so too did Gene Ronzani, Lisle "Liz" Blackbourn, and Ray "Scooter" McLean provide essential building blocks for the franchise: cautionary tales, teachable lessons, and essential growing pains. The God-fearing people of Green Bay—seat of a Catholic diocese, and a one-time major Jesuit outpost in the American interior—could appreciate this analogy.

Gene Ronzani, the 5'9" stout but muscled former running back for the Chicago Bears and later an assistant college coach, was another branch of the Notre Dame coaching tree, though one that bore no fruit. Despite a 14–31–1 record leading the Packers—the worst among all but one successor—he was an overlooked coach. In his first season, he took down the much-hated Bears in a home barnburner 31–21. A contrite and atypically humble George Halas remarked after the game, "They deserved to win and they did win. You can't take it away from them." Ronzani had at least passed a critical freshman initiation: Beat the Bears.

Occasional on-field glories weren't the only master strokes Ronzani orchestrated. He invented several plays, chief among them the spread formation featuring his signature "trips," an offensive design still commonly seen in today's NFL, in which three receivers line up on one side of the scrimmage line. Ronzani also invented double-flanker play and improved upon Clark Shaughnessy's now ubiquitous T formation. In addition to running a spread formation, which placed receivers farther apart along the line scrimmage, the plays opened up offenses and gave the quarterback plenty of downfield options to throw the ball. Pass plays to quick, lithe receivers making acrobatic catches satiated fans' thirst for exciting action.[17] Lavvie Dilweg and early Packers ends had set a high bar. Ronzani would also make one of the most consequential hires in Packers history.[18]

Before there were wunderkind general managers masterminding championship glory, like the Boston Red Sox's Theo Epstein or the Yankees' Brian Cashman, there was Packers scout and personnel man Jack Vainisi. "The man who did it all," as University of North Carolina general manager Michael Lombardi (no relation to Vince) said in a promotional video for Vainisi's candidacy for the Pro Football Hall of Fame.[19]

Ronzani hired Vainisi in the coach's first season in September 1950. The two had connections through the Notre Dame coaching tree—Vainisi played tackle under Hugh Devore, who went on to be a Packers assistant coach—and via the Bears organization. The Chicago native grew up next to the Halases and remained close family friends throughout life.[20] Though he made the Notre Dame squad his freshman year, Vainisi found himself in the Pacific Theater of World War II under General MacArthur after being drafted during his sophomore year. It was there that he contracted rheumatic fever, and complications from the illness would follow him the rest of his life.[21]

Vainisi was a "one-man personnel department and did the heavy lifting for some of the best drafts in Packers history," according to Packers historian Cliff Christl.[22] Indeed, Vainisi helped draft seven future Pro Football Hall of Famers, plus many more distinguished players, many of whom would play in the very first Super Bowl and whose names ring the mezzanine of Lambeau Field: Paul Hornung, Bart Starr, Forrest Gregg, Jim Taylor, Ray Nitschke.[23] Vainisi is credited with lobbying for and championing the hiring of Vince Lombardi, a little-known offensive coach for the New York Giants who had zero pro or college head coaching experience.

During the 1953 season the Packers had had enough with Ronzani's losing. At 2–7–1, with two games remaining in the season, Ronzani resigned. Assistant coaches Hugh Devore and Scooter McLean held the team together for the rest of the season.[24]

Southwest Wisconsin native Lisle "Liz" Blackbourn was selected as the Packers' third head coach on January 7, 1954. For four seasons he had led Marquette University, a nearby powerhouse that doubled as a Packers farm team (22 current and former Packers had played at Marquette).[25] It was a curious choice, given the search committee had pledged to cast a wide net and Blackbourn was just down the road in Milwaukee. He also had a mediocre college record of 18–17–4.[26]

At this time, most NFL coaches were pulled from the college ranks, including those leading successful teams in Cleveland and San Francisco. Perhaps they saw the next Paul Brown in Blackbourn? The Cleveland Browns legend had only coached high school and college before leaping to the pros and building a dynasty for a team that would bear his name.[27]

Blackbourn stands out because he handed his successors a roster that would anchor three NFL titles. According to longtime Packers historian Lee Remmel, Blackbourn "engineer[ed] the most spectacular trade" in its history in 1957: Don McIlhenny, Ollie Spencer, Jim Salsbury, and Lombardi-era standout Norm Masters for just two players, albeit one of them a starting quarterback, Tobin Rote. "We gave up a great quarterback to get what we had to have," Blackbourn shrugged. While Rote went off to Detroit and won the Lions an NFL title—a feat yet to be repeated by the club 69 years later—second-year Packers backup Bart Starr took the reins.[28] Starr would match his predecessor's meteoric achievement in short order.

Even as the NFL was entering its 37th season it remained a nascent league. Teams weren't making a lot of money, football continued to struggle against more popular sports like baseball, and 39 states were without a club. The Packers' stadium referendum of 1956 would quickly become about more than just the Packers and Green Bay. It would portend the survival of the NFL. If the Packers' stadium effort failed, it would undermine league momentum to expand and grow. This wasn't only about keeping the Packers in Green Bay but keeping the "National" in the National Football League.[29]

Unlike every other team in the league, Green Bay did not have a pro stadium because it was the only NFL city without a major league baseball team. All others played on their hometown baseball team's field. So, the five-time champs—who had settled for a glorified high school field—were always disadvantaged with low box office sales cutting into both the Packers' and the away team's take-home share. In 1955, the Packers made $261,000 on the road; visiting teams made only $161,000, which would have been even lower had the Packers not twice played at Milwaukee County Stadium.[30] This was the league's central and perennial argument for moving the team to the bigger city to the south.

Capacity at opponents' stadiums dwarfed tiny City Stadium. The Bears' Wrigley Field seated 47,000, the Giants' Polo Grounds allowed 55,000, and the Browns' Cleveland Municipal Field had a whopping 78,000. It wasn't until 1953 that the era of publicly financed stadiums truly got underway.[31] This was the year Milwaukee County Stadium opened for the Braves, the National League baseball team newly relocated from Boston. County Stadium was the first-ever wholly publicly financed stadium—every dollar and bond note came from the public treasury.

It was constructed ahead of any commitment from a team to move to Milwaukee. City elders were resolved to bring pro baseball to Brew City, and a shiny new stadium was certainly an incentive for pro sports owners. It had been about 25 years since the NFL's Badgers folded up in 1926, and on-and-off Packers games surely whetted the appetite of pro sports fans.

Football fans demanded stadiums, and a franchise's long-term viability was dependent on these concrete cathedrals. Before big-time television broadcasting contracts, tickets were the only source of revenue for clubs. With varying seating capacities and wide-ranging ticket prices came grave financial disparities among clubs—Green Bay was Exhibit A.

This was not a new problem.

Low ticket sales were the reason the team found itself at death's door in November 1922. Curly couldn't lure a team to Green Bay in this pivotal rain-soaked month. Had the patsy Duluth Kelleys not made the Thanksgiving exhibition game, then team president Andrew Turnbull wouldn't have cut his deal—play the game for a commitment from Turnbull to keep football in Green Bay—and the Packer legacy would've been reduced to a single bookshelf at the Brown County historical library.[32]

"They needed a new stadium, or they would be left behind," said Christl in *Legacy*.[33] In August of 1955, Packers executive board member Fred Leicht announced the club's intention to build one. An original stockholder from the 1923 sale, the stadium committee chair teamed up with the Green Bay school board to build a "new steel stadium" on the current stadium footprint next to East High School. Mayor Otto Rachals, whose city council would need to approve placing a referendum on the ballot, signaled support by announcing forthcoming architectural plans and cost estimates.[34] The *Press-Gazette* understood the time was fraught with uncertainty; the paper characterized the moment as simply "A Test for the Packers."

"Eventually the voters will be required to write on the ballot the final decision of whether or not Green Bay and the Packers are permanently a part of the national professional football scene. That decision will be final," the paper editorialized on August 25, 1955.

By January 1956, little progress had been made on a new stadium. At an impasse, the mayor created an ad hoc citizens committee charged with making a recommendation to the council on the "type and location of a new Packer stadium." The committee developed and considered four different proposals with different combinations of permanent and movable seats and locations, at either the current site or Perkins Park on the west side. Estimated costs ranged from $500,000 to $1,172,000.[35]

On February 2, the citizens committee recommended building anew at a separate location that included 20,000 permanent seats at a price of $960,000 to be paid 50-50 between the city and team. Twelve thousand auxiliary movable seats would be used for Packers games and taken down for the smaller high school matchups. The committee, however, was split on where to build it.[36]

On March 6, 1956, the Green Bay city council voted unanimously to hold a tax referendum on the following month on April 3.[37] It was a short turnaround. Spring election ballots were usually set by the first Tuesday of January when candidacy papers are due, with absentee ballots going out three weeks before Election Day. (Wisconsinites have been voting absentee since Abraham Lincoln sought re-election in 1864.)[38] Perhaps the decision was made late for strategic reasons; a successful referendum was not considered a lock.

Former All-Pro Packer Charley Brock, a center from 1939 to 1947, "doubted whether bonds for a new stadium would gain referendum approval." Brock singled out weak ticket sales and noted that "the stadium is filled to capacity only once a year."[39]

"One wouldn't believe that you'd have to do it, but it did take a referendum because the people thought it would raise their taxes," added board member Jerry Atkinson.[40] An analysis by the *Press-Gazette* soon after the campaign got underway showed the average property tax bill bumping up just $1.35 per year ($16.19 in current dollars).[41]

Unlike Brock and others, Coach Blackbourn was bullish. Having delivered countless halftime pep talks, he rallied the Green Bay faithful: "It looks like a tough battle… This is no half-way program; it's either for or against the squad."[42] A committee of 30 eager backers organized the "Vote Yes" campaign. Thousands of pamphlets were designed, printed, and distributed, enough for each voter. A little shoe leather and door knocking did the rest. The literature and face-to-face campaigning ginned up all range of conversation: "[T]he big topics are the stadium, money, taxes, television, crowds, parking and 101 other subjects all relating to construction of a new stadium," reported the *Press-Gazette* on March 27. Talk was indicative of the public debate to come, should the measure pass.[43] That people were thinking ahead was a good sign. On election eve, Packer backers packed the Columbus Club—once again. More than 1,000 fans joined the delirium.[44]

It all paid off.

Election Day was like no other. On April 3, a trio of tornados ripped through central and northeast Wisconsin, leveling the town of Berlin just outside of Oshkosh, injuring 50 and killing 7.[45] It marked one of the deadliest tornado touchdowns in state history.[46] A tornado warning went out for central Wisconsin from the US Weather Station at Austin Straubel Field in Green Bay, but Green Bay stadium voters were spared the brunt of the storm. Weather alerts extended beyond Wisconsin and into lower Michigan where the storm system made landfall near Traverse City later that evening, going strong for three hours before drying up outside Grand Rapids at 8:45 pm, just minutes before polls closed back in Green Bay. It was that powerful.

Punishingly cold December Sundays couldn't keep fans away from games; neither could unsettled spring weather deter Green Bay voters from making their voices heard in support of their team. Fans passed the million-dollar referendum on a near two-to-one margin.

Crucial to the measure's passage—in addition to the truncated campaign and no organized opposition—was a question that excluded sticky specifics: "Shall the City of Green Bay issue its General Obligation Bonds in an amount not to exceed $960,000 for the purpose of providing a stadium for said City?"[47]

Where to build it would be decided after the election.

There was no love lost between east- and west-siders. The roots of the feud ran deeper than the East-West high school football rivalries and the river that divided the two city halves. Until 1895, the west side was an incorporated community called Fort Howard, named after the local military installment established in 1816.[48] Remnants of yesteryear persist to the present day. A ban on saloons west of Broadway Street—which runs parallel to the river—from the 1895 charter remains in effect.[49]

Two main streets, two high school teams, and two separate histories. A lot of rivalry, a lot of bad blood.

Then again, the river wasn't all that deep, nor that wide; city fathers had figured out how to connect the two sides long ago. Likewise, the east-west rift could be bridged. Grievances healed and differences resolved, all for the sake of professional football in Green Bay. Indeed, in several respects, the river united the city. A shared economy of paper mills, coal piles, and shipping concerns dotted the river's banks on both sides. Packers stock drives extended to every neighborhood. Championship celebrations began at train stations on both sides of the Fox River and continued to the Northland Hotel downtown.

Curly Lambeau, who left football just four years after signing up with the Chicago Cardinals in 1950, returned home to rally support for his old team. The Packers couldn't have a better spokesperson. "You know I'm an east sider, strictly. But I firmly believe that a stadium on the west side is the best answer to bigger attendance," Lambeau told the *Press-Gazette*. "That super highway is a temptation for fans in Milwaukee, south of there and in the [Fox River] [V]alley to come. Same for fans coming from the north and west."[50]

He was right—and prescient. Today that "superhighway" is Interstate 41. At its Lambeau Field exit it bulges 10 lanes wide and carries so much traffic, it is encased with imposing sound barriers. One would be forgiven for confusing it with Cleveland, Minneapolis, or Buffalo. As for attendance, every seat would be sold out after 1960. As of 2024, there are 150,000 people on the season ticket waiting list.[51]

Two weeks from Election Day, Commissioner Bert Bell put the screws to the Packers, informing team officials and the city that Buffalo mayor Steve Pankow had been ringing Bell's phone off the hook to land the Packers or another franchise. "Buffalo is the more logical place," Bell teased Green Bay, according to a conversation with team general manager Verne Lewellen (1954-58). It sounded like Pankow had written the script for future mayors coveting their own NFL franchise by shelling out millions away from crucial public services and into billion-dollar temples of sporting glory. Not only was Pankow willing to build a new stadium, but he pledged to lease it back to the team for less than a home mortgage, about $1,000 per year.[52]

Pankow's audacity did not form out of thin air. He was building off MLB commissioner Ford Frick's recent declaration that municipalities would have to bear a bigger portion of the costs of Major League Baseball by providing the teams with publicly owned and maintained stadiums.

Buffalo versus Green Bay would be one of the first showdowns, soon to be followed in baseball by Brooklyn versus Los Angeles for the Dodgers in 1957 and New York versus San Francisco for the Giants in 1958.

After a couple false starts, the city and team moved expeditiously to get the stadium project underway. The team contracted with the Osborn Engineering Company of Cleveland, which had designed the newly constructed Milwaukee County Stadium, to select a site. On July 14, 1956, just over three months after the referendum passed, the city council approved Osborn's recommendation at the southwest edge of the city along Highland Avenue and Ridge Road in the town of Ashwaubenon (which would soon be annexed into the city).

It proved a perfect location and, like all major team decisions, seemed to follow Lambeau's direction. The new home was within a mile of Lambeau's "super highway," as he referenced U.S. Highway 41 during the campaign. Equally critical, commercial, industrial, and residential developments were sprouting up nearby, most significantly a 45-store shopping center to the north as well as an industrial park of sorts with a warehouse and paper converting company soon to be filled in with other manufacturing concerns.[53] Restaurants, grocery stores, and shops would soon pop up on Oneida Street along the property's east side. But those businesses were all in the town of Ashwaubenon, so Green Bay would not benefit from any added tax base. Serious commercial development around the immediate vicinity of the stadium wouldn't kick in until the following century. Incredibly, the bar scene around Lambeau wouldn't take root until the early 1990s, when fan-favorite Stadium View Sports Bar opened.[54] (Ban on bars west of Broadway in Green Bay didn't help; stadium-area bars are within the Ashwaubenon village limits.)

The project began immediately with design, followed by construction a few months later in February 1957. That summer, construction was completed on time and only slightly over budget. "Green Bay City Stadium" was christened on July 26. The stadium's inaugural game on September 29, 1957, began Saturday afternoon when Miss America Marilyn Van Derbur touched down at Austin Straubel Field and was escorted along a parade route through downtown before 80,000 onlookers—more people than the city itself. The evening saw a Venetian Nights boat parade along the Fox River. "Twenty-one brightly lighted yachts circled between the Mason and Main Street bridges before a riverbank crowd of about 15,000," reported the *Press-Gazette*.[55] Sunday, following Miss America's visit, Vice President Richard Nixon—a lifetime football obsessive himself—motorcaded to the stadium and joined football and state luminaries on the 50 yard-line. At the half-time dedication, Nixon offered up accolades.

"In Washington, we are used to hearing requests for federal aid. It is in the great American tradition that you people did it all yourself," Nixon said.[56] Indeed, the Packers got as much as they asked their congressmen. Future stadium drives in other NFL towns would learn from the Packers and lobby for millions in federal subsidies to supplement local and state taxes. Like the Packers, they'd get everything they asked for, too.

Chapter 6

The Pope

On February 2, 1959, the Packers found new life, a rebirth that would send the club soaring to new heights. Team personnel director Jack Vainisi scored a massive coup that would overshadow Curly Lambeau's great Hubbard-Blood-Michalske acquisition from 1929 that had launched the club's first three-peat championship. It came in the form of a heretofore unknown offensive coordinator with no head coaching experience, save for a high school stint, who had struggled to find a top job with any professional or even college team. He wasn't quite a late bloomer; just an overlooked talent who remained on the sidelines long past his due.

That Vince Lombardi failed to grab the attention of NFL front offices was mystifying. He had led the New York Giants' offense for five winning seasons, culminating in an NFL championship in 1956. In college, he anchored Fordham University's famed Seven Blocks of Granite offensive line. In between his playing and coaching career, he worked under the tutelage of Earl Blaik at Army, where the cadets posted four winning seasons and twice took home the Lambert Trophy, the annual award given to the best Division I program on the East Coast.[1]

Perhaps few people in American history would have better understood Vince Lombardi than President Theodore Roosevelt, who would no doubt nod along with Lombardi's timeless adage, "Winning isn't everything, it's the only thing." Indeed, it was Roosevelt who, 46 years before Lombardi called his first play as a Packer, wrote, "Nothing in the world is worth having or worth doing unless it means effort, pain, difficulty…"

Like Roosevelt, who lauded "the man in the arena whose face is marred by dust and sweat and blood," Lombardi dove head long into great battles on the football gridiron. But unlike Roosevelt, who suggested it was okay "to err…come up short again and again," Lombardi refused to accept failure. "Show me a good loser, and I'll show you a loser," Lombardi said.[2]

On day one, Lombardi took charge of the team as a general would his army. "I want it understood; I'm in complete command here," he told a luncheon of team directors on February 3, 1959. "I expect full cooperation from you. You will get full cooperation from me in return. I've never been associated with a loser, and I don't expect to be now. The Packers are steeped in tradition, and I expect with plenty of hard work, to bring them back to the position they once held."[3]

The new coach's message to his players was the same. "I'm not remotely interested in being just good," Bart Starr recalled him saying in the documentary *Legacy*. "We're going to relentlessly chase perfection…"[4]

Lombardi's most important relationship—with his players—was informed by his upbringing.

Despite his remarkable success, Vince's father, Enrico "Harry" Lombardi—who would outlive his son by one year—never really appreciated those accomplishments. Like the clichéd bull-headed, disapproving father, nothing ever seemed good enough for Harry, even after his son reached the pinnacle of success of his chosen profession—three consecutive NFL titles. The elder Lombardi would not mince words. "You made the biggest mistake of your life. You gave up the best job in the world," he told him on the occasion of Vince's announced retirement as Packers coach.[5] It seemed Lombardi carried over that never-good-enough worldview with his players, some of whom he considered sons he never had, like Paul Hornung.

"He rode me unmercifully, pointing out how slow I was, how weak I was, how stupid I was," wrote guard Jerry Kramer (1958–68) in a 1997 *New York Times* opinion piece.

Lombardi could be an SOB to his players. But there was another side to his gruff personality. His essence was in understanding the human condition and motivating his men accordingly. "I sat in front of my locker, head down, contemplating quitting," Kramer continued. "When Lombardi came up behind me, mussed up my hair and said, 'Son, one of these days you're gonna be the greatest guard in the league.' Suddenly I was 10 feet tall, ready to do anything for him."[6] Kramer would start 120 games for the Packers in a Hall of Fame career. Perhaps the best accolade, though, came from Lombardi himself, who called Kramer "the best guard in football."[7] That's something the coach never heard nor expected to hear from his father.

While family informed his relationship with players, Lombardi's Catholic faith shaped his core. His Jesuit education at Fordham University—built on his elementary and secondary Catholic education—drilled into him the value of learning and using one's God-given talents to the greatest degree possible, "a call to human excellence" as his college alma mater termed in its pedagogical philosophy.[8] Moreover, key tenants of religious practice comported with successful coaching traits. A good Catholic demanded constant vigilance: daily mass, devotion, prayer, self-reflection and improvement, confession, search for perfection, emulating one's savior, and, perhaps most important, sacrifice. Indeed, the word "sacrament"—a symbol of sacrifice such as the eucharist—is rooted in a Latin word (*sacramentum*) referring to an oath taken by soldiers. And Lombardi would drill his men like Roman gladiators.

Religion followed the coach wherever he went—literally. He had fastened a handmade string of rosary beads to the upper half of his car steering wheel to which he prayed every mile of every trip to morning mass, the office, practice field, and back home. Lombardi would need all the help he could muster—earthly or otherwise. At 45, this was likely his last opportunity to prove his mettle.[9] It was no accident that he devised his famous adage in this order: "God, Family, and the Green Bay Packers."

Training camp began the same way as his welcome address to the board of directors: with purpose, drive and resolve. "Three laps around the goalposts!" Lombardi commanded his men on the first day of camp, as author John Eisenberg recounted in *That First Season*.[10] It began and never ended. Two-a-day practices (with pads) felt like four. Six-a-week practices felt like seven. Once you arrived at training camp, there was no leaving. When Jerry Kramer and quarterback Joe Francis (1958–59) reported to camp, they mistook it for a chance to catch up with one another and hit the links. Lombardi was quick to dress them down. "If you sleep in this dorm, you're in the camp for good, and you make all meetings, practices, and curfews," he told them.[11]

Within two years the Packers had gone from the euphoria of opening a new stadium after winning a dramatic voter referendum to the depths of failure on the field. But there were two pieces of good news for Lombardi. First, he would have an easy act to follow. His predecessor, Raymond "Scooter" McLean (1958), had lasted just one miserable season, winning only a single game. Possibly the least demanding coach in team history, he had prided himself on strong camaraderie with players, hosting poker games for the fellas at night and running practice like a country club during the day. If the 1950s were a forgettable decade, 1958 would be its nadir.[12]

Second, the team that had barely escaped so many financial pitfalls had now posted a $200,000 surplus ($2.2 million current USD) after the 1958 season, setting a trend that would carry to the present day: the decoupling of on-field performance and financial success. They had been in the black for the seventh year in a row despite seven losing seasons.

Improved ticket sales and increasingly lucrative TV deals were adding up in the face of threats from CBS to drop Packers games because the network didn't want to lose money on small-market stations. Commissioner Bert Bell made quick work of that idle talk: "No Green Bay, no deal!" as CBS president Sig Mickelson recalled in *On Any Given Sunday*.[13] CBS quickly capitulated. By the end of the 1950s, the Packers were pulling down $80,000 ($890,000 current USD) in television revenue alone. And this was before the *really* big-money, shared-revenue deals that would begin in 1961.[14]

Lombardi's first season in 1959 began with a mid-fall rival matchup against the Bears at City Stadium before a sold-out crowd. Lombardi and his squad beat Chicago in a yawner 9–6. Green Bay would go on to finish the year with a respectable 7–5 record, marking their first winning season since the Lambeau era, and the new head coach earned AP Coach of the Year honors.[15]

The following season saw more improvement, and the Pack finished 8–4, splitting a pair with the Bears and sweeping the 49ers. The division title run was a tight one, with six teams claiming the lead at least once throughout the season. With San Francisco and Baltimore nipping at their cleats in Week 12, Green Bay arrived in Los Angeles enduring pressure that even the most secure shoulder pads could not hold.[16] Fortunately, the Packers felt some comfort from oddsmakers, who made them 10-point favorites, but not from their hard-driving taskmaster Lombardi, who would work his players to the nub if they were scrimmaging against some high school squad.[17]

At 4–6–1, Los Angeles had nothing to play for, only the spoiler. Under a brilliant California sun in an unusually dry December in the Golden State, traveling Packer backers weren't missing the 6-degree weather back home. But even with the perfect temps, the 100,000-plus seat Los Angeles Memorial Stadium sat nearly half empty with more than 40,000 open seats. Those bothering to attend would witness a Green Bay offensive clinic.

On paper, Los Angeles looked impressive, completing 22 pass attempts—over twice as many as the Green and Gold—and combining for 422 net offensive yards for the game. But where rookie coach Bob Waterfield's Rams were prolific, Lombardi was efficient. Quarterback Bart Starr, nearly perfect in the pocket, completed eight of nine passes including two touchdowns. Receivers Max McGee and Boyd Dowler combined for 216 yards off just five passes.

Perhaps the Packers' most spectacular play was their third passing touchdown, a 40-yard aerial to McGee from backfield virtuoso Paul Hornung, who had taken a pitch-out from Starr. The able running back and kicker, who lacked the innate passing talent of a marksman quarterback, nearly missed McGee as the end stretched out to make the catch while balancing just long enough before tumbling onto the end zone pylon for the score. The Hornung-to-McGee connection secured a commanding 28–7 edge going into halftime. They never surrendered their lead, finishing off Los Angeles 35–21.[18]

The final week victory over the Rams clinched the western division and punched their ticket to the NFL championship game, their first since 1944. "This ranks as the greatest comeback in NFL history," Art Daley of the *Press-Gazette* declared with no intended hyperbole. "The Packers are up there all alone, with an 8–4 record and worthy successors to the [1959 NFL champions] Baltimore Colts."[19]

The Vatican may not have sanctioned it, but the God-fearing Catholics and pigskin fans of Green Bay had no qualms about addressing coach Lombardi as they would His Holiness. Upon Lombardi's victorious return home from Los Angeles, Packer Nation bestowed a sobriquet that would last through the ages—one that a mother or favorite aunt might appreciate, but Family priest may have frowned upon as sacrilegious. "*There he is! The Pope! Look at the Pope!*" David Maraniss intoned in his Lombardi biography, *When Pride Still Mattered.*[20]

The 1960 championship game at Philadelphia was a nail-biter. Bart Starr threw for just one touchdown and Hornung split the uprights twice. Late in the fourth quarter and the Packers driving in Eagles territory, a would-be interference call on two Philly defenders against Green Bay receiver Boyd Dowler would have set up a seemingly sure score. But inside the 10-yard line, Eagles linebacker Chuck Bednarik tackled Packers fullback Jim Taylor and wouldn't let him up until the clock ran out. Ball game—Eagles 17, Packers 13. Unbeknownst to all, this game would mark the last Lombardi playoff loss.

The team—and city—would have to wait another year. In the meantime, the *Press-Gazette* wouldn't allow a mere technicality like the score to upset the party. Evincing a mother's unconditional love, reporter Art Daley incredulously declared Green Bay the real winner. "The Packers are the uncrowned 'world champions' of professional football—certainly in the eyes of Packerland," he wrote.[21] (As George Calhoun before him,

Daley was expected to cheer as much as inform on anything about the team.[22])

Rejecting overtures from his old team to return home and coach the Giants, Lombardi set his sights on the 1961 NFL championship. Having come close in 1960—nine yards to be exact—they were resolved not to come up short again in 1961. The team got off to a good start early in the year, shutting out the Bears in Week 3 and for the first time since 1935.[23]

By the regular season's end, the Packers were 11–3. Three days after claiming the Western Division title at Milwaukee County Stadium, where they took down the vaunted Giants on December 3, about 100 Green Bay business leaders convened at the downtown Beaumont Hotel to add another milestone to the Packers historical timeline. City and commercial leaders gathered in celebration and declared their city "Titletown, USA." An audacious moniker to be sure, but it was deserved. They were on pace to collect their seventh NFL title and held more championship trophies in any American pro sport save for the Yankees—and New York City already had the "Big Apple" nickname. The branding opportunities were limitless. How many other cities of 62,888 could boast a slogan bigger and better than Titletown, USA? Their wisdom would only grow with posterity. Today, the Greater Green Bay Yellow Pages list "Titletown" on no fewer than 17 businesses. (The team trademarked the phrase in 1990.)[24]

While the Packers would claim 13 titles in total, the 1961 championship game marked what Packers historian Cliff Christl called "the most eagerly anticipated game in the history of the Green Bay Packers;" more so than even the Ice Bowl in 1967, the 1996–97 NFC championship, or three subsequent Super Bowl appearances. The rematch against the Giants would be the first championship game held in Green Bay. This time the NFL wouldn't push the team to play in Milwaukee, as the league did in 1939. Nope, not with a big-league facility like City Stadium.[25]

City elders planned an entire month of partying, including a Christmas-themed revelry at the Brown County Veterans Memorial Arena, which had been constructed on Oneida Street across from the stadium in 1958. It would be "the biggest event to ever hit Green Bay," as Frank Shekore of the Green Bay chamber of commerce told *Press-Gazette* executive editor and Packers board member John Torinus. Bigger than Miss America and Richard Nixon? "The eyes of the world will be on Green Bay…the biggest little city in America," chamber general manager John Borgenson told Torinus.[26]

Among other recent milestones, the 1960 presidential election had represented generational change. The victor, John F. Kennedy, was the second youngest president in history. His age and youthful looks contrasted with the outdated and flailing Dwight D. Eisenhower, who had suffered several political missteps in recent years, including the downing of a secret U-2 spy plane over Soviet Russia and losing the first round of the space race with the USSR's launch of Sputnik.

The junior senator from Massachusetts had not been a favorite for the nomination and so had to battle his way through the state primary elections to become the party's standard bearer, as opposed to impressing party bosses in smoke-filled rooms where nominees were traditionally crowned. Kennedy won the crucial Wisconsin primary on April 5, 1960, which proved decisive in propelling him to the nomination. And for that, Kennedy had Vince Lombardi to thank.

Lombardi and Kennedy had much in common. Both were Catholics; each were sons of first- and third-generation ethnic Americans, respectively; both put up with their fair share of discrimination from the protestant and Anglo-Saxon eastern establishment; and most important, both loved football. Of course the stakes for each were a little different: Kennedy faced off against hyper-competitive brothers and cousins at the family compound in Hyannis Port, while Lombardi led pro teams in grand football stadiums of NFL cities against the game's and in time, history's best.[27]

It came as no surprise that Lombardi gladly endorsed the soon-to-be first Catholic president in his adopted state's primary. The outsider candidate earned nowhere near as much endorsement support as institutional favorite and neighboring US senator Hubert Humphrey of Minnesota, but what Kennedy lacked in quantity he made up in quality. Lombardi's validation proved decisive in Brown County, where the future president shellacked Humphrey three to one. Statewide, Kennedy polled strong in other Catholic enclaves and held his own in Protestant pockets where Methodist Humphrey did well, thereby beating Humphrey 56 to 44 percent.

At the time, religion was as divisive as partisanship is in today's elections. Kennedy was especially appreciative of Lombardi's support and passed along his phone number—just in case he ever needed it. Before the year was out, Lombardi would be crowned "Pope," and Kennedy president-elect. What Lombardi's endorsement did for Kennedy's presidential prospects in 1960, the latter's phone number did for Lombardi the following year.

Stars Paul Hornung, Ray Nitschke, and Boyd Dowler had been called up for service in the fall of 1961. Hornung was to fulfill his ROTC obligation, while the latter two needed to complete their service in the Army Reserve. These were three of Lombardi's star players, and a championship run was unthinkable without their participation. Eventually, each would be granted leaves of absence from their stateside bases on game day weekends. While no evidence existed in the form of a phone call between head coach and president, Hornung, Nitschke, and Dowler were clearly the beneficiaries of the First Fan's benevolence. Lombardi even penned a letter to top Kennedy aide Kenneth O'Donnell offering his thanks for his "help in obtaining leave for Paul Hornung so he could participate in the Championship game..."[28]

All favors aside, the team would have gotten along just fine without Hornung. The Packers and Giants faced off in Green Bay for the 1961 NFL Championship Game on December 31. The Green and Gold stomped New York 37–0. Starr threw for three touchdowns, tying the unstoppable Alabama gunslinger's season high from 1961. Hornung led the team in scoring with 19 points while claiming game-MVP honors. Giants quarterback Y. A. Tittle was thoroughly humbled by the Pack's defense, who forced him into throwing four interceptions. A record 39,029 fans turned out for the game, the largest ever in Green Bay. (It was a good thing that about 7,000 seats had been added in the offseason).

The Packers had returned to NFL glory, winning their first title since 1944 and marking Lombardi's first championship. But Green Bay had made it to the upper echelon of the league in more than one way. NBC had tripled its offer for broadcast rights over the previous season to cover the 1961 title game from about $200,000 ($2.1 million current USD) to $615,000 ($6.4 million current USD). Ticket prices were bumped up two dollars from $8 to $10 over the 1960 game. Despite being hosted by Green Bay, a town of just over 62,000—one-thirty-third the size of Philadelphia, the host city in 1960—the 1961 championship became the first title game to generate a million dollars.[29]

As for Kennedy, he was all too happy to have helped and showed his elation for the team. "Congratulations on a great game today," he wrote in a telegram from the White House that evening. "It was a fine victory for a great coach. A great team and a great town."[30]

Today, Super Bowl MVP winners go to Disney World; back then, championship-winning coaches traveled to Rome. Shortly after the season—just long enough for the Giants' wounds to heal—the Lombardis joined the Maras, owners of the rival Giants, on a European vacation. While in Rome, Wellington Mara[31] and Lombardi were granted an audience with Pope John XXIII, possibly the greatest honor a Catholic could experience. (Suffice it to say the Pope offered no comment on Lombardi's holy sobriquet.)[32]

While the NFL integrated in 1946, one year ahead of Major League Baseball, it was a dubious accomplishment: They were forced to do so. California state and local leaders had threatened to evict the Los Angeles Rams from their home stadium, the LA Coliseum, if they did not integrate. And so the Rams signed Kenny Washington and Woody Strode that year. Four years later the Packers crossed the color line—on their own volition—when they acquired their first Black player since the unwritten ban on players of color was initiated in 1933 by racist Washington Redskins owner George Preston Marshall.[33]

Few coaches did more to hasten integration in the NFL than Lombardi. It was a natural fit for a coach who experienced his share of bigotry growing up outside the religious and ethnic bounds of the East Coast establishment. "Lombardi deplored prejudice of any kind. As an American of Italian descent and a devoted Catholic who had grown up in Brooklyn, New York, hearing all sorts of demeaning slurs, Lombardi would not tolerate bigotry on his team," explained sports historian Johnny Smith.[34]

"He didn't see black or white; he just saw green and gold," said former NFL executive Joe Browne in the team's centennial documentary, *Legacy*.[35]

The first person of color to play for Green Bay predated the Packers by 22 years. Tom Skenandore of nearby Oneida Nation, a graduate of the famed Carlisle Indian Industrial School in Pennsylvania, suited up for Green Bay's semi-pro team in 1897. The crucial player was paid accordingly—a whopping $20 a game ($774 current USD)—and became Green Bay's first paid player.[36] By comparison, in the Packers first season each player received a total $16.75 ($300 current USD)—for the *entire* season.[37]

Eight years before the league's self-imposed color line precluded teams from hiring Black players, the Packers signed Walter Jean (aka Walt LeJeune, Walter LeJean), a player of Black and Cherokee descent who played multiple positions for Green Bay from 1925 to 1926.[38] In the middle of the 1950 season, the Packers signed Bob Mann, a receiver from the University of Michigan who the Lions had cut after the previous season.[39] Mann would lead the team in receptions in 1951 and rank second in the following two seasons. Notwithstanding the rampant racism that Black athletes suffered at the time, Mann had a good time with the Packers. "I didn't have any problems at all. Everyone treated me real well," he said in his induction to the Packers Hall of Fame in 1988.[40]

These and other key acquisitions of Black athletes turned the team into a championship franchise. Lombardi's visceral distaste for bigotry and racism secured his team's success for the coming decade. "[I]f not for his nondiscriminatory approach to building his roster, the Lombardi era almost certainly wouldn't have set the standard for NFL domination to the extent it did," said Christl in *The Greatest Story in Sports*. Five years later, on his Super Bowl I squad, Lombardi fielded six Black starters on defense alone, four of whom would be Pro Football Hall of Famers.[41]

Other personal experiences dealing with discrimination and bigotry shaped his outlook, too.

Vince's younger brother Harold was gay and came out to his family late in life. Their father, Harry, a "man's man" with ink-stained skin top to bottom and bulging biceps forged from tossing countless slabs of beef in Manhattan's Meatpacking District, was as unequivocal in his response: "I don't care. You are my son." Fatherly acceptance of a gay son was exceptionally rare in early- and mid-20th century America, let alone from a devout Catholic family.[42] But did Lombardi really discount Catholic theology? The coach's acceptance and enduring love for a gay brother certainly comports with popular Christian ethics like "Love thy neighbor" and even more so with Jesuit teachings. In addition to "a call to human excellence," Jesuits "examine the history of injustices subtly embedded within systems and cultures…" according to his alma mater Fordham's mission statement. "[T]o address significant world problems with courage, commitment, and good faith."[43]

Lombardi enforced his policy of non-discrimination and expressed a visceral contempt for racism loudly and clearly, though he tended to handle these delicate matters quietly and carefully. He would cover hotel bills when a Black player couldn't find housing. He inconspicuously got the word out among Green Bay's restaurants and other establishments that all players must be served—or be boycotted by the entire team. On a preseason trip to the South, he overnighted the team at a military base because hotels wouldn't accept Black players. After the trip, Lombardi adopted another rule: "[A]ny hotel that would not accommodate all

Packers would get no Packers," according to Maraniss. Lombardi's Black players would never forget the coach's indelible print on their lives.[44]

"I think about Lombardi every day," said cornerback Herb Adderley (1961–69), a five-time Pro Bowler and Hall of Famer. "I don't think of my father every day and I love my father because he was my father. But my father didn't instill in me the integrity that I have as a person and human being that coach Lombardi did."[45] By the time the 1964 Civil Rights Act was passed, one in five Packers players were Black and six such starters two years later. "Change was taking slow in the NFL, but not in Green Bay," said Christl in the team's centennial compendium.[46]

Adderley wasn't the only one who felt a kinship with the head coach. Bart Starr, the Packers' 17th-round pick in the 1956 draft and possibly "the least talented of the 25 modern-era quarterbacks in the Pro Football Hall of Fame," according to Christl, became one of the most famous players (and later coaches) in team history.[47]

Though blessed with few innate abilities—he wasn't even the most talented in his family according to his father[48]—Starr earned his position through hard work, discipline, and the help of an observant head coach. Starting quarterback Lamar McHan had lost his position to second-stringer Joe Francis in the sixth week of the 1959 season because of an injury; two weeks later, Lombardi then switched to Starr, who soon gained his coach's confidence despite having been written off by Lombardi's assistants. "A number two at best," one described him. (The assessment sounds much like that of a later Packers gunslinger from the University of Southern Mississippi, one who would also prove his mettle after a starting quarterback was knocked out with an injury.)[49]

Starr was a quick study who absorbed Lombardi's lessons from the sidelines to the point that he began to think like a coach himself. Against the 49ers in San Francisco to close out the 1959 season, Starr experienced a "quarterback epiphany," according to Maraniss. "[He] bent over center waiting for the snap, and as he looked across the line he read the defense in a nanosecond... One quick look and everything that Lombardi had taught him snapped into order."[50]

Starr is first and foremost remembered as one of the greatest Packers players of all time. While most if not all of his records have long since fallen, Starr left his mark with the Green and Gold by simply being the right quarterback at the right time, nearly "perfect" according to the NFL Hall of Fame—if not the best in team history. Among honors he held upon his retirement in 1971 included highest career completion percentage (57.6 percent) and most consecutive passes attempted without an interception (294). He earned the MVP in Super Bowls I and II and league MVP in 1966.[51]

As a Green Bay resident, his mark on the community would be equally lasting. Long after he tossed his last touchdown and called his last play as head coach, Starr's relationship with both the city and state only strengthened. He made lifelong impressions on those close to him. "I had all the respect in the world for him," said Jerry Parins, the Packers' security officer.

Starr would suffer more than his share of personal loss, including a son who struggled with drug addiction and died of an overdose at just 24 in 1988. He could relate to a lot of Wisconsin families, especially those who fell on hard times. He channeled this empathy and compassion into the Rawhide Boys Ranch in nearby New London, where young men caught up on the wrong side of the law could rehabilitate and get their lives back on track. Starr teamed up with founder John Gillespie in 1965 and helped seed the program with his Super Bowl II MVP Corvette; its mission continues to this day.[52]

The Packers would return bigger and better in 1962. Maybe it was a talented championship team hitting its stride—or a blessing from the pontific that made it so special. Wunderkind scout and personnel man Jack Vainisi had been essential to the team's growth; when Lombardi got to Green Bay in 1959, Vainisi had stocked the roster with 13 future Hall of Famers, including Bobby Dillon, Ray Nitschke, Bart Starr, Jim Taylor, Jim Ringo, and Jerry Kramer. To be sure, Lombardi was responsible for numerous important draft choices himself, including

Elijah Pitts, Ron Kostelnik, and Herb Adderley from the Class of 1961 alone. But where Lombardi truly shone was in developing superb *athletes* into Hall of Fame *players*, regardless of whatever position they played in college. In this manner he perfectly complemented the equally talented Vainisi.

"The power of Lombardi's coaching, the power of Lombardi's development, echoed the power of Jack Vanisi's ability to scout and procure talent," said University of North Carolina football general manager Michael Lombardi (no relation to Vince) in a promotional video for Vainisi's candidacy for the Pro Football Hall of Fame.[53] This is to say nothing of overlooked players who would have withered away had it not been for Lombardi. Exhibit A: Bart Starr, a late draft choice in 1956 who rode the bench his first four and a half years as a Packer before Lombardi tagged him his starter.[54]

"The 1962 Packers are widely viewed as the best of the Lombardi teams, if not the greatest team in Packers history," according to Christl in *The Greatest Story in Sports*.[55] If you didn't know better, you would think they'd switched over to a minor league schedule for 1962; the Packers laid waste to opponents. In September alone they outscored foes 100-7, beating new rivals the Minnesota Vikings (who had recently joined the league in 1960) and old ones too, like the St. Louis Cardinals and Chicago Bears. Green Bay went four for four in October, and in November they embarrassed Philadelphia in their own house 49–0. Save for a road loss at Detroit in November 1962, that year was a historically dominant season, just one of four single-loss seasons while in the NFL (1921–).

Starr claimed the year's passing title by leading the NFL in four categories: pass completions (62.5 percent), adjusted yards per pass attempt (7.98), lowest interception rate (3.2 percent), and most comebacks (tied-3).[56] Jim Taylor took home the Associated Press' MVP award with a league-high 1,474 rushing yards, his third 1,000-plus-yard season in a row, and 19 touchdowns.[57] On defense, the USC gunslinger-turned-safety Willie Wood led the league with nine interceptions.[58]

Despite claiming more NFL titles than anyone else in the maturing NFL, Green Bay had yet to receive the national acclaim they deserved. The franchise was still thought of as a quaint little town in a cold northerly outpost. That the NFL lay deep in the shadow of Major League Baseball for the previous four decades hadn't helped Green Bay build recognition. But Lombardi would change all that.

On December 21, 1962, less than two weeks before another NFL championship rematch against the New York Giants, the coach graced the cover of *TIME*. The publication that profiled few sports figures and even fewer football stars; Curly Lambeau never came close to appearing in a national publication like *TIME*. In a feature story, the magazine spun a hometown tale worthy of the Classics.[59]

Unfolding the story like a three-act Greek drama, the country's leading news magazine recounted the evolution of this miraculous franchise. The essence of *TIME*'s story resembled an extended haiku:

"Green Bay loved a winner, but it was next to impossible for such a small town to support one...

"In desperation the Packers turned to Vince Lombardi...

"Methodically, relentlessly, he set out to build his winner...

"'This is our year and our championship. Let's win it the way a champion should.'"[60]

Suddenly everyone was a Packers fan. Well, almost everyone.

On December 30, the Packers rode into New York in a charter bus that could be mistaken for a team of horses, the Big Apple a town in the Old Wild West, and the game a shootout at high noon. As they pulled to a stop just outside the game's venue, Ray Nitschke tumbled out and marked his territory.

"Welcome to Yankee Stadium, home of the world champion Packers!" he shouted.[61]

Nitschke's unbound chutzpah must have tweaked the all-business Lombardi, especially in the latter's hometown full of friends and family. The last thing he wanted was a showboating all-star mouthing off. He hated those types. "When you get in the end zone, act like you've been there before," the coach would admonish his players.

Not only did No. 66 possess a one-of-a-kind sense of humor but held key defense records and honors. His physicality was as intense as his humorous one-offs. "Ray played with such a recklessness and fierceness that he developed a reputation fast that here was a guy you avoided, if at all possible," according to Starr. Nitschke was inducted into the Pro Football Hall of Fame in 1978, about five years after his retirement—the minimum time lapse before a former player is eligible for the honor.[62]

The 1962 title match was set up to be a real donnybrook. Shut out and humbled by the Packers a season ago in Green Bay, the Giants were resolved to return the favor. "We will absolutely kill (them)… It's the only way we can atone for what happened to us last year," Giants defensive end Andy Robustelli said in the lead up to game day.

The '62 Packers led the league in 11 offensive categories; not only were they more well-rounded in moving the ball, but they had their pick of strategies, making it difficult for head coach Allie Sherman's squad to plan their defense. Even so, game day wind gusts would push 40 miles per hour, tempering the offense and forcing Lombardi to run the ball. He leaned hard on his recently crowned league MVP Jim Taylor. The fullback would earn his pay, running the ball a mind-blowing 31 times, more than all Giants backs combined (26). On the other hand, New York's Y.A. Tittle connected twice as many times as Starr with 18 pass completion. Starr hit Boyd Bowler four times, Taylor three, and receiver Max McGee one.

Perhaps the real drama was not on the field but off. Taylor nearly bit off his tongue after absorbing an especially hard tackle in the first half. He'd remember it all day as he swallowed down his own blood. At halftime, team doctors sewed up his cut arm, without Novocain. Players could hear the screams from the adjoining medic room. Taylor had also been playing sick; he was diagnosed with hepatitis a week later. "Taylor isn't human. No human being could have taken the punishment he got today," said Giants linebacker Sam Huff. Then again, Huff didn't play for Vince Lombardi.

The Packers defense held the Giants to no offensive scores (New York recovered a blocked punt in the end zone) and forced three turnovers.

Y.A. Tittle was stuck with a miserable 48.5 QB rating, missing most of his passes and throwing one interception.[63] Tittle's mishap occurred early on when the Giants appeared poised to take back lost momentum after the Packers drew first blood with a Jerry Kramer field goal (Hornung had injured his knee and did not kick). Tittle's bungled pass and other missed opportunities affirmed the taunts of happy Packers fans: "New York Can Have Tittle, Green Bay Has The Title." It wasn't a blowout like that of the previous year in Green Bay, but the Packers never surrendered their lead, even when the Giants came within a field goal of tying it up. With a pair of Kramer field goals from 29 and 30 yards out in the second half, the Green and Gold put it away 16–7.

Nitschke wasn't all talk and had a good day; he recovered two fumbles and was responsible for Tittle's interception by deflecting an otherwise decent pass.[64] The Packers were now two-for-two against the coach's old team in championship matchups during the Lombardi era.

The Wellington Mara–Vince Lombardi relationship was a fascinating chapter in Packers history. Each personified the American immigrant experience. Wellington's father, Tim, who founded the Giants in 1925, was born into poverty and grew up on New York's then-hardscrabble Lower East Side. Harry Lombardi, a first-generation Italian American, struggled hard to provide for his family. Both Wellington and Vince were devout Catholics and would attend mass together when both were in New York, Milwaukee, or Green Bay. They shared a love for football, a classic American work ethic, and a deep sense of faith. It's easy to see how, despite the rivalry, their relationship took root and flourished. Mara delivered Lombardi's enshrinement speech at the latter's posthumous Hall of Fame induction in 1971.[65]

Lombardi–Lambeau, who crossed paths intermittently when the former helmed the franchise, was an entirely different matter. "Two extreme opposites," according to Christl in the documentary *Legacy*. One hailed from the nation's largest metropolitan area; the other grew up in a small town in America's heartland. One lived his faith; the other had no time for church. One remained faithful to his wife and family; the other was thrice divorced and largely ignored his sons.[66] Despite clashing priorities in life, both valued football above all else.

Their legacies stand tall outside Lambeau Field. Literally. Two equally sized 14-foot bronze likenesses guard the stadium's north entrance like centurions at the gate. Lambeau's statue defiantly points east as if summoning troops to the goal line. Lombardi's looks straight ahead, serious and confident. A slight smile creaks out of the edges of his pursed lips.

But whose house is it really? The stadium bears the founder's name, though Lombardi's presence permeates the building and his namesake trophy stands 50 feet high inside the atrium. Is it not surprising, then, that a franchise so rich in tradition and unique in origin would have room for two dynastic legacies: The creator who started the team and kept them in business early on, and the second coming who forever sealed the franchise's name in NFL history?

On June 1, 1965, Curly Lambeau passed away unexpectedly; he died much as he had lived—with a girlfriend. While courting Mary Jane Van Duyse, a Packers majorette half his age, Curly relieved her father from mowing their front lawn in Sturgeon Bay, Wisconsin. After a turn, he collapsed from a massive heart attack and died immediately. Earl "Curly" Lambeau was 67 years old.

For Curly, life had slowed down—if not his libido. He had retired from coaching in 1953 over a falling out with George Preston Marshall of the Washington Redskins, his last assignment. Two years later he divorced his third wife, Grace Garland. In retirement, Lambeau spent most of his time at his home in Door County's Fish Creek. His public persona was muted; only on special occasions did he resurface. One exception was his indispensable assistance in passing the stadium referendum in 1956 and later rallying support as an "East-sider" for building the new facility on the west side which would be closer to new development and more accessible to Highway 41. In short, when the Packers really needed him—he was there. Always.

Mayor Don Tilleman and a retinue of city fathers and ex-players dedicated City Stadium in Lambeau's honor, renamed it Lambeau Field, the following season on September 11, 1965. Curiously, the team made little of the occasion, a move out of character for a franchise that celebrated every milestone with overwhelming fanfare. Coach Lombardi was conspicuously silent that day and did not participate during the halftime program. Maybe it was the stress of the new season for the coach, or Milwaukee's latest campaign to upstage Titletown and land its own pro team? Perhaps it was a complicated matter of legacy? Or maybe it was Occam's Razor, in which the simplest explanation is the best one: Lombardi simply did not like Lambeau. (Later in the season, when Lombardi learned that he would share the cover of the Green Bay Packers Yearbook with Lambeau, "he flew into a rage" and he refused to talk to its editor for the rest of the season.)[67]

Lambeau's contribution to the Packers in particular and pro football in general cannot be overstated. The Packers simply would not have existed without him; the NFL would have taken on a much different color. Lambeau challenged and beat the rich guys from the big city showing the league and country you didn't have to be in a New York, Chicago, or Los Angeles to compete—and win. His underdog persona inspired dozens of owners and coaches; his compelling backstory (small town denizen, modest means, college dropout) and larger-than-life charisma made the careers of hundreds of players who may very well have peaked in college or fallen to the wayside had Curly not saw the potential that seemingly everyone else missed on draft day. Neither Green Bay nor the NFL would ever be the same.

In the 1960s, the Packers came close to winning six consecutive NFL titles, an accomplishment that could very well have altered the fabric of the game itself. Other sports leagues over the years have changed rules to rein in dominant teams or players. Indeed, that's exactly what Major League Baseball did to the Yankees in 1939 after New York completed a World Series four-peat by giving the reigning league champion last dibs on waiver claims on players. Every other team would have a chance to take someone off waivers before the World Series champ could put in an offer.[68] The NHL and NBA did likewise when a uniquely special player upturned the playbook, namely the "Gretzky rule" (in place from 1985 to 1992) and the "Illegal Offense" rule (instituted 1987), respectively.[69] Imagine not just the Lombardi Trophy but the Lombardi Rule—though what could the league possibly do to hamper the Packers without banning them outright?

It wasn't from any slip-up on the gridiron but rather an unforced error off the field that would come back to bite the Green and Gold in the 1963 season. Paul "Golden Boy" Hornung's bachelor lifestyle was the stuff of legend; only A-list movie stars or monster rock stars could exceed his partying. Hornung could have put on a tutorial for Curly. "He freely admits that he and wide receiver Max McGee led the Packers, and maybe the NFL, in chasing women, hanging out in bars and nightclubs, and generally trying to circumvent the strict rules of Vince Lombardi," said author Billy Reed in the foreword to Hornung's autobiography, *Golden Boy.* A slow night meant getting home before 4 AM and having fewer than 30 drinks.[70]

It was only a matter of time before his unseemly habits caught up to him and the NFL authorities caught on. On April 17, 1963, just over three months since the Packers claimed the 1962 league crown, Commissioner Pete Rozelle handed down an indefinite suspension to Hornung for betting on NFL games and "associating with gamblers." Division rival Alex Karras of the Lions faced similar sanctions for betting, too, albeit unrelated to Hornung's indiscretions.[71] Well-practiced in getting out of personal fixes, Hornung immediately apologized. He would be reinstated the following season and later inducted into the Pro Football Hall of Fame in 1986. The Packers proved resilient in 1963 and continued to play strong even without Hornung and despite missing Starr for four games and Nitschke for two due to injuries.[72] Green Bay ended the season 11–2–1. Both losses came from an overwhelming Chicago Bears squad who went on to win the league championship over the New York Giants. Had the Packers split their two meetings, they would have made it to the championship game. But the damage had already been done in the offseason. Said Lombardi after the season, "Injuries hurt us, as they will anybody. But our most significant loss—and I've never said this before—we were injured in not having Hornung."[73]

Despite a healthy, full roster the following season in 1964, the Packers came up short of the championship again, settling for a distant second place at 8–5–1 versus the division winner Colts, 12–2–0. They would start afresh in 1965.

The '65 season marked the first sign that Lombardi might not stick around forever, despite the success of the past seven magical years and the longevity of his legacy competitor, Curly Lambeau, who had coached the team for 31 seasons.[74] Rumor had it the expansion Atlanta Falcons had approached Lombardi to take over as general manager and head coach and according to an Atlanta area radio DJ, Lombardi had even agreed! When asked about the reports, Lombardi simply said he "had a contract to live up to in Green Bay," according to the *Press-Gazette*. (Here, he didn't deny the rumor outright.) Fortunately for the Packers, on November 4, 1965, team president Dominic Olejniczak announced that Lombardi had re-upped his contract for another nine years, extending his tenure out to 1974. Packer Nation breathed a sigh of relief.[75]

The following January, the first branch of the Lombardi coaching tree sprouted. Offensive line coach Bill Austin went to Pittsburgh.[76] Following him was defensive back field coordinate Norb Hecker, who took the open position in Atlanta.[77] Later in Lombardi's tenure and beyond, four other assistants would follow Austin and Hecker into the head coaching ranks: Phil Bengtson (Packers), Jerry Burns (Vikings), Tom Fears (Saints), and Mike McCormack (Eagles, Colts, Seahawks)—two coaches shy of coach Mike Holmgren's (1992–98) record.[78]

Lombardi's team would bounce back from frustrating campaigns in 1963 and 1964 to honor their franchise's proud tradition in the only way they knew how, winning not just one but three consecutive NFL championships, including the first two Super Bowls. The record of most NFL championships remains unbroken. For all the accolades afforded Vince Lombardi as a tough-as-nails coach who took nothing less than the very best, Lombardi's twin Super Bowl trophies were essential to his legacy.

The Packers' second three-peat began with a grind of a 1965 season. Weak on offense and overly reliant on defense, Green Bay managed to notch wins the first six games, but the arch-nemesis Bears destroyed them 31–10 in Week 7 and put the Packers in a first-place tie with the Colts in the Western division.[79] Chicago had dominated the run with 212 rushing yards, quarterback Rudy Bukich threw for one touchdown, and Gale Sayers ran 10 yards for the second Bears' touchdown. Halas per usual delighted in the Packers misfortune. Papa Bear bragged at his post-game media availability that the Packers had unloaded the defensive playbook but nowhere near offset the Bears' "great team effort." When one reporter asked Rozelle, who was in town for the match, if he would prefer an undefeated team in the league, the commissioner demurred. At which point Halas, who was still coaching at age 70, piled on, "Neither do we," as reporter Lee Remmel recorded for the *Press-Gazette*.[80] The Green and Gold would lose the following week at home against the Lions, then finish the rest of the regular season with four wins, one loss, and a tie, ending up with a strong 10–3–1 record.

The Colts' and Packers' season-long horse race ended in a tie, which meant a division run-off, the last such tiebreaker playoff game in NFL history. That game was almost as close as their regular season records. Referees evidently gave Packers kicker Don Chandler the benefit of the doubt in the final seconds of regulation, when his kick veered high and right. Had the game been played the following year in 1966, when goal posts were extended upward 20 feet, it could have hit the pole.[81] At least one person was convinced it missed. "There is no question the field goal wasn't good," Colts coach Don Shula said in the documentary *We Wuz Robbed*. But he heaped praise on Green Bay's game-long performance: "That probably in my entire coaching career, that was the best effort from a team that wasn't supposed to be able to do it."[82]

The Green and Gold grinded it out for 13 minutes and 39 seconds in sudden death overtime, coming out on top with a 25-yard field goal by Chandler. This time there was no controversy; the pigskin nearly split the uprights perfectly. Green Bay 13, Baltimore 10.[83]

For the NFL title, the Packers took on the Cleveland Browns, who finished 11–3 and outpaced their nearest competitor by four games, claiming the league's best regular season record. Returning from the locker room after halftime with a razor-thin 13–12 lead, Green Bay kicked into gear immediately.

On the Packers' first possession of the third quarter, Starr marched down the field 90 yards in 11 plays. On second-and-8 from the Cleveland 13, Starr rested on the famed Packers sweep. With Hornung set on Starr's right side, the halfback clutched the pigskin and ran left, gracefully stepping on the mud-soaked sod like a tight rope artist avoiding a fall. The quick, sure-footed right guard Jerry Kramer, just a stride ahead, cut off Hornung and took out a Cleveland defender beneath the knees. Hornung stepped over Kramer and darted into the end zone. The Green and Gold would not surrender the lead, only adding a field goal in the fourth for a 23–12 hard-fought, well-earned victory.[84]

The *Press-Gazette* characterized the win as the "most satisfying" championship of their nine titles to date. "They were counted out and even jeered during the grueling Western Division race," wrote Art Daley. "It was a 23–12 chapter in the 46-year history of the Sports Wonder of the World."[85]

On December 1, 1966, Commissioner Pete Rozelle announced that the newly merged American Football League (AFL) and NFL would play in the "World Championship" the following month. As the name suggested, it would match the champions from each league. AFL founder and Kansas City Chiefs owner Lamar Hunt thought the game's name too bland, so he suggested a play on words of a child's toy: a Super Ball. And so, the "Super Bowl" was born.[86] Not everyone was enamored of the name. "Super Bowl. It sounds like a comic strip," Lombardi said.

As the team from the long-established league with more star players and experienced franchises, the Packers were 13-point favorites to win the newly christened big game.[87] In this respect, arguably the "real" contest for the 1966 season title remained the NFL Championship Game, a matchup between the Packers and Cowboys on New Year's Day, 1967.

Vince Lombardi had much in common with his Dallas counterpart Tom Landry, who took the helm their inaugural year in 1960 and had coached alongside Lombardi when both were assistants with the Giants in the 1950s. Unlike Lombardi, however, Landry had struggled through his first six seasons, failing to post a single winning season. His fortunes finally came around in 1966, when the Cowboys finished first in the Eastern division with a 10–3–1 record.

On a 41-degree day with a light southern breeze blowing beneath a low winter sun—chilly for Dallas but perfect playing weather for Lombardi's squad—the Green and Gold jumped out with a 7–0 lead on a 17-yard touchdown reception by Elijah Pitts. It took Bart Starr's offense eight plays to go 76 yards. On the ensuing kickoff return, Cowboys cornerback Mel Renfro fumbled the ball; Jim Grabowski scooped up the floundering pigskin and carried it 18 yards back for another Packers score, the second touchdown in 12 seconds of play. But instead of waving the white flag, Dallas bounced back. By the end of the first quarter, the Cowboys would score a pair of rushing touchdowns to tie it up 14–14.

Dallas and Green Bay went back and forth the rest of the game in a barn burner between two otherwise middling offenses (Dallas and Green Bay finished seventh and eighth, respectively, in a 14-team league in total offense in 1965.)[88] The combatants combined for 42 first downs, 785 yards from scrimmage, eight touchdowns, and 61 points. Dallas smartly relied on the run against the league's best pass defense, scoring a pair of touchdowns on the ground. The otherwise prolific quarterback Don Meredith would play second fiddle to the run game—that is, until the fourth quarter, when he fired a 68-yard strike to Frank Clarke.

The Packers, meanwhile, scored four aerial touchdowns. Starr completed an impressive 19 on 28 attempts with no interceptions and an astounding 143.5 QB rating. And yet Dallas came within three feet of upsetting the favored reigning NFL champions.

With just over two minutes to go, the Cowboys marched 45 yards to the Packers 2-yard line. With every ounce of strength Landry's squad could muster, the Cowboys bore down on the league's No. 1 defense like the indigenous longhorns of the vast Texas plains. But Meredith and his squad got stuck at the goal line, failing to punch it in off five tries. On fourth down, Packers linebacker and future Hall of Famer Dave Robinson drove a stake into the heart of the Cowboys when he shot out like a jack in the box from the line of scrimmage, chasing down Meredith. The 6-foot-3 playmaker nearly sacked the luckless Cowboy, who flubbed a pass into the waiting arms of Packers defender Tom Brown to end the game. Final score: Packers 34, Cowboys 27.[89]

Sunday evening, the Packers' 727 chartered plane touched down at Austin Straubel, where a delirious crowd of 15,000 greeted the conquering heroes. The city hadn't witnessed such a reception since Curly and his band of brothers won its first championship 37 years earlier. Plenty of patrol officers were on hand and the Civil Defense was called up. It was the "largest crowd ever" at the airport, according to one county traffic cop recorded in the *Press-Gazette*.

As the plane circled the runway, Bart Starr witnessed a line of headlights from the airport entrance to Lambeau Field—four miles as the crow flies. Despite a frigid 15 degrees, the atmosphere was electric. Offensive lineman Fuzzy Thurston "broke into an impromptu dance up and down the ramp," Len Wagner reported.[90] Fans were forced to ride out the elements and were denied safe haven in the terminal, having trashed it two weeks earlier during another welcome-home ceremony for the Western Division champs.

If the 1966 season were a Greek drama, then Super Bowl I would be its denouement. Kansas City never had a chance. Despite the Chiefs heaping a lot of trash talk on the Packers during the one-week leadup, Green Bay shellacked the helpless AFL champs 35–10. Never a stickler for gracious-winner etiquette, Lombardi delightfully returned the favor to head coach Hank Stram's squad. "I don't think that Kansas City compares with the top teams of the NFL," he stated plainly at his post-game presser.

Few pro football contests sold out at Los Angeles' Memorial Coliseum. On January 15, 1967, the NFL-AFL matchup had 30,000 open seats.[91] It could have been the weakest turnout for a major sports championship game, an unfathomable phenomenon in today's age of the modern Super Bowl, when tickets average $8,076 a pop,[92] viewing audiences exceed 127 million,[93] and commercials cost $233,333 per second, 233 *times* more than in 1967.[94]

Poor ratings aside, the Packers had now gone back-to-back for the third time in franchise history. Starr shone brightest among his teammates, nabbing Super Bowl MVP honors for throwing a season-high 250 yards and a pair of touchdowns with a sterling 116.21 QB rating.[95] Backup receiver Max McGee subbed in for an injured Boyd Dowler and took honorable mention for catching two touchdown passes, including the Super Bowl's first-ever TD, along with 138 yards.[96] Legend has it McGee got little sleep the night before and showed up hungover. McGee maintained the tale to his dying day, though trainer and bed check captain Dave Hanner disputed the story.[97] It certainly wouldn't have been a surprise for the one Packer who could keep up with Hornung's extracurriculars to make the most of a free trip to California. And he wouldn't have been the first Packer to put fun ahead of business on the West Coast.

No doubt the Pack were bone-tired on the way home; it was the 21st game of the year.[98] But with another repeat championship in the books, a third consecutive title in 1967 was there for the grabbing. They'd have to once again battle their way through the NFL Championship Game first.

The 1980 US Men's Olympic ice hockey showdown against the Soviet Union, dubbed the "Miracle on Ice," lives on forever in the pantheon of greatest-ever American sports victories. The game's enduring legacy is twofold: The squad were huge underdogs, and the victory came at a perilous moment in United States history. Fresh off defeat in the Vietnam War, President Jimmy Carter had declared a crisis of confidence, inflation had broken double digits, and a bungled rescue to bring home dozens of American hostages in Iran was in the works. American soft power was flagging.

Save for die-hard hockey fans, few realize the Miracle on Ice was not the final match; rather it was the semifinal before the team made quick work of Finland in the gold medal game. So too was the case with the Packers in another fabled ice-themed match.

If everyone who said they went to the 1967 NFL Championship Game on the afternoon of December 31 did in fact attend, then the Ice Bowl at Lambeau Field would have hosted at least 200,000 fans—a number that grew in proportion to its legendary status over time. A warm front above Green Bay had contained a polar vortex for days. But around midnight on game day, the front gave way and freezing Arctic air gushed down onto Lambeau Field and the rest of Wisconsin.

The visiting Dallas Cowboys, eager to avenge the previous year's NFL championship shootout, were rustled awake by the front desk operator at their hotel in nearby Appleton. "Good morning. It's 7 o'clock and 16 below."

"Sixteen below what?" quarterback Don Meredith asked.

"Step outside, honey, and you'll find out," the operator answered.[99]

Amazingly, Packers fans poured into Lambeau Field hours before game time.[100] "Not as many tailgaters as usual, but they were still out there. Folding chairs, card tables, brats and beer," wrote David Maraniss in *When Pride Still Mattered.*[101]

One thing that could have made the conditions tolerable was a recently installed "electric blanket" beneath the turf. But when the field tarp was pulled back, a thin layer of water and mud quickly froze into an "ice glaze," making traction difficult if not near impossible. The electric grid had broken down, earning the stadium its enduring moniker, the Frozen Tundra, a line NFL Films producer Steve Sabol wrote into the script of his highlight reel. Lombardi, embarrassed that his $200,000 heating system failed, did not appreciate Sabol's clever term: "They showed [the highlight reel] to all the stockholders," Sabol recalled. "He didn't want them asking about the heating system."[102]

Metal whistles froze up and were unusable. Refs would have to call it the old-fashioned way with hoarse voices over chapped lips. NFL Films brought extra cameras just in case; a handful of the 12 stopped working.[103] Press box windows were wide open to accommodate TV cameras. "It's the coldest field I have ever seen for football," NBC analyst and former Giants receiver Frank Gifford—an early Lombardi acolyte—reported from the sideline.[104] Later in the booth, he quipped, "Excuse me, but I'm going to take a bite out of my coffee."[105]

A young fan named John Des Jardins wasn't supposed to go, but when his grandpa came up with an extra ticket, the teen and future Outagamie County judge was all in. "We didn't have really the best gear. I couldn't feel anything below my knees," DesJardins recalled. "I was in so much pain at the end, but I was joyous."

Future actor and Appleton native Willem Dafoe attended the game too and recalled weather conditions well. "My father was a doctor, put me in a hot bath right away [when I got home] to kinda thaw [my feet] out. They were very close to frostbite," said Defoe in an *NFL Films* short.[106]

The Packers started out strong. "Starr operated flawlessly with almost mechanical brilliance," according to *A Chilling Championship*. Receiver Boyd Dowler caught the game's first two touchdowns, and by the second quarter they had plowed ahead 14–0. But Dallas was by now accustomed to the punishing cold and slowly clawed their way back, holding the Pack scoreless for the next 41 minutes. The Cowboys would grab the lead eight seconds into the fourth quarter and hold on until the final 13 seconds. For some time, it felt the Packers would not make it.

Recalled *Press-Gazette* reporter Warren Gerds watching from the sideline that day, "The Packers were trailing and struggling. My feeling was this was going to be the end of the Packers story."[107]

Just as Dave Robinson freelanced on the final play of the NFL championship the year before, so too did Bart Starr pull a wild card on the final play of this game. The circumstances were eerily similar.

"We had run out of ideas," Starr said later.[108] He trotted back to the sideline to consult with his coach. Starr settled on the play: Brown right, 31 wedge. Oddly enough, Lombardi seemed indifferent—perhaps because the punishing temps were too much even for a tough New Yorker who grew up on a similar parallel as northern Wisconsin. The coach caught his quarterback off guard. "Well run it and let's get the hell outta here," as Starr recalled with a chuckle in *Vince Lombardi: A Football Life—The Ice Bowl.* "And I'm laughing like I am now—going back to the huddle—and I'm trying not to let anybody see me laughing because it just broke me up. That was his response!?"[109]

Neither Lombardi nor anyone else on the field knew what Starr was going to do next. It was the last thing Dallas coach Tom Landry expected. "I thought Starr might roll out and throw or run," he said, adding, "It was a dumb call. But now it's a great play."[110] Landry must not have done his homework; Starr had called an audible sneak the year before against the 49ers in Milwaukee. The Alabama gunslinger gambled that he could pull it off. It worked then—and it'd work today.[111]

Under center, Ken Bowman snapped the ball to Starr, who charged the line. Bowman and guard Jerry Kramer each took a shoulder of 6-foot-6 defensive tackle Jethro Pugh and plowed him over to clear a path for the ball carrier. Starr lunged through the opening. Behind him came would-be hero fullback Chuck Mercein caught unawares. (He was the "3," which referred to the fullback position, in the play call.) Mercein thought fast and threw up his arms not to signal the score but instead to show the refs he hadn't pushed the quarterback—a sure illegal use-of-the-hands penalty.[112] Touchdown. Final score: Packers 21, Cowboys 17.

Little did they know at the time they had won the greatest game in team history. Too bad most of the city hadn't seen it; the game was blacked out in the Green Bay market.[113] At least the rest of the country did, as nearly 31 percent of households with TVs tuned in and discovered what Green Bay and Wisconsin had known for almost a half-century.[114]

"The Ice Bowl define[d] the city to the rest of the world," said author Mark Beech in *The People's Team.*[115] Just as coach Herb Brooks' 1980 squad was counted out before the puck dropped, so too was Green Bay many times over. But not that day.

The Ice Bowl was not without controversy. Debate over playing sport in inhumane conditions peppered news casts and articles in the wake of the match. This extended to upset spouses of Dallas players like Willie Townes, whose wife, Sandra Clark, later claimed her late husband's skin had peeled off a few days after the game. There were bright sides, however. Though Bob Lilly suffered lung damage, he ended his smoking habit. "I've never been able to smoke a cigarette again," the former defensive tackle told the *Dallas Morning News* in a 2017 retrospective. One Packers fan, however, paid dearly. An elderly fan died of exposure, perhaps the first—and only—casualty claimed by the Frozen Tundra.[116]

So it was a welcome respite that the second Super Bowl would be held in sunny Miami where Lombardi and team would meet up with the AFL's Oakland Raiders. An 81-degree improvement over sub-zero temperatures of the Ice Bowl, Florida's Orange Bowl was a veritable paradise for the football sojourners from Green Bay. Still two years away from the consummation of the country's two pro football leagues, the Ice Bowl technically marked the Packers' second NFL three-peat since the 1929–1931 titles. But for good measure, a second trifecta wouldn't be secured until the final seconds ticked off the clock in Super Bowl II.

The outcome was never in doubt. Green Bay was a two-touchdown favorite (minus-13.5 points) at kickoff. So good were their chances, bookies had stopped taking bets for the Packers the day before the big game.[117] Oakland came within a touchdown of Green Bay in the middle of the second quarter. That was the closest Raiders' coach John Rauch—with youthful defensive prodigy John Madden at his side[118]—would get to Lombardi's squad. By early fourth quarter, the Green and Gold had blasted ahead 26 points. With 11:35 minutes remaining, typical mid-winter southern Florida weather—no rain, high 60s—carried both refreshing trade wins and a Super Bowl trophy. Packers: 33–14. Not all was lost for Oakland, in fact the opposite. The Raiders had a strong lineup from veteran George Blanda to rookie stand out Gene Upshaw—thanks in part to a journeyman scout in the front office with a promising career himself, Ron Wolf—and the legendary managing general partner Al Davis would be ready for future postseason matchups.[119]

News of the win was inexplicably buried in the hometown paper. A cursory mention of the victory figured inconspicuously below news-of-the-day. Under "Quakes Kill 250 In Sicily," *Press-Gazette* reporter Dave Devenport captured the zeitgeist: "Wild Receptions of Past Missing As Fans Meet Packers at Airport." Late Sunday evening at Austin Straubel Field, there were no civilian patrol to sort out bumper to bumper traffic from downtown; no inebriated Fuzzy Thurston dancing down the gangway; no cheerful bands and packed risers with local dignitaries prepping speeches. Just the spouses, family and die-hards. Deeper in the paper lay the real news: "Retirement? 'No Announcements,' Vince." That, not the second three-peat in pro football history lay heavy on the minds of Packer Nation. For those fans holding their breath, it wouldn't be long before they could exhale.[120]

Chapter 7

The Sorry '70s

The year 1968 was not a good one for the Packers. But then, it wasn't a good year beyond Green Bay, as well.

On January 30 of that year, American GIs in Vietnam were caught off guard by the Viet Cong, who launched the Tet Offensive. The North Vietnamese show of force surprised a lot of Americans back home, who then reconsidered their country's involvement in the war. The following month, for the first time Pew Research registered a plurality of Americans who opposed the US intervention.[1]

At the end of March, President Lyndon Johnson told a national television audience that he would "neither seek nor accept" the Democratic nomination for president and instead focus on the US military's spiraling fortunes in southeast Asia. A few days later, the Rev. Martin Luther King Jr. was gunned down outside a motel in Memphis. Two months after King's tragic demise, New York senator and presidential candidate Robert F. Kennedy was assassinated inside the Ambassador Hotel in Los Angeles after pulling off an upset win in the California primary.[2]

Things weren't quite as apocalyptic in Green Bay, but Titletown, USA, was facing a reckoning of its own after coming off its three-peat Super Bowl victory that January.

Bart Starr, the Packers' first-string quarterback, was entering his 13th season, during which he would only start nine games. The average

age of the starters was 30—primeval for the times. Special teams were ranked second-last in the league. Most critically, the defense, which had consistently made up for its flagging offense, was hemorrhaging talent.[3] In the 1967 Super Bowl season, the Packers were third in the NFL in overall defense and No. 1 in pass defense.[4] Their offense was middling at best, however, placing ninth among the league's 16 franchises.[5]

On February 1, 1968, just a couple of weeks since landing the franchise's second Super Bowl trophy, Vince Lombardi dropped a bombshell that could be felt across professional football. Not since Curly Lambeau's decision to leave the club he birthed 31 years earlier, had the ground shudder beneath football fans in general, Packers fans in particular. Lombardi would announce that he was stepping back from coaching the team—one secret in life is knowing when to leave. In Lombardi's case he had accomplished as much as any single individual in his position. Plus, he didn't want to follow the tortured path his rival traveled. And the Packers weren't Lombardi's baby. To be sure he made his bones as head coach of Green Bay and in turn solidified the club in football lore for generations to come. On the other hand, his decision-making process tracked Lambeau's in that the Lombardi sought ownership stake in the club which was dismissed out of hand.[6] It was now only a matter before The Pope cut ties.

While Lombardi would hang on as general manager for the 1968 season, he devolved into a crazy uncle of sorts, armchairing games from the press box. In the end, it proved too painful for the old man to watch his team pile up loss after loss, finishing the year with a disappointing 6–7–1 record, the first losing season since the infamous Scooter McLean year. On February 6, 1969, the Packers agreed to release Lombardi from his contract. Tears hadn't welled up in too many eyes, and it wasn't due to a dry winter day. In fact, some corners of Packer Nation seemed relieved. "So the Green Bay Packers have lost a general manager…and gained a coach," wrote longtime *Press-Gazette* reporter and columnist Len Wagner. "And thus the releasing of Vince Lombardi can optimistically be looked at as blessing in disguise." Nor more "looking over the shoulder" of coach Bengtson, as Lombardi said in a letter to the team's board of directors in the third person. "Losing him now is not nearly as much of a loss," Wagner continued.[7]

Lombardi then signed on with the Washington Redskins as coach, general manager, and part-owner and did yeoman's work in his first season in 1969, leading the team to a 7–5–2 record, their first winning season in 14 years.[8] But it would fall to someone else to build a dynasty in the nation's capital. Lombardi was diagnosed with terminal colon cancer in early June 1970. When Bart Starr visited his old coach, the great Lombardi lay wasting away on a bed at Georgetown University Hospital. Although he would not suffer alone—far from it. A parade of well-wishers streamed in to visit the coaching legend including fellow coaches, players, broadcasters, owners, fans, and dignitaries. Richard Nixon, who had ascended to the presidency the year before, phoned in his good wishes.

On September 3, 1970, one of the greatest coaches of all time passed away. Vincent Thomas Lombardi was just 57 years old. Starr, along with former players Willie Davis, Paul Hornung, and Tony Canadeo served as pallbearers. A retinue of NFL royalty joined them at New York's St. Patrick Cathedral, where 3,000 gathered to mourn this terrible loss. Another 3,000 well-wishers lined the motorcade route to Mount Olivet Cemetery in Middletown Township, New Jersey where he was buried.[9] Encomiums poured in around the world. In Wisconsin, fans took it hard, no doubt. Indeed, The Pope was only two years removed from his tenure in Titletown. "It is a gray day in Green Bay, Wisconsin, a city which shouted itself hoarse for the teams of Vince Lombardi," intoned radio host Paul Harvey at the start of his daily editorial on September 3, 1970, seemingly overlooking the fact his subject was coaching a different team at the time of his demise. In Green Bay, it must have felt like the Packers were losing their identity with the sudden loss of two giants, Lombardi and Curly Lambeau just five years earlier. No doubt some tears were not those of happiness for a life well-lived nor sadness for one who was cut down all too early in life at age 57. Rather, a different kind of sadness hung like a pall over the city as if a new era was on the horizon. Green Bay had lost an icon; and they had lost their way.

Of course, after five championships and sterling 96–34–6 regular season record, Lombardi had left his legacy intact.[10] But there was one blemish: hiring Phil Bengtson. Despite the swiftness in which Lombardi had appointed as successor his former defensive coordinator, for whom he expressed high praise and confidence, he did have second thoughts.

"[Lombardi] had misgivings about Phil. But he was almost stuck with elevating him," recalled former player personnel director Pat Peppler 35 years later as if Bengtson was a default successor.[11] Many more, however, gave Bengtson the benefit of the doubt. The '68 roster had not been replenished with equal or greater talent, and the club had continued to rely on some of the old horses like Bart Starr, Bob Skoronski, and Forrest Gregg, who had a combined 36 years of service. Seven starters had played at least 10 years in Green Bay.[12] "[Lombardi] knew. The Packers were dead," tight end Gary Knafelc (1954-62) told David Maraniss in *When Pride Still Mattered.*[13]

Regardless of Bengtson's flaws, it's hard to imagine the Packers executive committee saying no to Lombardi's recommendation. It quickly became clear, however, that Bengtson was not up for the job, posting a losing record in his first year the worst in 10 seasons—no wonder Lombardi was pulling his hair out in the press box. Save for some solid defenses and effective special teams they wouldn't get much traction elsewhere. By 1970, the inaugural year of the AFL-NFL merger, Green Bay had posted one of the league's worst offenses (24th), sat dead last in kicking and punting (26th), and struggled at 19th in defense overall.[14] Off the field, matters were worse. In October 1969, Bengtson raided a local hangout when he suspected players broke curfew.[15] He was right, but the coach had crossed a line by intruding on the players' private lives. Crucial player-coach trust evaporated into pillows of cigarette and cigar smoke hanging over the party. Respect and professionalism were equally ill-fated.

And then there was his own love of alcohol.

"I remember going to out-of-town games and the poor guy was up all night drinking," said former *Milwaukee Sentinel* reporter Bud Lea in the team documentary *Legacy*. "He'd show up the next morning unshaven, smoking like crazy."[16] Back home, it wasn't much better. According to Christl, citing linebacker Jim Carter (1970–75, 77–78)[17] as well as others, Bengtson would show up to team meetings drunk.[18]

The Bengtson years harkened back to another set of dark days, the 1950s, when the team hung on to has-beens and never-would-bes for far too long. Scooter McLean, the denouement of that decade's wreckage, was the biggest coaching debacle. Then there was the team's board of directors, rank amateurs who didn't know what they didn't know. "None of them [were] football people," front office administrator and future franchise chairman Bob Harlan said in *Legacy*. "It's like asking somebody who runs a hardware store to go run a hospital."

The board allowed Bengtson to bungle the operation for three seasons, from 1968 to 1970. This would prove to be only one of many of the board's sins as the team closed out the decade.

Between 1969 and 1970, Packers president Dominic Olejniczak and the board missed out or lucked out on not one but *three* opportunities to land generational head coaches. First, they passed on Don Shula after he left the Colts in 1969. Shula, who still holds the all-time NFL coaching win record with 347, was ready to accept an offer to coach the Packers. "I understand I was being considered; why wasn't I picked?" he reportedly asked the wife of Packers vice president Dick Bourguignon.[19]

Next up was future Hall of Famer George Allen, who showed serious interest in the Packers job, and at one point was the team's first choice for the top job according to longtime Allen assistant Joe Sullivan. Penn State legend Joe Paterno was also in contention and would have accepted an offer. In the end, the team went with the president's first choice, University of Missouri head coach Dan Devine.[20] The hire would set the Green and Gold back a couple of decades before they would bring home the Lombardi Trophy again.

Passing on three top-tier coaches for someone who ran a second-rate college program remains not just a catastrophe but a cautionary tale on a glaring downside of a community-owned and *operated* club. Without a Jack Vainisi or a legit personnel director in the front office, nor a strong president willing and able to override a coffee klatch of armchair local businessmen, politicians, and old-timers, the team would suffer a setback that would take more than 20 years to correct. An entire generation! This is what happens when the right incentives are not aligned at the right time. With flagging leadership and no one individual or group with a financial stake in the franchise, it was easy to allow dysfunction and mediocrity persist. This is why the Packers of late have sustained success for so long: quality leaders in important decision-making positions for long tenures. Former president Mark Murphy helmed the franchise for 17 years (2008–2025); before him, Bob Harlan held the presidency and/or chairmanship for 19 (1989–2008)—both were experienced football executives, with Murphy also a former player and union representative. The Packers have benefited from solid, long-tenured coaches (five) and have boasted remarkably low quarterback turnover—just three primary starters since 1992. Continuity, consistency, and quality cannot be stressed enough. The previous three presidents which covered a similar length of time, 36 years, included a judge, realtor and car dealer. And while there were no doubt good teams in that time period, those presidents posted records of .317 (Russ Bogda [1953–57], .524 (Dominic Olejniczak [1958–81]), and .406 (Robert J. Parins [1982–88]),[21] Between 1992 and 2024—under full-time, professional presidents—Green Bay held a .631 overall record.[22] As Harlan told me, "You can't bring in someone from a hardware store when you're in the hospital business. You can't bring a good insurance man to run a football team. You're not qualified."

Devine was an unmitigated disaster, arguably worse than McLean, who only coached one season and thereby minimized long-term damage to the club. With the single exception of hiring an unknown Major League Baseball public relations executive in 1971, who would become the Packers future chairman and president, Devine's tenure was distinguished by a series of bad coaching *and* life choices.

One of Devine's specialties was pulling off impolitic practical jokes that ended in thuds—literally. At practice, he once dared defensive back Doug Hart to spin around ten times and then try to kick the ball. Hart fell, and the team laughed…sort of. More crucially, Devine lacked much technical expertise in the game. He leaned heavily on assistants, most of whom he'd brought along from his old college coaching days. In that regard, Devine was the opposite of Bengtson, who was "more of an X and O guy," said former Packers public relations director Chuck Lane, referring to Bengtson's penchant for absorbing himself in the nitty-gritty details of play calling. Devine also made the absurd claim he had invented Vince Lombardi's signature sweep play.

Devine was just lazy—and plain weird. He pretended to watch game film, but when staff caught on to the lark, they rigged film cases with stubbed toothpicks, which never fell out and proved that the film went unused. Devine would also sneak out of the office in a rental car to eat sandwiches and drink champagne in a Howard Johnson room by himself.[23] (This was the guy who kept Joe Montana on the bench at Notre Dame because the future Hall of Famer "rubbed him the wrong way."[24])

Two bad omens early in his first season portended Devine's rough tenure. First, in his inaugural game with the Packers, not only did he fail his freshmen initiation by losing to the Bears in a preseason matchup, but he dropped the game by a rare score of 2–0. (Only five regular seasons games in NFL history have ended 2–0.)[25] Then, in the first regular season game, Devine's squad gave up a close one to the visiting Giants. In the fourth quarter, while Green Bay was storming back, safety Doug Hart intercepted Fran Tarkenton, who was then knocked out of bounds by Giants guard Bob Hyland, a former Packers player. The latter lost his balance and tumbled into an unsuspecting Devine, who sustained a double fracture to his left leg. The coach was whisked away to St. Vincent Hospital for emergency surgery.[26] In the meantime, the Packers failed to close the gap and lost 42–40—the first of eight losses in Devine's forgettable 4–8–2 debut season.

The Devine era, from 1971 to 1974, had one bright spot. While they posted losing records in 1973 and 1974, Devine took the squad to the playoffs in 1972, losing in the first round to George Allen's Redskins. (It took Washington just three post-Lombardi seasons to reach the Super Bowl). The remainder of the postseason left a bitter taste in fans' mouths and would be remembered as the year that two Packers coaching prospects—Shula and Allen—matched up in the Super Bowl. The Miami Dolphins would prevail, claiming the first-ever undefeated regular season and playoffs in NFL history, a record that still stands today.

In the summer of 1974, more than a year after the last American GI left South Vietnam,[27] striking NFL players at the annual Hall of Fame Game in Canton, Ohio, expressed their grievances to owners. The theme: "No Freedom, No Football." Their beef: the hated "Rozelle Rule," which limited player free agency by adding another hurdle to the process, requiring the acquiring team to compensate the other franchise for the loss of a player albeit at the discretion of the commissioner, hence "[Pete] Rozelle," the NFL commissioner at the time. *Sports Illustrated* characterized the atmosphere as "strange" and "funky." Indeed, former Packers center Bill Curry (1965–66), who started in Super Bowl I and led the strike as union president, said, "It was the '70s, after all."[28]

In Green Bay, veteran players picketed practice at a preseason Bears game. Always sticklers for enforcing the law (except during Prohibition), Green Bay police nabbed striking players for trespassing on Packers property. Arrested players tossed into a paddy wagon recalled images of Haymarket and other labor unrest flashpoints in late 19th century Chicago, though instead of cries of solidarity, playful smiles and understanding cops with just-doing-my-job defenses kept matters peaceful.[29]

On August 10, one day after President Nixon left the White House under the dark cloud of the Watergate scandal and looming impeachment, NFL players returned to work.[30] They had lost the strike. Too many veterans crossed the picket line, fans largely sided with owners, and NFL alumni looked askance at union tactics. None of the union's 63 demands were agreed to, and players would go without a collective bargaining agreement for the next few seasons. Despite these setbacks, the '74 strike would be a steppingstone to future labor victories.[31]

Before the year was out, Devine would commit one more blunder, this one proving fatal. This capstone pratfall would go down as *the* worst trade in team history and a doozy in the annals of bad NFL transactions.

True to form, Devine ignored professional advice and went behind scout Bill Tobin's back to land quarterback John Hadl from the Los Angeles Rams. In exchange for two first-round draft picks, two second-rounders, and a third-round selection, he got a 34-year-old balding gunslinger with a history of championship success with the AFL's San Diego Chargers but well beyond his prime. "He couldn't throw a ball out of a phone booth," recalled Chuck Lane in *Legacy*. "His arm was shot."[32]

Hadl put up a dismal 54.0 passer rating in his first year with the Packers and 52.8 in his second and final season in Green Bay, logging a grand total of 7 wins in 19 starts. (Hadl's salary was never publicly released, sparing the team further embarrassment.) Meanwhile, the Rams would dominate their division for the rest of the decade, making the Super Bowl in the 1979 season.[33]

Tobin was shunted aside in early 1975 after losing out on a bid for general manager. But he'd have the last laugh. The Bears wisely picked him up and the prodigy proceeded to build a championship franchise in Chicago, nabbing the all-time great running back Walter Payton and constructing one of the most explosive defenses of the 1980s—all while stymieing his old team. The Packers lost 24 times while Tobin worked in the Bears front office, first as director of scouting and ultimately as vice president and de facto general manager.[34]

Thanks to the *Press-Gazette* and its editor George Calhoun, a franchise cofounder, the Packers had been getting free press for more than half a century. Had it not been for Calhoun and his daily columns, the team likely would have been stillborn. Local news dailies had a near monopoly in those days, especially in a small city like Green Bay, making the *Press-Gazette* the paper of record.[35] For decades Calhoun's paper would beat the Packers drum every week, beginning on Monday with news updates, inside gossip, and opinions that build to a crescendo by Sunday morning, when fired up fans would flock to Hagemeister Park in the afternoons, tossing whatever change they had left over from their church tithe into Calhoun's hat.

But it was now the 1970s and well past the moment to get with the times. The national body politic had been convulsing through Watergate after *Washington Post* Metro reporter Bob Woodward and colleague Carl Bernstein exposed President Nixon's role in covering up the 1972 break-in at the Democratic National Committee in Washington, DC. Faith in public institutions had crumbled, congressional approval ratings had fallen. General skepticism, compounded by the country's recent ignominious exit from Vietnam, became contagious. By summer's end, Nixon had resigned, Woodward and Bernstein were American heroes, and journalism school enrollment had skyrocketed. For the Packers, the timing could not have been worse.

Longtime reporter Lee Remmel departed the paper in March 1974 to head up the Packers' public relations, opening the door to Cliff Christl, a hungry young reporter who would cover the team for about 36 years, first for the *Press-Gazette*, and later for the *Milwaukee Journal* and *Milwaukee Journal Sentinel*.[36] "This was the beginning of the contemporary coverage of the Green Bay Packers," explained former *Press-Gazette* reporter Jeff Ash in *Legacy*.

Other than the shimmer of an embedded ear stud in his left lobe, Cliff Christl looks all the part of a crusty, seasoned journalist. His pursed lips with dead-on stare that could coax a confession out of a killer—or an underperforming quarterback—signals all business to his targets. One measure journalist-skeptic and five parts sports-savant, few denizens of Packer Nation or figures in team history know more about the franchise than Christl. If his reams of news coverage of the Green and Gold over a nearly 36-year journalism career[37] and countless essays and Q-and-As as team historian were not enough, he authored a four-volume encyclopedia set of the franchise and served as a central interview subject for the team's centennial ten-part documentary *Legacy*.

"Cliff was a young, aggressive reporter who knew his stuff, who wasn't afraid to ask hard questions, who wasn't afraid to ask questions that nobody wanted to answer," Ash described the reporter's early years to me. "Cliff took a harder edge, a kind of straight journalism approach…in a way that the old-time reporters that Lee [Remmel] and Art Daley were not."[38]

This was also the time the team's sorry situation, with deep dysfunction both on and off the field, came to light. Was it just the awful truth that the Packers had hit their nadir (so far)? Or was the team being covered differently and more critically—and accurately? Or was it a function of downbeat times in both Packer Nation and the country itself?

By the end of the 1974 season, the team had devolved into warring factions fueled by drunken outbursts and fisticuffs, bonuses and payouts to favorite players and coaches without disclosing the transactions,[39] and a near boycott that unfolded at Austin Straubel Field on December 14. Players had talked up skipping the team charter to Atlanta for the last game of the season. According to team trainer Domenic Gentile, "Several players were actually going to skip the team flight to Atlanta and force the Packers to forfeit."[40] In the end, everyone made the flight. The game proceeded as usual, with the Packers handing the helpless Falcons just their third win of the season.[41] Devine resigned from the team that evening to take over as head coach at Notre Dame. He had finally gotten the message. A few years earlier, Devine's farmer-neighbor in rural Oneida shot (and killed) Devine's dog. Just as his pooch had wandered across the fence line upsetting chickens one too many times, so too did Devine overstay his welcome in Green Bay—though the now-former coach escaped relatively unscathed.[42]

If Bengtson's hiring had been an attempt to extend the Lombardi era, then Bart Starr's selection as the team's eighth head coach—the fourth within a decade—was a return to Camelot.[43] "A favorite son to come home to be our coach," was how *Press-Gazette* reporter Jeff Ash put it to me.[44]

A major expectation of the Packers' new leader would be to repair the damage that the team had done to its own brand and to Green Bay itself. In his quest to turn the team around, however, Starr was disadvantaged in three ways. First, he was inheriting a franchise that had fallen from grace having bled talent, a reputation tarnished, and prestige, lost; second, he had no head coaching experience; and third, quarterbacks turned head coaches had terrible track records. Starr's hiring felt like the Packers had once again listened to their heart and not their head.

Starr's first press conference didn't inspire a lot of confidence.

"I'm not as qualified as I'd like to be, but I'm willing," he told the assembled media on Christmas Eve, 1974.[45] Lombardi, 16 years earlier, had used the same occasion to set a much different tone: "I've never been associated with a loser and I don't expect to be now." But the people were in a joyous mood in welcoming back their old hero and new leader. The *Press Gazette* daily Bible quote on the page opposite of Starr's news coverage with the Prayer of St. Francis of Assisi, a favorite of the local Catholic faithful, read, "Lord make me an instrument of thy peace…where there is despair, hope; where there is darkness, light; where there is sadness, joy."[46] Few prayers or bible verses could capture the prevailing sense of hope in Green Bay, despite a truly awful year.

Contemporaneous accounts suggested Packers president Dominic Olejniczak and the board had no choice but to hire Starr. "There was no stopping the groundswell," said Christl in *The Greatest Story in Sports*.[47] This was the man who delivered five league championships and two Super Bowl victories to Green Bay under a master head coach's tutelage.

Starr's nine-year tenure would prove to be a painful example of how the team badly needed a disciplined, professional front office. Future general manager Ted Thompson (2005–17) comes to mind. Thompson stood firm against the popular tide in 2008, refusing to bring back a recently retired and diminished Brett Favre. Thompson prevailed upon his contemporaries and within three seasons returned the Lombardi Trophy to its rightful home.

Bob Harlan knew his old boss Bart Starr was out of his depth. "He just was so raw in the position; he probably got the job too early," Harlan recalled in a 2019 interview with ESPN.com.[48] *Press-Gazette* reporter and columnist Tony Walter seemed to agree: "There was the general feeling that the Packers threw him into that situation sooner than they should have."[49]

The coach himself would later concur. "The greatest mistake I made in my life was to coach," Starr would say later in his life.[50] For a man known and respected for his humility and selflessness, taking a head coaching position before he was ready was a puzzling decision. Starr nevertheless soldiered on as something between a white knight and a neophyte.

Green Bay would finish out the decade with losing records in four of the next five seasons.

On the plus side, the Packers were gaining financial ground. The federal antitrust exemptions that Commissioner Rozelle had successfully lobbied Congress for in 1961 allowed the teams to negotiate national broadcast rights collectively and split the proceeds among franchises accordingly. This law would bear much fruit. Instead of cutting up proceeds from the Green Bay and Milwaukee markets only—two of the smallest in the league—they were partaking in a bonanza of broadcast revenue from the largest markets in the country: New York, Los Angeles, Chicago, Houston, Miami. The Packers weren't just making more money; they were now getting paid New York prices!

Packers president Dominic Olejniczak worked closely with Rozelle and NFL officials to keep the rules intact. Olejniczak also banned no-cut contracts, in which Devine had indulged. Devine's final years were the fiscal low ebb of the club with a $128,425 operating income. In Starr's first season as head coach, finances rebounded and operating income shot up to $784,803, largely due to eliminating Devine's salary giveaways.[51]

The Pack posted a miserable 4–10 record in 1975, the worst since the infamous Scooter McLean year. Starr responded by putting quarterback John Hadl on a one-way flight to Houston along with Pro Bowl safety Ken Ellis and two draft picks—fourth (1976) and third (1977), since they'd already surrendered their top-round picks in the coming 1976 draft to Los Angeles in 1974. In return, the Packers landed 26-year-old former Kansas State standout quarterback Lynn Dickey.

Just as Packers fans had placed all their hopes and dreams on their old quarterback of Ice Bowl fame, so too did Starr pin his hopes on Dickey. It was a puzzling assessment, and it would turn out to be costly decision. Dickey had a "first-round arm" according to Christl, despite going in the third round of the 1971 draft, but a "crippling" left hip and socket injury had knocked the gunslinger out of the Oilers' 1972 season.[52] The severity of this type of injury cannot be overstated; it's one of the more severe a quarterback (or any player) could experience and has been a career-ender for many. But even if Starr discounted the bum hip, there were still three post-injury seasons to evaluate Dickey—none of which stood out, save for the red flags.

Why hadn't the Packers heeded this obvious warning? Were the NFL ranks so depleted of quality quarterbacks? Or was this yet another bad front office decision?

At least he had good looks. At his introductory press conference Dickey appeared like a dream boat. With tinted aviators and a leather jacket over a fashionable butterfly collar, he could have passed as Greg Brady's Johnny Bravo in *The Brady Bunch* or as country singer Mac Davis. Coach Starr sat next to him like an old high school coach welcoming home a local boy done good. Just as Starr would call Green Bay home, so too would Dickey.[53]

"[A] fine student of the game with size, strength, agility, and poise—all the qualities we think it takes to make a good quarterback," Starr told the assembled press corps.[54] Yet the coach seemed to gloss over Dickey's recent season-ending injury, nor put a lot of stock into his middling stats. Over four playing seasons with the Oilers, Dickey threw for 1,953 yards and completed 155 passes in 294 attempts, with only eight touchdowns against a jaw-dropping 28 interceptions—a 43.18 passer rating, lower than Hadl's rating with the Packers. Starr didn't need sabermetrics to make a good prediction on Dickey as a prospect—a pocket calculator would've done just fine.[55]

Still, Dickey would have his moments, living up to a portion of the hype heaped on him upon his arrival in Green Bay.

"He was the most accurate deep thrower I've ever seen," said former Packers center and team captain Larry McCarren in *Legacy*. McCarren's compliment was no throwaway line. McCarren worked as a color analyst for the Packers radio network when Brett Favre took snaps under center, hitting wide receiver Sterling Sharpe over and over in tight corners of the end zone. Future Hall of Famer James Lofton would agree. "There were things [Lynn] could do with a ball that were kind of like what Magic Johnson could do on a fast break," said Lofton, who considered Dickey the best quarterback he ever played with.[56] As for Dickey's penchant for tossing interceptions, McCarren seemed dismissive. "That's just the price you paid to have that kind of quarterback," he said.[57]

Despite assurances from the patient himself—"he says [the injury] is totally healed now," the *Milwaukee Sentinel* reported on April 3, 1975—Dickey's body would eventually give out. That day came two seasons later on November 13, 1977.

At Milwaukee County Stadium, trailing by 18 points with 17 seconds remaining in the game against the Los Angeles Rams, one of the toughest defenses in the league,[58] Dickey was hit hard in the pocket and fell to the ground. As time expired, the quarterback lay crumpled and motionless at midfield with a torrent of boos raining down on him after a dismal performance that day. He had sustained a double fracture in his lower leg and would miss the rest of the season.[59] Starr's decision to leave a vulnerable Dickey in the game, well after it was lost, would haunt him for the rest of his coaching days.

When the cast was sawed off the following spring, Dickey still felt shooting pain in his leg. He went for a second opinion and learned that his surgery from the previous fall had been botched, leaving his fibula and tibia still broken.[60] He would miss the entire 1978 campaign, despite a follow-up surgery to correct the first. Dickey would miss 44 games in his 10 seasons as a Packer, playing only three complete seasons, including the nine-game strike season in 1982.[61]

The 1970s would end the same way it began: with a big, missed opportunity. The Packers had fielded 18 different quarterbacks (including 14 different starters) over the decade, and just as Olejniczak passed on hiring Hall of Fame coaches like Shula, Allen, and Paterno, Starr would miss out on another golden prospect. This time, however, it would happen despite pleas from the front office, who had since learned their lesson. Inside the Packers draft room at the Waldorf Astoria Hotel in New York City on May 3, 1979, long-time scout Red Cochran was ringing the five-alarm bell. On the board was a can't-miss player who could revolutionize the Green and Gold and perhaps return the Lombardi Trophy to its rightful home. But no one was listening.

The moment was soon lost.

The Packers had just passed on Joe Montana.[62]

Chapter 8

Darkest Before Dawn

It wasn't easy being a Packers fan in the '80s.

Like the biblical Job tested by the Devil, Packers fans withstood the football gods' every taunt and temptation: draft busts, injuries, scandals, playoff droughts. Nevertheless, Green Bay never lost its faith in the team. Games remained sold out, the season ticket line still stretched out years, and folks planned their summer vacations around preseason mini-camps.

In some respects, the Packers faithful had it harder than the biblical figures and prophets whose trials lasted days or weeks, not years. Despite all the championships and legendary games of yore, the Packers had also suffered some truly dark days, and the '80s weren't without precedent. Recall the 1922 do-or-die Thanksgiving matchup with the Duluth Kelleys, where nothing less than the future of the franchise rode on the outcome. Or the third stock issuance in the wake of Curly Lambeau's departure in 1950, which forced the team to grow up fast or drift into irrelevance. In both cases, the struggles were worth the pain; the former led to an established NFL franchise in a still-fledgling league, while the latter offered sound financial footing to rebuild in a new era in the 1950s.

For fans in the 1980s, however, this brand of losing felt totally different. There were no signs of hope. The '80s teams were characterized by the bad, the ugly, and the uglier. There were "flagrant misdeeds on the field—and repellent ones off of it," as Packers historian Cliff Christl put it including a Packers defensive lineman body slamming a helpless quarterback long after a play was called dead; and an alleged sexual assault committed by another player a few weeks later. Such regrettable behavior combined to give the team a black eye and the city a reputation that would take years to repair.[1] Disappointingly, they occurred on the watch of, and were sometimes condoned by, the giants of the Lombardi era: Bart Starr, Forrest Gregg, and team president Dominic Olejniczak, among others. The franchise's bad habits didn't change, either, and committee members displayed breathtaking degrees of unprofessionalism. Personnel were held on for too long because "it was hard to fire your neighbor," as then attorney John Zuidmulder put it in Frank Deford's 1987 hit-job in *Sports Illustrated*;[2] or the executive committee couldn't come up with a better plan.[3] Bar softball leagues were run with better business acumen and ethics than the Packers of the 1980s.

The culprit?

The team simply couldn't move on from the Lombardi era. Three coaches and players from that time—Phil Bengtson, Bart Starr, and Forrest Gregg—had led the team 16 of the past 19 seasons (1968-87). Despite their success as Lombardi assistants, the three underwhelming coaches compiled a miserable 97–134–5 record (1968–70; 1975–87). They also left no mark with the talent they drafted and tried to develop. While 13 future NFL Hall of Famers played under Lombardi, just three donned the Green and Gold in the '80s.[4]

Before quarterback Lynn Dickey even took his first snap in the 1980 preseason, things were off to a bad start, foreshadowing a tough year in Green Bay. The new decade portended yet another dark era.

While the front office had learned lessons from past trades gone awry (like double-checking the health of a new player), they still managed to make wrong calls in fresh and creative ways. For the 1980 draft, the team selected defensive end Bruce Clark from Penn State with the fourth overall pick. The 1979 consensus All-American passed his physical check-up—and then passed on Green Bay, signing with the Canadian Football League's Toronto Argonauts.[5] Clark told Starr and his staff in advance he would not suit up for the team.[6] The official reason: he didn't want to move to middle guard.[7] Unofficially: the Packers were losers, Clark said two years later, when he had had enough of losing in Toronto's punishing winters and decided to join the NFL.[8] And so, the Packers would begin the 1980 season without a first-round pick and having failed to fill their biggest hole: the defensive line. Green Bay had the worst run defense in 1979, and they had missed their chance in the draft to make a big improvement.[9]

If there was one game that epitomized the Packers of the 1980s, it was an otherwise forgettable preseason matchup with the Denver Broncos on August 30, 1980.

The preseason had gotten off to an inauspicious start when they tied the San Diego Chargers 0–0 on August 2, proving there were fates nearly as bad as losing to an opponent 2–0 (as Dan Devine did in his first season in 1971). The Pack then came into the annual Bishop's Charities game having lost three in a row. (This exhibition match was established in 1961 as a benefit for favorite causes of the local Catholic diocese.[10])

Outside Lambeau Field for the Packers–Broncos matchup on a brisk though refreshing late summer evening after a punishingly hot August,[11] unwashed masses covered a sea of asphalt dotted with Weber grills, swirling plumes of charcoal smoke, and coolers loaded up with beer and Brandy Old Fashioned mix—a tailgating tradition that dated back decades. "Each year, legions of Packer zealots make an annual trip to Lambeau Field that is akin to a Christian's pilgrimage to Jerusalem," wrote Don Langenkamp of the *Press-Gazette*. Preseason games tended to attract more unruly fans because tickets were more available (and affordable) and were played at night. Even with the late kickoff time, tailgaters would assemble as early as 9:30 AM and stay until the small hours the following morning. (Some things don't change.)[12]

Though 1980 would be Lynn Dickey's first season at full health starting every game, the inaugural preseason home game left much to be desired. Denver drew first blood in the first half with two touchdowns after a pair of Dickey interceptions, followed by a third TD from generous field position after a 14-yard punt by David Beverly. (Beverly would go on to post the league's second-worst yards-per-punt average of the regular season.)[13] Green Bay's run offense combined for just four yards.

The second half was more of the same. Denver twice punched it into the end zone and the Broncos' Fred Steinfort nailed a 44-yarder early in the third quarter. Denver racked up just south of 400 offensive yards and 97 return yards off seven punts. The Packers lost 38–0 and went winless in the preseason for the first time in 26 years.

"Boo birds" had flocked to Packers games in the past. Disappointed fans were known to channel the foul temperament of their rowdier football cousins in Philadelphia and elsewhere, and some even chucked beer cans and whiskey bottles at players on at least one occasion.[14] But the Bishop's Charities game was anything but charitable. Fans let their team know exactly how they felt. On a Broncos pick-six late in the fourth quarter, Packers fans actually cheered, then reverted to booing when the play was overturned on a penalty. This level of scorn was a first for Starr, whose tenure as a player and coach spanned four decades.[15]

It seemed as if the players had all but given up, as well. Defensive end Ezra Johnson was caught eating a hot dog on the sideline between possessions. He was fined and later apologized. That was apparently good enough for Starr, but not so for defensive coordinator Fred von Appen, who was aghast as his head coach's leniency and resigned over the incident.[16]

Distraught fans filed back into the stadium a week later for the regular season opener against the Bears, filling 54,381 seats, ready to give their team another chance. At least for one brief moment of glory that year, they would not be disappointed.

After finishing regulation tied 6–6, the Packers found themselves in field goal range on the second series of overtime, thrusting kicker Chester Marcol into the spotlight. Marcol, who made just 40 percent of his field goal attempts in 1979, didn't exactly inspire confidence, even on a makeable 34-yard attempt. When the former Pro Bowler booted the ball, it smashed into the facemask of defensive lineman and former longtime Viking Alan Page, then bounced back into Marcol's waiting arms. The kicker, who could easily be mistaken for Buddy Holly with a football helmet, tucked the pigskin under his stubby arms and zipped 25 yards for the touchdown.

Packers win 12–6 in a wild overtime thriller.[17]

It would be the highlight of a season that ended with a 5–10–1 record and a tie for last place in the division with the lowly Tampa Bay Buccaneers.

Christmas in 1980 was anything but a joyous holiday season. American hostages were still locked away at the occupied US embassy in Iran, a sitting president had lost reelection for the first time since the Great Depression, and the country was struggling through another winter energy crisis. In Green Bay, the dismal national mood may have contributed to the Packers reaching a breaking point.

Two days after Christmas, the executive committee called a meeting to discuss Bart Starr's fate. Inside the gathering, matters went quickly south.[18] In the end, the committee chose a half measure, stripping Starr of his general manager title while keeping him on at head coach and failing to resolve the team's underlying problems—and perhaps creating more. Christl called it the "worst possible [choice]" and "an unworkable situation."[19] After missing Joe Montana in the 1979 draft and losing out on their first-round draft pick for 1980, sticking with a proven loser at head coach made little sense. "They were throwing the organization away," explained Bob Harlan, who, despite holding a junior position in the front office at the time, had a front row seat to the 1970s and '80s debacles.[20]

Two mediocre seasons later, it seemed the Packers might actually catch a break. After winning the first two games of the 1982 season, including a *Monday Night Football* matchup against their old rivals, the Giants, NFL players went on strike. While the strike caused fissures in most teams, the Packers rallied and hung together for the duration of the work stoppage, practicing and conditioning at nearby St. Norbert College. When it finally ended after 57 days, the union had a new collective bargaining agreement with the league and the players won a few concessions, including back pay and additional medical protections.[21]

The break also allowed the Pack to rest up and prepare for a quick run to the postseason. They would finish out the truncated 1982 season at 5–3–1, making the playoffs for the first time in ten years. Facing an upstart Cardinals squad led by freshman quarterback Neil Lomax, a future Pro Bowler who the Packers passed up in the previous year's draft[22], Green Bay pounded St. Louis mercilessly, outgunning and outhustling the visitors and crushing them 41–16. The Packers had earned their first playoff win since Super Bowl II, 15 seasons earlier.

"Tear down the goal posts. Hell, tear up the field. You deserve it!" the *Press-Gazette* cheered after the victory. The win was cathartic. "It's over and so are the goal posts."[23] Fans indeed rushed the field and tore down the goal posts. A particularly excitable group hauled one of the uprights out of the stadium and dragged it along Lombardi Avenue. No doubt the old man would have had a chuckle.

The celebration would end the following week in Dallas. Despite putting up an admirable fight and coming within a touchdown of taking the lead in the fourth quarter, the Pack succumbed to the Cowboys 37–26. True to form, Green Bay outran and outpassed their opponent with 466 total yards but turned the ball over five times, including three interceptions by the untamable Lynn Dickey. Packers center Larry McCarren was right: "It's the price you pay with the kind of quarterback you have."[24]

Starr's final season in 1983 would be a roller coaster, one that featured a record five overtime games and peaked with a classic against the reigning Super Bowl–champion Washington Redskins on a Monday night, October 17. Not quite the Miracle on Ice just three years earlier, yet this ABC special still felt like there was more riding on the game than let on. The world Doomsday Clock was ticking closer to midnight. Within a week terrorists would bomb a Marines barracks in Lebanon, killing 241 US service members, followed by a US invasion of the tiny Caribbean

Island nation of Grenada.[25] The Cold War had cooled to a deep chill, as did the brisk air on this late autumn showdown in Green Bay.

The Redskins rode into Green Bay having written off the Packers long before they arrived. "The game will be a rout," taunted longtime Washington tight end Don Warren. (Warren would go on to make just four receptions and score no touchdowns despite the highest-scoring Monday tilt at the time.)

"'Warren thinks it's going to be a rout, but he never said which way,'" Dickey recalled Bart Starr saying in his pregame pep talk. "'Now let's go kick some ass!'"[26]

It was off to the races.

"[Offensive coordinator Bob] Schnelker is unloading the playbook… we are going for the throat, everything we got we're laying out on the Redskins," recalled Dickey in the team's centennial documentary *Legacy*.[27]

The assistant coach did not disappoint. Green Bay's offense proceeded to run the Washington defense ragged as Dickey passed for 387 yards and three touchdowns. The gunslinger commanded the squad as surely and efficiently as he managed the clock, although the quick strikes on offense were exhausting his own defense, who were on the field for almost 40 minutes of game time.[28]

It all came down to Washington kicker Mark Moseley, whose 39-yard attempt with three seconds left in regulation was long enough but not straight. It was as if the capacity crowd of 55,255 at Lambeau Field willed the kick left for the miss. Final score: 48–47, Green Bay.

"I'm going to remember tonight for a long time and so will all those people who watched us," said receiver John Jefferson. His prediction withstood the test of time. (The ecstatic though exhausted eight-year-old version of this author would agree.)[29] Meanwhile, up in the ABC booth, color commentator and former Cowboys quarterback Don Meredith, who had suffered defeat at the hands of Starr in the Ice Bowl, serenaded his old rival's squad. "Turn out the lights, the party's over…"[30]

When the hoopla settled down after the conclusion of the 8–8 season, Judge Robert J. Parins—who had been elected president of the team's executive committee in 1982—unceremoniously dumped Bart Starr. The coach and former Lombardi-era legend was informed the day after a heart-wrenching 23–21 final-game loss to the Bears. One field goal separated the Green and Gold from the playoffs—and perhaps Starr from his job.[31]

Parins acknowledged the decision was "difficult" but assured media at a hastily assembled press conference the next morning that it was "not made out of emotion or frustration, but on an overall evaluation of the needs of the franchise." Starr, who was never well equipped with situational awareness—at least as coach—was caught by surprise.[32]

After eight mediocre seasons and a .408 overall winning percentage under Starr, a change was undeniably in order.[33] Some argued that Starr may have been right on the cusp of turning around the franchise, but nine years is nine years. The losing trend and lack of player accountability was clear from early on. The team had missed several opportunities to fix coaching problems but demurred each time, and the board, skilled micromanagers that they were, had their way with the front office repeatedly, meddling in matters of all range of import. Parins was resolved to put an end to the cycle. He then worked quickly to assemble his own search committee for a new coach.

But what the firing meant to the players and fans can't be overstated. Even after more than 30 years, Dickey was still piping-hot mad about the decision. "[Parins] knew nothing about football," he said in the 2019 team documentary. Larry McCarren shared his quarterback's sentiment. "It's almost like your mom and dad firing you from the family," he said.

Packers staff saw it differently; Bob Harlan supported his boss' decision. "We had waited long enough," he said. "It had to be done. Bart did have nine years."[34]

For just the ninth time in the team's 64-year life, the Packers were on the market for a new head coach. Two Lombardi legacy hires had fallen well short of returning Super Bowl glory to Titletown. None of the three subsequent head coaches posted an overall winning record, either. But there were two pieces of good news. First, after 16 disappointing, mostly playoff-less seasons, Green Bay had had plenty of time to process what could work moving forward—and what definitely would not. Second, they were well positioned to land a top coaching prospect despite their abysmal recent track record. According to then CBS analyst John Madden, the Packers' head coaching position was one of the best available jobs in the NFL, and he was confident it would get filled in short order. "I don't think they are going to have any problems whatsoever," he told the *Press-Gazette* shortly after the Starr firing. (Madden himself was fully retired from coaching and unwilling to return to the game.)

The Packers seemed not to have been too much of a reclamation case to scare away top talent; despite a terrible defensive squad, they had an explosive offense, and any pro coach worth his salt could diagnose—and hopefully fix—the problem. Some of the names floated for the opening included former Philadelphia Eagles coach Dick Vermeil, Penn State's Joe Paterno (again), and a bumper crop of up-and-comers in the college ranks like the University of Miami's Howard Schnellenberger.[35]

But the allure of another Lombardi descendent returning Titletown to glory was still too strong for the front office to turn down. The Packers went with their former perennial All-Pro offensive tackle Forrest Gregg (1956, 1958–70). One season earlier in 1982, Gregg came within six points of winning Super Bowl XVI as the Cincinnati Bengals' head coach. He checked a big box: experience. He had four years under his belt as an assistant coach and eight as a head coach, as well as five championships and three Super Bowls as a player with the Packers (1961–62, 1965–67) and Cowboys (1971). But over the 12 coaching seasons Gregg was a hot potato, tossed among five different teams.[36]

Team president Parins was head over heels, as was the local press corps and his former team. "To a man, [Bengals players] said they will miss him," said *Press-Gazette* reporter Bob McGinn.[37]

Ignoring the clear lessons from past head coaches, Parins nevertheless agreed to Gregg's bottom line demand that he be granted "total say over all personnel matters: the draft, trades, waivers," as well as "everybody who comes on the plane: players, fans, everybody," according to director of player personnel Dick Corrick, who witnessed the negotiation. Then again, he must have become immune to the team's poor decision-making (see, again, the Joe Montana draft miss four years earlier).[38] Corrick would have to stomach it yet again when Gregg passed over quarterback Boomer Esiason in the first round for Alphonso Carreker, a defensive end from Florida State who'd blend into the scenery as another first-round bust.[39] This, despite an aged and off-and-on healthy Dickey having obviously run his course in Green Bay

But contrary to McGinn's glowing report, not every Cincinnati player fawned over Gregg, at least not publicly.

When Gregg's hiring was announced, Cincinnati quarterback Ken Anderson offered his Green Bay counterpart a tongue-in-cheek warning: "You met Forrest yet? Let me know what you think," Dickey recalled Anderson telling him.[40] The Cincy QB was onto something.

Corrick, who didn't agree with Parins giving Gregg general manager duties, suspected something was amiss, too.[41] "[Cincinnati] pulled the ploy, 'We're only going to give you 24 hours.' So that forced us to speed everything up… We either had to say yes to him without looking at anybody else or making comparisons," recalled Corrick in an oral history with the team.[42]

"Forrest tore the team apart," tight end Paul Coffman (1978–85) told me. Coffman, along with Dickey, middle linebacker Mike Douglass (1978–85), and tackle Greg Koch (1977–85), were shown the door the following season in 1985. "He basically came in and said we weren't going to be 8–8 around here anymore." Gregg was wrong. The Packers did in fact go 8–8 in his first two seasons, followed by 4–12 in 1986 and 5–9–1 in his final year as coach.[43]

In addition to losing, Gregg could be remembered for his sadistic qualities, who focused less on player development and more on beating up on his own guys. "Forrest would come in [saying], 'You stupid m—f—ers. I'm searching the waivers every day to replace your asses. You guys suck,'" Coffman recalled. "It was so negative."[44] And it was far worse for opposing players. The NFC Central had the reputation as the "black and blue" division for playing hard and taking no prisoners, but under Gregg, the Packers took it to a different level. Parins wanted someone tougher than Starr, and he got it.

Everything came to a head on November 23, 1986, when the Packers matched up with the Bears in Chicago. Following the latter's 1985 Super Bowl victory, in which they demolished the Patriots 46–10, the largest margin in Super Bowl history at the time,[45] the 9–2 Bears were riding high in the NFC.[46]

Meanwhile, the Packers were in the doldrums of another losing season. On their last visit to Chicago in 1985, they suffered a punishing loss. Defensive tackle William "The Refrigerator" Perry subbed in at fullback and stuck it to the Pack—literally and figuratively—by punching through a butter-soft Green Bay defensive line to seal a 23–7 victory. Gregg and the Packers were thoroughly embarrassed on national television on *Monday Night Football*.[47]

In the second quarter of the '86 game, Bears quarterback Jim McMahon was rolling out of the pocket to his right on third-and-10 when he threw the ball away and into the hands of Packers cornerback Mark Lee. As McMahon stopped to process his interception, Packers nose tackle Charles Martin came up behind him, scooped him up, and slammed the QB to the turf. Martin was ejected immediately, and a midfield scrum of Packers and Bears players and coaches traded verbal barbs and came close to fisticuffs.[48]

Despite the flagrant nature of the infraction—an attack on a defenseless quarterback—Gregg dismissed the foul's severity. "I don't see really why there would be a suspension," he said. Ditka and the Bears were rightfully beside themselves and continued to spar with Gregg in the media the following week. McMahon, who would miss the rest of the season because of the cheap shot, didn't hold back. "I'd hang [Martin] upside down and take turns kicking the crap out of him," he said, when asked how NFL commissioner Pete Rozelle should handle the situation. Though McMahon was recovering from a previous torn rotator cuff injury, Martin's hit set back any recovery, disabling his throwing arm completely. Martin's two-game suspension without pay was the most severe on-field penalty that Rozelle had handed down in his 25-year career.[49]

Perhaps the harshest criticism for the Packers came later in the week from Ditka: "It's interesting to me that one of the really class organizations in pro football has fallen on some hard times. Those hard times are a direct indication of the character of the people they have."[50]

And it got worse from there.

Three weeks later, All-Pro receiver James Lofton was arrested on charges of sexual assault at a local night club. "The city's image has been tarnished severely…" wrote staff writers of the *Press-Gazette* on December 19, 1986. Former player Charley Brock (1939–47) spoke for the many: "It's a disgrace to the team and the people."[51] Lofton was suspended the following week and missed the final game of a season that ended 4–12 for Green Bay. After nine seasons, it would be his last year as a Packer.[52]

It was an embarrassing and tragic pronouncement because one year earlier, on November 4, 1985, first-team All-American cornerback Mossy Cade was arrested on similar charges, though in his case for *three* counts of second-degree sexual assault.[53] Like Lofton, Cade was a standout player at his position, having gone sixth overall in the 1984 draft. Over the 13 months between the two assaults, the *Press-Gazette* had followed the Cade case like a hawk, referencing it in no fewer than 41 articles between his arrest and the Lofton arrest on December 18, 1986.[54] The two cases would soon track one another as the players went to trial at the same time across the hall in the Brown County courthouse. While the spotlight was growing brighter on the disgraced players, the Packers' reputation was growing dimmer, and the two victims were finding their lives upturned before a widening audience across the football universe. Cade would be found guilty on two of three charges; Lofton judged not guilty. Cade was sentenced to two years in prison.[55]

On May 25, 1987, *Sports Illustrated* put out an exhaustive account of the arrests and state of the team.[56] Its author, the respected and colorful Frank Deford, did not restrain himself. With his signature too-smart-to-be-a-sportswriter style, flowery prose flowed from his pen as he introduced his subject, "[Green Bay] made charming what was provincial, romantic what was obscure, quaint what was merely small."

"Don't do a hatchet job on us," former Packers center Ken Bowman turned local attorney implored Deford as he was interviewed.

Deford didn't listen.

Turns out the arrests and subsequent trials were an excuse for Deford to belittle the city by characterizing it as a bunch of hick racists who would be best served by surrendering their franchise to the city of Milwaukee or liquidating it and funneling proceeds to the University of Wisconsin–Green Bay athletic department. It was a fitting piece for a publication renowned for making awful season predictions. (The Cleveland Guardians have still not won a World Series.)

Deford even dredged up the 65-year-old story of Curly Lambeau illegally fielding college players in the 1922 season. He afforded former Packers linebacker Mike Douglass plenty of space to air out grievances. Douglass—who left the team on bad terms—claimed there was a "cottage industry in Green Bay for local girls…to set up players and blackmail them," according to Deford. The latter provided zero evidence to Douglass' sordid accusation. The scribe even threw in a few digs about the city's smelly smokestacks: "[T]here are paper mills and cargo ships and all the ugly effluences of maritime commerce."

Back in the front office, Parins finally wised up that 1986 season and hired an executive vice president to share power with Gregg. Why not? The coach had yet to record a winning season and the team had plenty of money to pay for the new role; the Packers had turned a record profit of more than $3 million in 1986.[57] Parins interviewed worthy applicants, including Los Angeles Raiders player personnel director Ron Wolf. The longtime scout and executive took himself out of consideration soon after learning he would not have complete control over team operations, a dealbreaker in his book.[58]

Wolf knew what he was talking about. Without well-defined job responsibilities, overlapping roles with Gregg, and still no structural changes to the front office, any new administrator would be at a severe disadvantage. Former Falcons personnel staffer Tom Braatz, who did not distinguish himself in a similar role with Atlanta over a 22-year career, took the reins as executive vice president on January 31, 1987.[59] His first order of business: unload Lofton, whom he quickly dealt to Wolf and the Raiders.[60]

The Packers would then drop their opening day game at Lambeau Field against those very same Raiders, whose newly acquired star receiver would receive a hero's welcome—more "cheers" than "jeers," with many fans offering a "standing ovation," according to the *Press-Gazette*. Then again, popular opinion seemed to have already turned in favor of the shamed receiver; both Bart and Cherry Starr had attended Lofton's trial as a show of solidarity the previous spring. (The prosecuting attorney was rightfully furious.[61])

The reception at Lambeau stirred up fond memories for Lofton. "It was kind of reminiscent of when Bart took the players around the stadium in appreciation for the fans," he said. "They're a really classy group."[62]

The 1987 season featured another players' strike that would last for 24 days. Like the 1974 strike, the players would return to work without any demands met, although this time only 15 percent of the players crossed the picket line compared to one in four in 1974. The solidarity would provide essential momentum for members to one day realize the elusive dream of free agency; but that day was still a few years off.[63]

Under cover of night and without even telling his assistant coaches, Forrest Gregg left his adopted hometown on January 13, 1988, less than a month after the Packers' 5–9–1 season ended. He was bound for sunnier skies and greener pastures at Southern Methodist University in Dallas.[64] Never one to follow rules, go along with a ref's decision, or accept a recent court ruling (Gregg panned the Mossy Cade verdict, saying, "I can't believe that conviction. There was no basis."[65]), Gregg seemed an appropriate candidate to resuscitate his alma mater's fall from grace. One year earlier, in February 1987, SMU suffered the NCAA's so-called "death penalty" for illegal recruitment and payments to current and prospective players. They had sat out the 1987 season and would again in 1988, Gregg's first year.[66]

Tom Braatz, the Packers' new executive vice president, took the team in a different direction. For the first time in 13 years, the club opted for a coach not from the Lombardi era. After a three-week search, Braatz offered the job to Cleveland Browns offensive coordinator Gelindo "Lindy" Infante. Braatz's first choice was Michigan State University's head coach George Perles, fresh off a win in the 1987 Big Ten championship and the Rose Bowl, who would have been a prize catch (he remained with MSU).[67] Even still, Infante looked like a good bet to rekindle the team's lost spark on offense. The Packers landed third-last in overall offense in 1987 after being one of the league's hot offensive machines under Bart Starr in 1983.[68] Infante masterminded Cleveland's Bernie Kosar–led offensive marches into the AFC championship in both 1986 and 1987.[69] It seemed like an ideal fit.

The new head coach got off to a shaky start, posting a 4–12 record in 1988 and remaining near the bottom of the league in total offense.[70]

Infante's first draft showed incredible promise when he landed future Hall of Famer Sterling Sharpe in 1988.[71] That soon proved the exception—not the rule. In 1989, the Packers flubbed the granddaddy of them all at the spring NFL draft. With the No. 2 overall pick, Green Bay had carte blanche to select any player save UCLA quarterback Troy Aikman, who was destined for Dallas at No. 1. The Packers were high on their young quarterback Don Majkowski anyway, a 10th-round pick in 1987 who had exceeded all expectations and was destined to be a starter. Braatz would not go with the best available player on the board—Oklahoma State's Heisman Trophy–winning running back Barry Sanders—when it was time for the Packers to pick. (The team hadn't yet given up on running back Brent Fullwood, who had talent despite a history of contract holdouts, fumbles, and scoring a 1 out of a possible 50 on his Wonderlic cognitive ability test.[72]) The Packers also looked past future Hall of Famers Deion Sanders and Derrick "DT" Thomas.

And so, the Packers went with Michigan State University offensive lineman Tony Mandarich.

Today, "Mandarich" is a cruel euphemism in Green Bay for poor decision-making. At the time, however, Mandarich was lauded by scouts and sports nerds alike. *Press-Gazette* sportswriter Bob McGinn called him "the most celebrated offensive lineman since…1968."[73] *Sports Illustrated* put the unanimous All-American on the front cover that April, crowning him "The Incredible Bulk," presaging yet another poor prediction. Mandarich was a George Perles acolyte at MSU and played on his 1988 Rose Bowl championship squad. For a team that respected Perles as much as Green Bay did—at least Parins and the front office, that is—it wouldn't be a bad move to grab a player from a respected college program with a good, winning culture.

Of course, there *were* warning signs—in addition to Mandarich's receding hair line and pimples, telltale signs of steroid abuse. Mandarich wouldn't travel to Green Bay ahead of the draft to meet with team officials, betraying his true feelings about the small-town team. And he publicly demanded more money than first overall pick Aikman, a no-no in rookie etiquette.[74] Meanwhile, Sanders had knocked the socks off a Packers scout with a "phenomenal workout" the previous week.[75]

Despite desperately needing a breakout draft selection, the Packers whiffed. What the team lacked was not something a lineman alone could deliver. A quarterback? Absolutely. A running back or wide receiver? Sure. Offensive tackle? Maybe not. "[Mandarich] was supposed to be a gamer changer at a non-game-changing position," said former center Larry McCarren, who had become the sports anchor for local ABC affiliate WFRV-TV in 1988.[76]

Shortly after the Mandarich pick, Judge Robert Parins called it a career and stepped down as the Packers' first full-time president. In his place he recommended promoting his chief lieutenant, Bob Harlan, to which the committee agreed in a unanimous vote.

As another lost decade wrapped up, there still felt like reason to hope. The torch had been passed not just to a new president, but to a new team showing promise. In 1989, Lindy's resurgent Packers squad managed to blunt the fallout from the Mandarich draft and claw their way back to the top of the NFC Central, along with the Vikings. They edged out favorites, survived cliffhangers which earned them the endearing sobriquet Cardiac Pack, and immortalized comebacks that would inspire future teams and honor the memories of earlier Packers eras.

After a rough start in the preseason, which included a record-low attendance of 30,218 at the Bishop's Charities game and a dismal showing at the regular season opener, in which they lost to the lowly Bucs 23–21, the Packers got their act together.[77] In front of a forgiving capacity crowd the following week, Green Bay pulled off a 35–34 squeaker against the visiting Saints after falling behind 21–0 in the first half. Quarterback Don Majkowski had the best showing for a Packers quarterback in six years. The crowd's approval at the end of regulation was deafening. Said veteran linebacker Brian Noble to the *Press-Gazette* after the game, "I have never heard this stadium rock the way it rocked. Never, never, never, never…"[78]

The highlight of the season, however, was yet another classic matchup against the Bears, this one at home on November 5, 1989. Having lost the last eight games against their longtime rival, the Packers were hungry for a win—and so were the fans. With a 4–4 record and a thrilling overtime win against the Lions the week before in Milwaukee, the Pack liked their odds against the slightly favored 5–3 Bears.

With just seconds to go in the fourth quarter and the Packers down by six and staring at a fourth down inside the 15-yard line, Majkowski rolled right to evade a defensive line in hot pursuit, pump faked a few times and hit wide receiver Sterling Sharpe in the end zone to tie the game. Watching with seemingly eagle eyes from the opposite side of the field, line judge Jim Quirk flagged Majkowski for crossing the line of scrimmage before he threw the pass. The penalty nullified the touchdown, turned the ball over to Chicago, and effectively ended the game.

But the replay official upstairs in the booth knew better and called for a review.

As the crowd waited for the call, seconds grew into minutes; minutes felt like hours. With no replay board in the stadium, fans had to wait in agony. They remained on their feet cheering. To CBS color commentator Dan Fouts, the decision seemed obvious. "I don't care what size [review] screen you're looking at, that appears to be a touchdown…I don't know what's taking them so long," he said.

In a line that would be quoted in media guides, repeated on sports talk shows, and memorialized on novelty T-shirts, referee Tom Dooley announced, "After further review, we have a reversal. Touchdown."

The "Instant Replay Game" remains one of the most memorable, if not controversial, of the Packers–Bears rivalry. In 1988, fewer than 10 percent of reviewed calls in the league were overturned, making the decision all the more improbable, but one that most assuredly kept Packers and Bears fans equally engaged to the very end—and passionately in argument for years to come.[79] "This is what makes this the all-time rivalry in all of football—NFL, college, whatever," said Fouts as the CBS producers rolled the replay one more time.[80]

Twenty-five years later, however, Pete Dougherty of the hometown *Press-Gazette* maintained the original call was the right one. "[T]here's no way to tell, and no justification for replay official Bill Parkinson to overturn the call," said Dougherty.[81] But at the time, it didn't seem to stir up much anger. *Press-Gazette* reporter Jim Hayes claimed neither head coach Mike Ditka nor his players were particularly hung up on the call. From the sideline, with a fashionable Bears sweater and old-time newsboy cap, Ditka just stood there, cross-armed and still. Only his slapping jowls from chewing a ubiquitous stick of gum moved under his push-broom mustache. If anything, Hayes reported, "newfound respect greatly outweighed any leftover feelings of bad blood…" The sentiment was hard to process after the same club effectively ended the career of one of their franchise's all-time quarterbacks not three years earlier.

"I think they've got a very good coach… I think they've got a lot of classy players here," said Bears guard Mark Bortz. Bortz, a veteran of the 1986 offensive line that protected Jim McMahon—at least during play—found a silver lining in the loss. "They're a different team than they were when Forrest Gregg was here," he added.[82]

Another Bears player gave credit where it was due. "The replay didn't kill us. [Sharpe] caught the ball. That's what killed us," said safety Dave Duerson, who was one of four players in on the coverage of Sharpe on the play.[83] Though the game seemed to assure the future of instant replay review in the NFL it was not to be. After a new two-minute limit for review was implemented in 1990, the system was scrapped after the 1991 season. It would lie on the ash heap until the end of the decade.[84]

The Packers finished the year 10–6, their first winning season since the strike-shortened campaign in 1982, and missed the playoffs due to a tiebreaker with the Vikings, who finished with the same record. Infante walked away with AP Coach of the Year honors. Majkowski, who would dominate his position outpacing all other quarterbacks in completions (353), passing yards (4,318), and first downs (204), took second in MVP balloting. More impressive, the "Majik" Man lead the league with five comebacks and an astounding seven game-winning drives according to Pro Football Reference.[85] No wonder his squad was called the Cardiac Pack. Meanwhile, Mandarich played 14 games with no starts, infamously suggesting on the eve of his debut that someone else on the depth chart should take his spot.[86] He continued to air his grievances off the field. "I wish the mall was a lot bigger," he said.[87]

The last year of the decade was the first good one in many for the Packers, a fortuitous bookend to one of the franchise's worst decades. The team had yet to get a handle on drafts and still relied on an imbalanced offensive-defensive attack, but rather than sulking on the bench chomping on a wiener, the Packers were standing tall and proud like champs waiting in the wings. Maybe in the next decade, things were finally going to change.

Chapter 9

Coronation

Like many institutions, the Packers have been defined by their once-in-a-generation leaders. These figures found ways to survive treacherous waters, and where others saw certain doom, they saw opportunity. The same phenomenon manifests elsewhere in society.

In politics, parties coalesce in times of profound desperation—often against a stagnant or oppressive status quo—around inspirational figures who with vision and sheer force of will lead a country to victory on the battlefield or in the halls of Congress and public commons. Two prominent examples include President Franklin D. Roosevelt, who brought 20th-century liberalism to the political mainstream with the New Deal, and President Ronald Reagan, who shepherded the rise of American conservatism in the latter half of the century.

Similarly, religions organize around prophets and even second-comings who inspire a wayward flock with compelling orthodoxies and, above all, salvation. Rarely do they appear in times of certainty but at moments of great despair. Figures like Mohammad, Moses, and the Dali Lama come to mind.

And then there are the Green Bay Packers, one of the most prominent institutions in professional sports, a team that fans seem to follow as if governed by a theology or an inflexible ideology.

There are three main eras in the team's history named after the defining leader of that time: Lambeau, Lombardi, and Harlan.

Earl "Curly" Lambeau founded the Packers and led the team as player, coach, and manager for 30 years. During his tenure, Green Bay won six championships, including titles in back-to-back-to-back seasons (1929 to 1931). In perhaps his greatest feat of all, he kept the team afloat; this at a time when every other small-town NFL squad in the country shriveled up and melted away.

Vince Lombardi returned glory and prestige to Green Bay and, through his unyielding commitment to excellence on the gridiron, earned the city its moniker, "Titletown, USA." He knew only winning over his nine seasons, securing five championships, including another franchise three-peat from 1965 to 1967.

Enter Bob Harlan, who served the team from 1971 to 2008. Before he took over as team CEO and president in 1989, he watched a moribund franchise spiraling into oblivion across two decades that featured only three winning seasons and two playoff appearances. As a junior administrator with little clout—but one with enough savvy to catch and keep the eye of his former boss who recommended him for the spot—Harlan saw the team hire the wrong coaches and make ridiculous draft picks, leading to predictably dismal performance on the field and an atmosphere that condoned embarrassing antics off it. But with three swift, successive hires—general manager Ron Wolf, coach Mike Holmgren, and quarterback Brett Favre—all made in a span of three months (November 1991 to February 1992), Harlan put the Packers on terra firma and positioned the team to become one of the winningest and most respected franchises of the last several decades. It was an accomplishment second only to the team's founding and its 1960s reincarnation under Lombardi.

The first non-Wisconsinite to become Packers president, the Iowa native more than established his bona fides as a full-blooded Cheesehead during his 37-year tenure in the Packers front office. What Harlan was not, however, was a Green Bay good ol' boy along the lines of predecessors Robert Parins, Dominic Olejniczak, and Andrew Turnbull, each of whom emerged from the city's business or civic community. Harlan was certainly a creature of the organization, but not its governance "club."[1]

If the team's new top dog learned anything from his forebears and co-workers during his first 18 years with the Packers, it was how *not* to run a football franchise. (Perhaps not surprisingly, it could be argued that Harlan is the most successful president and CEO in pro sports to climb to the top *without* a decent mentor.) Harlan famously said the Packers had failed in previous decades because the club was run by amateurs: "You can't bring in someone from a hardware store when you're in the hospital business. You can't bring a good insurance man to run a football team. You're not qualified."[2] (Incidentally, Lambeau sold insurance in the offseason.)

Gross mismanagement had corrupted the club, as had a deeply flawed governance model without appropriate checks and balances. This revealed a downside to a locally owned and operated football franchise. Unlike a wealthy owner with money and reputation at stake, some Packers board members seemed to act like a pro football franchise was no different than any other community service opportunity, like the Rotary or Kiwanis or high school varsity football clubs; it was just another group that you volunteered for. To be fair, there are sports owners who are completely unserious about fielding winning teams and hold onto a franchise merely to accrue money and build cultural capital. See: John Fisher (Oakland/Las Vegas A's) and former owner Donald Sterling (San Diego/Los Angeles Clippers).

Harlan's contemporary and erstwhile competitor for the presidency, Thomas Olejniczak, son of the former mayor and team president Dominic, had a slightly different perspective. "It wasn't like hardware people were trying to run a hospital. It's that the doctors in the hospital weren't very good," he said in a not-so-subtle defense of his father.[3] Team historian Cliff Christl would agree: "The Packers' 24-year slog stemmed more from incompetence at the top of their football operation than any interference from the corporate side of the company."[4]

At his introductory press conference, Harlan announced that things were about to change, sounding a lot like Lombardi at his first presser 30 years earlier. "I'm the one in charge," Harlan told the state press corps. "It's up to me to make the decisions that are right or wrong, to move the franchise ahead in every area."[5] And not a moment too soon;

the Packers had just drafted Tony Mandarich, who was holding out and demanding $1 million more per year than what the Packers were willing to pay, news that took top billing over the Harlan hire on the Sports page of the *Press-Gazette* on June 6, 1989.[6]

Back on the football field, the 1990 and 1991 seasons (6–10 and 4–12, respectively) confirmed that 1989 (10–6) was an aberration. Coach Infante's team finished fourth in the division both years, not even coming close to the playoffs.[7]

Harlan made the unusual step of dumping Executive Vice President and General Manager Tom Braatz in the middle of the 1991 season, "a very strange time" by his own admission, and a move that wasn't easy.[8] "Resting with this single decision is the Packers' next decade…beneath his well-cut suit and carved, confident expression, Bob Harlan's hands were ever so slightly shaking," *Press-Gazette* reporter Kevin Isaacson observed at the press conference.[9]

Harlan had seen enough, but there was another motive for sacking Braatz. He wanted to snatch the one that got away, personnel director Ron Wolf, winner of two Super Bowls working for the Raiders, before other teams got to him first.[10] Assuming Harlan could get his man, he also wanted Wolf to have a few weeks to get to know the club, "to travel to games and find out what the scene was," as Harlan put it.[11] So certain was he of his decision that he unloaded Braatz before even speaking with Wolf, let alone getting a verbal commitment.[12]

One week later, on November 27, 1991, Harlan hired Wolf away from the New York Jets, for whom he'd been personnel director for less than two years. Harlan's opening press conference promise to clean house and be decisive with his hires was something to be taken seriously.

Those efforts would now be at the sole discretion of the new general manager. "Wolf will have 'full authority' over the Packers' football operation," reported the *Press-Gazette*, citing unnamed sources at the time of his hiring. "That includes authority to hire and fire members of the scouting and coaching staffs, including head coach Lindy Infante."[13]

The message was clear as day: Lindy wouldn't be around much longer. But Wolf had more pressing matters to deal with, namely getting his hands on a raw third-string gunslinger from the Falcons who Wolf believed could become not just the Packers' next quarterback in 1992, but maybe the franchise's future. Wolf had scouted Brett Favre at a pre-draft workout at the quarterback's alma mater Southern Mississippi the year before, along with Infante and future Green Bay coach Mike Holmgren. The latter, then San Francisco's offensive coordinator, didn't need an additional quarterback, with Steve Young taking over for an injured Joe Montana and yet another promising QB, Steve Bono, third in the depth chart. Still, Holmgren was "a passing junkie, and he wanted to see what all the fuss was about," author Jeff Pearlman explained in his Favre autobiography, *Gunslinger*. "Somebody will probably take you fairly early. I wish you luck," Holmgren told Favre.[14]

Serendipitously, the Packers were matched up with the Falcons the following Sunday. Wolf was giddy. "The football gods were giving us an opportunity," he said.[15] Wolf was utterly convinced Favre was his man, though he never put eyes on him that day. Wolf attempted to watch Favre warm up before the Falcons-Packers game got underway—he was not slated to play in the game nor would he—but on his way down to the field from the press box the Milwaukee and Green Bay media mobbed the new Packers GM with questions. Despite the aborted trip, Wolf's mind was made up. "Ron comes back [to the press box] and he says, 'We're gonna make a trade for Brett Favre,'" Harlan recalled. "It was just that blunt."[16]

Quarterback, check. But what about the head coach?

Shortly after taking the helm, Wolf broached another issue with his new boss. "'Bob, you got a problem on the practice field. This is like a country club,'" Harlan recalled.[17] Wolf saw none of the discipline necessary for a successful pro team—in practice or on game day. His prognosis: losing had become a habit for the Packers.

On December 22, after less than a month on the job, Wolf fired Infante.

But what seemed an obvious decision in hindsight was not as easily made, especially for the team. The move was met with a "somber" mood, according to the *Press-Gazette*.[18] Indeed, the charismatic Infante was a fan favorite despite his losing ways. Incredibly, he had been voted best coach in team history in a TV poll a year earlier according to Packers historian Cliff Christl. Without a doubt, an illegit barometer for public opinion.[19]

"When you play a sport like ours you get to be a kind of family. It's kind of tough when a member of the family is asked to leave," said one player.[20]

Within 24 hours of Infante's departure, Wolf had identified a "top candidate" for the open coaching post, one who the *Press-Gazette* revealed to be Bill Parcells. In fact, Wolf was on the phone with the former Giants coach and then-NBC analyst a few days before Infante was released. Both general manager and prospective coach were coy about a potential deal and would not comment publicly, but Wolf did state that salary requirements were not a problem for the team.[21]

The stars appeared to be aligning. But once again, the team missed out on a top coaching talent, albeit through bad luck. Parcells was set to undergo open-heart surgery and could not take the job for health reasons, according to Wolf.

A few days later, the GM phoned San Francisco offensive coordinator Mike Holmgren, who Wolf believed was *the* up-and-coming coach in the league. (It wasn't until many years later that Wolf learned that Holmgren came to Green Bay because of him.)[22] Other highly sought-after coaches were also in contention, namely Seahawks head coach Chuck Knox, Cowboys defensive coordinator Dave Wannstedt, and Jets defensive coordinator Pete Carroll, whom Wolf had worked with in 1990 and 1991.[23]

But in the end, the team got their man. On January 11, 1992, Mike Holmgren was introduced to the sports world as the 11th coach of the Green Bay Packers. A longtime protégé of 49ers coach Bill Walsh, Holmgren ran the so-called West Coast offense in San Francisco. Though in vogue at the time, the offensive strategy really was just a more contained version of run-and-shoot offenses that emphasized passing over running, albeit with shorter, simpler throws and routes. It was credited as key to San Francisco's run of three Super Bowl wins under Walsh in the 1980s.

Holmgren immediately felt the weight of expectations in Green Bay, as evinced by his measured comments at his first press conference. He nonetheless gave players and fans comfort in knowing that they had a professional who knew exactly what he was doing. "The quick fix, neither Ron nor I are in," Holmgren said. "We're in it for the long haul, so I'm going to hold off on any predictions." Wolf had wisely given Holmgren the latitude necessary—including a five-year coaching contract—to build a dynasty in Green Bay.[24] That included assistant coach hires. Unbeknownst to Wolf and Holmgren, the new head coach was planting a coaching tree that would one day dominate the league ranks.[25]

Wolf made good on his promise and acquired Brett Favre from Atlanta on February 11, 1992, in exchange for one of the Packers' two first-round draft picks that year. The move was met with fierce criticism within Packer Nation. Rosie's Water Works, a Milwaukee bar and institution, spoke for many fans when it posted a top 10 list on the wall as to why the Packers had hired Wolf. **Number 2:** "[Wolf] can give away draft choices better than anyone else in the NFL." And **Number 1:** "Green Bay needed more no-talent quarterbacks."[26] The Favre trade would not be the only player acquisition by Wolf that team president Harlan would have to defend.

A couple of months later, Wolf selected Florida State cornerback Terrell Buckley as the team's first round choice in the 1992 draft. Buckley had put up impressive numbers for the Seminoles, including 21 interceptions despite a height disadvantage. Buckley stood just 5'9"—considerably shorter than most wide receivers he'd be defending in the NFL.[27] Wolf would rue the "mistake" of using a high draft choice on a questionable prospect, but the GM learned a lesson: Never second-guess personal standards, especially the rules that had served you well in the past. "If you start making exceptions to your standards you soon become a team of exceptions," Wolf often said. Like his mentor, Raiders owner Al Davis, Wolf liked to acquire players based on three qualities: height, weight, and speed.[28] Buckley was undersized in both height and weight, and his selection would haunt the team for years to come, especially in the playoffs.[29]

One personnel choice Wolf would not rue was Favre, though the quarterback certainly had his doubters at first. The Atlanta Falcons weren't the only team that had given Favre short shrift. In fact, it's a surprise that Favre even ended up at the University of Southern Mississippi at all. When USM recruiter Mark McHale was assessing high school quarterback prospects in Mississippi and New Orleans, Favre didn't make the list. It wasn't until a scouting trip when McHale heard from one coach, and then another, and yet another, about the gunslinger from Kiln, Mississippi. McHale decided to check out Favre even though he still had an entire state and the second-largest city in the Deep South to scout. There were only so many Friday nights in the fall to watch players.[30]

McHale came away unimpressed with Favre. It wasn't because of the young quarterback's play, but rather a dashed opportunity to show what he could do on the field. Parents who coach sons or daughters are often ribbed for favoring their kids over other players, generally by giving them extra playing time. It was the opposite for Irv Favre, Brett's father and coach at Hancock North Central High School. Irv was a true believer in the run offense, to a fault. Despite a Division I scout in the stands, Irv allowed his son to throw the ball just four times in the entire game.

Irv then promised McHale he'd allow his son to throw the ball more in an upcoming game; even then, he didn't give Brett many passing plays, waiting until late in the second quarter to show off his boy's talent. With the game tied 8–8, Favre presaged his pro football career with a stellar drive, capped with a 21-yard strike for the go-ahead touchdown. McHale recalled the pass like it was yesterday. "The ball had flames and smoke coming off of it," he told Pearlman in *Gunslinger*. "[The receiver] caught it and I could hear the crack." Favre's Hawks would go on to win 29–21. McHale was on board "100 percent." It was a breathtaking assessment since the scout had but a handful of passes to make his judgement. It goes to Favre's indelible mystique, which had captured the attention and imagination of fans across the football universe—and made Wolf the GM *sine qua non* of his generation.[31]

It would take some coaxing on McHale's part to convince Golden Eagles head coach Jim Carmody to bring Favre aboard. Carmody eventually acquiesced to his scout. Despite landing seventh on the Southern Miss quarterback depth chart (while also playing safety, as he did in high school, in addition to other duties as assigned like kicking and punting),[32] Favre found his way to the top very quickly. The rise was meteoric. Not only was he a freshman but, at 17, one of the youngest players on the roster. Something about the rookie caught the coach's attention, not unlike McHale's first impression a year earlier. "I heard this noise, a whooshing sound. I turned around and said, 'What in the world is that?'" Carmody recalled in Mississippi's *Clarion-Ledger,* referring to his first practice with Favre. "I coached a long time, and I never heard a ball sound like that."

In the second game of the season against Tulane, Carmody pulled his struggling starter and put Favre in during the third quarter. Favre responded by completing 6 of 10 passes, including a pair of touchdowns in a come-from-behind win. Carmody never looked back—and neither did his new first-string quarterback. Favre would start for the rest of his college career, leading Southern Miss to memorable wins over powerhouse programs such as Florida State, Alabama, and Auburn.[33]

Only two quarterbacks went before Favre in the 1991 draft. It wasn't considered a notable class, but the Falcons needed a quarterback and evidently Favre met their needs. He was drafted 33rd overall in the second round, though against the wishes of Atlanta coach Jerry Glanville. General manager Ken Herock overruled Glanville who didn't like Favre and never would.[34] He considered Favre a drunk, a criticism Favre admitted was fair.[35] Glanville proceeded to slot Favre at No. 3 on the quarterback depth chart, allowing him to see game action just twice in his first and only year with the Falcons. He threw four times, was intercepted twice, made zero completions, and was sacked.[36] So, when the Packers came knocking, Glanville was more than happy to answer.

As the 1992 season dawned, despite Favre's expected role of change agent tasked with the heavy burden of turning around a legendary franchise, there was no set plan or path for the quarterback to become the starter. (Holmgren teased starting Favre in Week 1, but it never came to be.[37]) Regardless, Wolf seemed sure it would ultimately happen. "[Holmgren] wanted to give Majkowski a chance to seize the job," said Wolf. "Let's face it, Don couldn't do that. He wasn't as talented as Favre was."[38]

In Week 2 against the Tampa Bay Buccaneers on September 13, Favre got his first real chance as a pro. Holmgren pulled Don Majkowski after a dismal first half and put in Favre to start the second. The upstart made the most of the opportunity, completing 8 of 14 passes and just missing two oh-so-close throws to Sterling Sharpe that could have led to a pair of touchdowns. Not great, not awful. His QB rating was close to Majkowski's for the game.[39]

Freshman jitters appeared to get the best of Favre. But Favre had made an impression. By the fourth quarter, color commentator Matt Millen said: "I think if you're a Packer guy watching this team play right now you gotta be impressed with Brett Favre. It's clear to me he doesn't have the system down 100 percent…but when he can see what is happening and know his arm can work for him, [he's] gonna be a good player."[40] The future Detroit general manager was onto something. Over his seven seasons from 2001 to 2007 with the Lions, the team won just twice against Favre.[41]

Nevertheless, Holmgren second-guessed himself and put Majkowski back in against Cincinnati in Week 3. It would be the quarterback's last game as a Packer. In the first quarter, Bengals nose tackle and Wisconsin native Tim Krumrie made short work of Green Bay's crumbling offensive line and took down Majkowski, knocking him out with a sprained ankle and torn ligaments.

The Packers would be Brett Favre's team for the next 15 seasons.

The metamorphosis from third-rate franchise to Super Bowl winner didn't happen overnight, but it began in that game against Cincinnati.

Without many old hands in the room—Holmgren and his coaching staff of several future head coaches were still brand new in their roles—Favre looked to his veteran teammates for help. In particular, he targeted fifth-year receiver Sterling Sharpe, to whom he tossed the majority of his passes in that game, including seven completions for 109 yards and a touchdown. It is not a stretch to argue that future Hall of Famer and one of the greatest Packers receivers of all time Sterling Sharpe made Favre who he is today—one of the greatest quarterbacks in NFL history. Indeed, Favre connected with Sterling Sharpe for 41 touchdowns over their three years together (1992–94) or about 14 each season. To say Favre relied on Sharpe to pad his TD stats would be an understatement. In 1992 Sterling caught 12 of Favre's 18 touchdown tosses; in 1993, 11 of 19; and in his final season with the team, 18 of 33. Though Favre hit Sharpe for no fewer than half of his touchdown passes in his first three seasons with Green Bay—including two of every three in 1992—Favre's receiver-codependency ended in his following three MVP seasons. By 1996, only one of four touchdown tosses went to the same player. Or, as the *Los Angeles Times* reported that year, "With Favre, It Doesn't Matter Who Packers Have at Receiver." Two decades later, in 2014, the *Milwaukee Journal Sentinel* ranked the Favre-Sharpe tandem the second "most productive quarterback-receiver touchdown combination" in team *history.*[42]

"[H]e was getting better as the day wore on," said NBC color analyst Ahmad Rashad in the third quarter, before play-by-play announcer Jim Lampley seemingly jinxed the team, calling Holmgren's decision to put Favre in the previous week (ostensibly to prepare him for this game) a "piece of genius." On the following play, however, Favre fumbled, in what would become a familiar high followed by a low for Packers fans. Lampley summed it up perfectly before it would become a mantra in Green Bay: "You live and die with someone like Favre."

With just over a minute to go in the fourth quarter and the Packers down six, deep in their own territory and with no time outs remaining, Favre began to write the score to the theme he would play time and again as the team's quarterback for the next decade and a half.

Meanwhile, Holmgren, the conductor, would call every play of the series, an arrangement the two would keep for the rest of their time together. The first of many more to come.

Starting at his own 8-yard line, Favre tossed a screen pass to running back Harry Sydney for a gain of three, then wasted no time connecting with Sharpe for 42 yards on second-and-7. On the next play, Favre hit running back Vince Workman across center for a gain of 11 yards. Sharpe clutched his gut in obvious pain—either from the Favre missile that nearly took out his arms or collateral damage from the fall—and lined up on the wing, only to be relieved by Favre, who spiked the ball to stop the clock. Three plays in the chamber.

With his Pro Bowl security-blanket receiver Sharpe now tucked away on the sidelines, Favre had to look elsewhere. On second down on the Cincinnati 35-yard line, the Southern Mississippi gunslinger dropped back, pumped once toward the middle, then fired a rocket toward the right sideline and into the waiting hands of receiver Kitrick Taylor, who caught it and glided into the end zone.[43]

For 36 long seconds, the TV booth went silent as delirium took hold in Lambeau Field, echoing through television sets and radios across Packer Nation. Favre ran around in circles on the field, pumping his helmet as Taylor joyfully fell into the arms of his receiver corps. It was the first touchdown of his six-year career in the NFL. (It would also be his last.)[44] Tears streamed down the face of exhausted Packers center James Campen, while frustrated Bengals head coach Dave Shula kicked up a chunk of sod on the Cincinnati sideline. Chris Jacke, who would kick for 8 seasons for Green Bay and come within three points of beating Don Hutson's team scoring record with 820 points, chipped in the extra point for the lead.[45] With no timeouts and 13 seconds left on the clock, the Bengals were out of options. Packers 24–23. No one could have known for sure at the time, but it was the start of a new epoch for Titletown. Indeed, Favre-to-Kitrick Taylor marked the coronation of the Harlan era.[46]

Chapter 10

Return to Titletown

As a new era dawned in Green Bay, the league was still experiencing growing pains. It had been 36 years since NFL players organized as a union, yet free agency remained elusive in 1992.[1] The right to choose who to work for—a right many take for granted—was the subject of strikes in 1974, 1982, and 1987, with each action ending in disappointment for the players.

Fed up, frustrated, and out of options, the union decertified in 1989 and re-established itself as a professional association. The purpose was to retain the right to sue NFL owners for free agency as a violation of antitrust law, something they couldn't do as a union as the result of a 1989 federal court ruling.[2]

In the spring of 1990, the NFL Players Association filed a lawsuit, *McNeil vs. NFL*, that singled out "Plan B," a free agency system owners implemented in 1989 that offered little benefit to players. Jets running back Freeman McNeil was chosen as the lead plaintiff because his Christian name so matched the cause.[3] (Don Majkowski was listed as one of the co-plaintiffs.) Under Plan B, up to 36 players on a 53-person team roster would be restricted free agents. They would be subject to "the right of first refusal/compensation system," that is they would have to stick with their current team and if a contract could not be agreed upon, the new, acquiring franchise would have to compensate the old team, hence the term "first refusal/compensation." The rest of the squad would be unrestricted free agents, the status all players sought and had sought for decades.

On September 10, 1992, a federal jury ruled in favor of the players. The *McNeil vs. NFL* ruling said that Plan B was too restrictive, and according to the jurors, NFL players were owed compensation. The Players Association then filed a class action lawsuit seeking damages and new free agency rights.[4]

But who would lend their name to such a controversial, high-profile case? One that drew the collective ire of every owner in the league, save one.

Abortion rights activists had Jane Roe; segregation foes were championed by Linda Carol Brown. NFL players had Reggie White.

Like most kids, Reggie White knew exactly what he wanted to be when he grew up. Though unlike most kids, Reggie became precisely what he said he would: a minister and a pro football player. While his peers were partying and goofing off, White was ordained as a pastor at 17 and earned All-American honors at nose tackle and tight end for his high school football team in Chattanooga, Tennessee.

He'd find himself in a pulpit soon enough, but first he'd make his mark in football—on and off the field.

White built his legend at the University of Tennessee, where he became the school's all-time sack king, logging 32 over his collegiate career, a record that would stand for 33 years. He chose not to enter the NFL draft in 1984, instead signing with his home state's Memphis Showboats of the upstart United States Football League (USFL). White's deal with Memphis was for a five-year, $4 million guaranteed contract—equal to five times the average salary of an NFL rookie. Understanding his worth and not settling for less was a lesson White would carry throughout his life.[5]

When the USFL folded the following year, White signed with the Philadelphia Eagles in a supplemental draft for considerably less than his Memphis deal, earning $1.7 million over four years. He would later re-sign with Philadelphia in 1989 for a lucrative four-year, $6 million contract.[6] Over his eight seasons with the Eagles, White would become the franchise's all-time sack leader, racking up 124 across 121 games, including 21 in the strike-shortened 1987 season.[7] By 1993, if not 1987, he was arguably the best defensive player in the league.

As fond as White was of Philadelphia—a city full of rabid Eagles fans who truly cared for him—it seemed like it was time to move on. He wanted to leave his mark not just on another city and team but the league itself and perhaps American labor history in general—not to mention earn a nice payday.

In addition to spreading the Gospel and sacking quarterbacks, White's life purpose was to lead his fellow man on a basic human right, the ability to choose whom to give one's labor. Players needed a leader in the fight for free agency, and the good Lord nominated Reggie. Indeed, what better spokesperson for the free agency movement than an outspoken preacher and a brilliant player beloved by fans and fellow players alike? White never sold himself short and always held out until he got what he believed he was owed. It was a big reason why he opted for the upstart USFL over the established NFL, the former offered a far superior contract. Now, he would do likewise for his brethren. And White's convictions went well beyond words. During the 1987 strike, he stood in front of the bus of replacement players to prevent them from entering training camp.

Said his son, Jeremy, "My dad was brash. He was going to bring some conviction. So, he put his name on it," referring to the lawsuit *White v. NFL*. "He knew what he was doing was right for people..."[8] *White* built on the success of the *McNeil* case by seeking from team owners a whopping $1 billion in damages caused by repressive measures put in place after the 1982 CBA expired in 1987. (The fiduciary amount trebled the actual damages because antitrust law called for tripling awards.[9]) Owners quickly capitulated and the two parties agreed to a robust series of free agency rules, as well as salary caps—"an equalizer in response to free agency," according to the NFL. All players other than those given a designated "franchise tag" or "transition tag" would be free to sign with the club of their choosing after three years of service with their current team.[10]

Players were beyond grateful.

"I can maximize my earning power because a guy was willing to take a chance and sue the league," said former Minnesota Vikings wide receiver Cris Carter.[11]

But if there was one player who might have benefited more from free agency than any other, it was White. The All-Pro and 1987 Defensive Player of the Year was the most sought after player and had been paid well under true market value, which no doubt factored into his calculus in pursing the lawsuit so publicly—notwithstanding his principled stand of labor solidarity over the years.[12] Shortly after the NFL and players union settled on new personnel rules in early 1993, offers poured in from around the league.

"It was crazy. He was the homecoming king, and everyone wanted to be his date," recalled Sara White, his wife and mother of his two children.[13]

But one team stood above all the others.

Teams from big cities wined and dined the Whites at upscale restaurants and gifted them leather jackets, mink furs, and other luxuries, but the Packers' modest offer to go out to a chain restaurant endeared them to Reggie and his family. "We discovered Reggie liked catfish. What better place to go than Red Lobster?" recalled Ron Wolf. "That's one thing we did have."[14]

On April 6, 1993, White signed a four-year, $17 million contract with the Packers. The deal would make him the third-highest paid player in the NFL behind quarterbacks John Elway and Dan Marino. Reggie claimed God told him to sign with the Packers; the Green Bay offer also happened to be the highest.[15]

With White anchoring the team's defense and Favre helming the offense, two main ingredients were now in place for the Lombardi trophy to return to Titletown. Coming off two lost decades, the turnaround was so complete it was almost inconceivable to Packer Nation. Though success would not come quite overnight.

White was the final link of an iron chain that provided Green Bay the strength and durability to dominate the NFL ranks for the foreseeable future. It all began with former team president Judge Robert Parins handing over operational control to Bob Harlan and a new generation of legit football minds. Over a five-year period, crucial links would hook together one after another: Harlan (1989)—Wolf (1991)—Holmgren (1992)—Favre (1992)—White (1993).

The latter two would find themselves on the covers of national sports and news magazines and in local and state newspapers nearly every week—sometimes daily. Few pro teams featured a marquee offensive maestro and defensive juggernaut like Green Bay. In 1992, the Packers were 17th in offense, 15th in defense overall. In White and Favre's first year together in 1993, offensive and defensive team ranks leapt to 6th and 9th, respectively. Three years later in their 1996 Super Bowl season, both ranked No. 1.[16]

Playing on Favre's team was an early factor that piqued White's interest in joining the Packers. "[T]he vivid memory of Brett Favre playing straight through the punishment I put on him stuck in my mind," the defensive end said, referring to Philadelphia's matchup with Green Bay in November 1992.[17] On the Packers' second possession, White hit Favre hard, laying him out in the pocket after disorienting tackle Tootie Robbins with his signature hump move where he scoops up a lineman with his forearm/hand by the blocker's armpit, tosses him aside and sacks the QB. Favre shook it off and proceeded to lead his squad downfield, ultimately hitting Sterling Sharpe on a five-yard screen toss for a touchdown. Before and after each down, Favre had grabbed his separated left shoulder wincing in obvious pain. Nevertheless, he soldiered on through the drive and the rest of the game to win it 27–24. The sold-out Milwaukee crowd had witnessed another classic Favre come-from-behind victory—further proof that their new gunslinger was no fluke.[18]

The club had needed a football man—not a money guy—to pry loose the purse strings and invest in players, coaches, and facilities. Harlan resolved that the Green and Gold under his watch would finally come of age.

"This goldmine of fresh cash, plus the still-swelling nest egg handed down from the years of Dominic Olejniczak's and Robert Parins' frugal guardianship, allowed the Packers to remain a player in this high-stakes bidding war," said team historian Cliff Christl, referring to sky-high reserves that Harlan's predecessors built up over their tenure[19] There was a reason the Packers consistently posted profits year in and year out in the dark days of the '70s and '80s. Green Bay's city fathers and mothers were of the old-school variety. Olejniczak, Parins, and their contemporaries valued hard work and understood that success in business was never a given. No doubt that above every cash register in every diner, haberdasher, or hardware store was a framed one-dollar bill from their first sale, reminding them and every customer of this ethos.

But they were also cheap. They sat on money and wouldn't spend it if they didn't think they had to. The Pack were in the black, and that's all that seemed to matter.

Reggie White was the franchise's crown jewel. The dominant defender was what neither Favre nor Holmgren were: proven. "Now we have legitimacy," explained *Press-Gazette* reporter Jeff Ash in the team's centennial documentary, *Legacy*, referring to the overall significance of acquiring White. One of the league's greatest defensive ends now complemented two offensive powers—a promising young quarterback and a star apprentice of the West Coast offense. Throw in one of the league's top receivers, Sterling Sharpe, along with one of the best third-down conversion rates in the league,[20] and you had the makings of an offense ready to explode. Indeed, the team's passing offense jumped from 19th in 1991 to ninth in 1992, with just three other NFC teams ranked higher than Green Bay that year.[21] Meanwhile, the defense was positioned to grow and strengthen exponentially with key acquisitions due largely to the team's attracting new star and the league's free agency rules. The following year, Green Bay signed defensive end Sean Jones, and two seasons later, tackle Santana Dotson; both would help White anchor the NFL's number one defense in the 1996 Super Bowl season.[22]

The transformative 1993 season marked the beginning of the team's winningest era. From 1992 to 2024 they would post a .631 winning percentage (best in the NFL in that span) with 24 playoff appearances. It was pointedly appropriate that 1993 marked the Packers' diamond jubilee. It had been 75 seasons since Curly first took snaps under center at Hagemeister Park while his marriage vows were still fresh, his tonsillitis in remission, and his vision of football glory just a glimmer in his eye. The franchise had traveled a long, winding road in the interim, with pitstops, occasional breakdowns, and a few checkered flags.[23]

Reggie White singlehandedly turned the defense around in his first year with the team. In 1992, the Packers ranked 23rd overall in stopping the pass. At the end of 1993, they were second best in the league. On the offensive side of the ball, Brett Favre threw for more than 3,000 yards and led the NFC in completions—though he also threw the most interceptions. Receiver Sterling Sharpe finished another 1,000-yard season with 1,274 total yards, just behind future Hall of Famers Michael Irvin and Jerry Rice. It was enough to earn the 9–7 Packers a playoff bid, ending an 11-year drought.[24]

January 8, 1994, the day the Packers squared off against the Lions in the NFC Wild Card game, marked the moment when John Elway—star of "The Drive" from the 1986-87 AFC Championship—surrendered his sole claim as the offensive auteur of late fourth-quarter, game-winning drives. As Green Bay logged its first playoff win in a decade, Favre not only snatched the unofficial title from Elway, but he made dramatic marches to victory something to expect. It was now clear that this team was never done until the clock hit zero.

With 2:26 to go down 24–21, the quarterback began his late fourth quarter march on the Packers' own 29-yard line. Like Elway in 1987, Favre began cautiously, tossing a screen pass to a reliable back, Edgar

Bennett. That's where the comparison to Denver ended. Whereas Elway took his time with conservative handoffs, Favre let 'er rip—quick, decisive, and efficient—making two completions in a row followed by a fourth and final play, one that should have gotten its own name in football lore.

To say Favre's winning play was improbable would be such an understatement that even the quarterback himself has questioned his own wisdom in trying to pull it off. "I would never tell my quarterback not to make that throw because my quarterback would never make that throw," he said years later, thinking back on the play through the eyes of a hypothetical Coach Favre. On second-and-4, Favre rolled left, thinking Sharpe would be running down that side of the field. But when Favre quickly scanned the field, he spotted his go-to receiver on the opposite sideline racing for the end zone. He planted his left foot and wound up for a 75-yard (as the crow flies) bomb that he launched across his body. Most mortals would have blown their rotator cuffs and ended their careers. Not Favre.

"With daylight and time Favre goes for the whole thing!" shouted play-by-play announcer Brent Musburger. The ball's arc and distance were perfect. "Touchdown!"[25]

The improbable playoff win, Green Bay's first since 1983, was spectacular, but the euphoria was short lived. Favre and the Packers dropped the NFC Divisional Game at Dallas the following week. It was one of many losses to the Cowboys and quarterback Troy Aikman, the team's most frustrating rival of the 90s. Flummoxed by the repeated high-stakes losses, general manager Wolf would turn to superstition. "Every time we'd lose to the Cowboys I would change hotels," he said in *Legacy*. "I would tell the [travel agent] we're changing hotels, and, well, about the eighth time we're out in Amarillo!"

Fans and local press were understanding. "The Green Bay Packers know they have a ways to go. But thanks to the Dallas Cowboys, they also know how far they have come," wrote the *Press-Gazette*'s Kevin Isaacson.[26]

Ron Wolf would spend the offseason orchestrating brilliant acquisitions that didn't get much attention in the short run but proved definitive. In 1992, he nabbed free agent Frankie Winters (center), traded a low draft pick for Tootie Robbins (tackle), and brought on George Koonce (linebacker) from the World League. He repeated the feat in 1993 by acquiring Gilbert Brown from the Vikings and then, in 1994, Sean Jones, both proved indispensable in reinforcing White on the defensive line.[27]

Wolf had a penchant for picking really good quarterbacks who would go on to blockbuster careers. It was a result of brilliant draft acumen and a lot of practice. If there's a good quarterback on the board, take him, he would say. Wolf drafted seven QBs in his ten drafts; four of the seven would go on to start in the league.[28] All of this after Favre had established himself as the starter.

The Packers GM would further enshrine his reputation as a draft king with key moves that rivaled those of Jack Vainisi and even Curly Lambeau. Just as Vainisi was credited with stacking Lombardi's championship team, so too would Wolf for the 1996 Super Bowl season. Starters drafted by the GM included: Edgar Bennett (1992, 4th round), Mark Chmura (1992, 6th), Earl Dotson (1993, 3rd), Aaron Taylor (1994, 1st), William Henderson (1995, 3rd), Antonio Freeman (1995, 3rd), and Adam Timmerman (1995, 7th).[29]

"My focus was let's get the best players we can," Wolf said in *Legacy*. "When I talked to Mike [Holmgren] about coming to Green Bay, [I said,] 'Mike we're going to stir the pot, we are going to keep changing the roster.'"[30] And stir the pot he did.

Under Wolf, the Packers cranked through players by the dozen. "Even after we started winning… Ron always made a point of bringing in free agents," said Harlan in *The Greatest Story in Sports*.[31] "He looked under every rock to find the right people to fit the program," former Packers assistant coach Jon Gruden said in *Legacy*.[32]

"It was like a Greyhound bus terminal here for a while. I didn't want to remain stagnant," the GM said.[33]

Wolf's relentless pursuit of continuous improvement reflected an ethos inherited from his mentor, Al Davis, who stamped an adage atop Raiders stationery and draped it over the field wall at the LA Coliseum: COMMITMENT TO EXCELLENCE. "If you're not getting better, you are getting worse," Wolf said.[34] By 1995, just four of the 45 players on the 1991 roster were still around.[35]

The 1994 season saw a marked improvement and, on their way to their second straight playoff appearance, the Pack were able to settle some old scores. At the top of the list, as usual, was Chicago.

When the Packers and Bears match up, it's easy to feel the pull of a time warp. Both play in old stadiums, their team colors and logos have remained unchanged, and players hit each other hard, as age-old rivals do.

If you could pinpoint the game in which pride finally returned to Packer Nation, it was the October 31, 1994, Monday Night matchup in Chicago. At 3–4 for the season, the Packers had gotten off to a slow start. Some fans were still questioning whether Favre was the future of the franchise. This game put an end to those habitual, irritating doubts.

The game's setting was appropriate. An eerie fog hung over Soldier Field on Halloween night, while rain-wrapped surges of wind topped out at 53 mph. "Some of the worst weather ever seen for a football game," wrote Glenn Swain in his 1996 account of the rivalry.[36] The field slowly deteriorated into a morass of mud and water, earning the game its moniker: the Mudder."[37] Throwback uniforms, donned for the first time since the 1920s, added to the age-old mystique of the rivalry. The Packers wore tan khaki pants and starched white jerseys (well, starch-white only for the first few seconds of play), while the Bears sported dark navy-blue jerseys with vertical orange stripes, making them look almost like jailed convicts—a physical manifestation of what Green Bay fans envisioned as their sworn enemies.

The Packers figured out early that the run game would win the evening and opted to carry the ball 45 times for 223 yards and a quartet of rushing touchdowns. The Bears, however, were slow to adapt to the horrible field conditions and leaned heavily on the pass—attempting 35 and completing 21 for a single touchdown. Bears quarterback Erik Kramer—who suffered at the hands of the Packers defense much as he had as the Lions' starter in the 1993 Wild Card Game—went 5 for 10, throwing two interceptions and getting sacked twice. He was replaced in the second half.

But what made the matchup most memorable wasn't during the game but between the halves, when the Halas family retired the jerseys of the franchise's most storied players: Dick Butkus and Gale Sayers. Dressed in ponchos, the two rain-soaked Hall of Famers struggled to speak to the crowd over the din of the elements. Not only did they have to ride out the crummy weather—just like the good ol' days—but they had to do it while watching a crushing 33–6 defeat. The Packers' win would become a habit that lasted for most of the decade, and the Green and Gold would best the Bears in the next nine games.

"I'd hate to have been the Bears tonight," said defensive tackle and Illinois native John Jurkovic, summing up the evening perfectly.[38]

In 1994, a tradition nearly as old as the franchise ended: Packers games in Milwaukee, which dated back to 1933, just weeks after the team filed for receivership in Brown County court in August of that month. Some, like Packers historian Cliff Christl, viewed the arrangement as a "lifeline." "If Milwaukee had not become a second home to the Packers…they almost certainly would not have survived," Christl said.[39] The Green and Gold would play 167 games over 62 seasons ending in a 107–61–3 record.[40] But Green Bay's relationship with its bigger cousin to the south wasn't necessarily innocent and one of pure intentions. It had been complicated. How exactly this big city failed to retain a football team while the small-town franchise to the north survived had mystified and flummoxed Cream City's elders for years. Milwaukee had several times tried to poach the Packers—often in cahoots with the league—though neither Milwaukee nor the NFL could break Green Bay's bond with its team. Like any deep and lasting relationship, Green Bay had seen its Packers through the good and the bad and never gave up on them.

Now team President Bob Harlan decided it was time to cut ties with Milwaukee. Green Bay was more than capable of managing a full season at home. So controversial was the decision that officers from the Milwaukee Police Department escorted Harlan out of County Stadium the last time the Packers played there—in case the angry crowd took its frustration out on the team president himself. Harlan nonetheless struggled with the decision. For someone who appreciated history, he knew that Milwaukee fans had hung tough with the Packers in dark days, too. And so he offered to honor Milwaukee season ticket holders for the traditional three games at Lambeau Field. Nearly every Milwaukee ticket holder took Harlan up on his offer (97 percent).[41]

For the Packers' Milwaukee swan song, Favre would give their home away from home a sendoff they'd never forget. With 21 seconds to go on the visiting Atlanta Falcons' 9-yard line, Favre rolled right and made an ill-advised scramble, evading two defenders and then launching headfirst into the end zone to score the winning touchdown. The successful 67-yard, one-minute-and-44-second drive kept the team in playoff contention and Favre's reputation intact. "It's vintage Brett Favre," declared kicker Chris Jacke. "Dumb and brilliant at the same time." A fitting farewell.[42]

The Packers once again finished a respectable 9–7 for the 1994 season, just enough to make a wild card playoff appearance, but not without suffering a devastating loss: Sterling Sharpe. In Milwaukee against the Falcons, the Pro Bowl receiver had taken a hit from Brad Edwards when Sharpe blocked the defensive back on a running play. He fell backward, hurt his neck, and lay motionless on the turf for more than three minutes, not unlike what happened to quarterback Lynn Dickey 17 years earlier when the chronically injured gunslinger took a hard hit in the pocket. That ended the season for Dickey; Sharpe had one more game in him, however. He helped close out the season with a win against the Bucs the following week where he caught three touchdown passes while piling up 132 receiving yards. His heroics secured the team its second playoff appearance in as many years; but Tampa Stadium would be the last venue he would ever play. He reinjured his neck late in the game. When he officially ended his playing career the following March after the Packers waived him, Sharpe had laid claim to several Packers records, including most career pass receptions (595), most consecutive games with a reception (103), and most touchdown receptions in a game (4), a record he shared with the great Don Hutson.[43]

After grinding down the Lions 16–12 at home in the famous "Sanders Held to Zero Yards" game (minus-1 yards, to be exact) on New Year's Eve, it was back to Dallas the following weekend.[44]

The team learned some tough lessons from the previous season's divisional playoff loss to the juggernaut Cowboys—but not enough of them. One of Wolf's biggest mistakes as GM was his very first draft pick, Terrell Buckley. While the cornerback picked off a pass in the 1993–94 divisional playoff game, renewing some confidence among coaches and teammates, his performance across the 1994–95 season was less than spectacular.

"Buckley struggled down the stretch matching up with bigger receivers," declared the *Milwaukee Journal Sentinel,* which graded his season with a D.[45] Indeed, opponents knew well that the best way to stifle "T-Buck" was with a taller receiver. "A good big man usually beats a good small man," noted *New York Times* sports columnist Frank Litsky. "A combination of size and untimely mistakes by the Green Bay Packers helped the Dallas Cowboys whip them 35–9," Litsky continued in his post-game coverage.

In two devastating plays in an eight-and-a-half-minute window, Troy Aikman lobbed passes to oversized receivers Michael Irvin and Alvin Harper that led to touchdowns, the latter against the 5'9" Buckley, effectively wrapping up the game.[46] The *Press-Gazette*'s Jim Hayes' pregame analysis proved prescient. "Look for Dallas to try to exploit its height advantage in the passing game by throwing the ball high to Irvin

(6'2") and Harper (6'3")."[47] In Buckley's defense, however, cornerback bookend Doug Evans missed key plays, too. But their Achilles' heel had been exposed and exploited.

The Packers made progress beginning in April 1995 by dumping Buckley off to the Dolphins in return for "past considerations."[48] In other words, Wolf was happy just to get rid of the former first-rounder, even if it meant not getting anything real in return.

The Green and Gold finished the '95 season 11–5—their best record since 1966—and clinched the NFC Central division on Christmas Eve, when Steelers receiver Yancey Thigpen dropped a six-yard touchdown gimme from quarterback Neil O'Donnell giving Packers the win 24–19.[49] It got even better. The following week on New Year's Day not 48 hours after Favre led his team to a first-round playoff victory, dropping Atlanta 37–20,[50] he earned a lifetime achievement award of sorts at age 26. "He was just like a kid winning his first trophy ever," then girlfriend Deanna Tynes recounted of her future husband. Favre had just been voted the NFL MVP by the Associated Press, the first Packer to earn the league's highest individual honor since Bart Starr in 1966.[51] Not a bad year.

In the second round of the 1995–96 postseason, the Packers traveled to San Francisco where they upset the reigning Super Bowl champion 49ers at Candlestick Park. For Holmgren it was a homecoming like no other. Action picked up on the second possession when Packers linebacker Wayne Simmons jarred loose a screen pass from 49ers running back Adam Walker halfway into the first quarter. Craig Newsome—Buckley's replacement in the 1995 draft—scooped up the live ball and returned it for six points. The breakout offensive play on the Packers' second possession was an over-the-middle bullet to tight end Keith Jackson—the "past consideration" of the Buckley trade. (Jackson had been acquired from Miami a few weeks prior to the transaction in March of 1995.) Three plays later, Jackson was in the end zone on a three-yard toss from Favre.[52] The Packers rolled the 49ers in the first half 21–3 and kept the lead in the second half, finishing 27–17. All of this before San Francisco born-and-raised Holmgren's hometown audience, including family, friends, and old players and coaches.

The Pack had punched their ticket to the NFC Championship Game, and the diaspora could hardly contain itself. "For this generation of Green Bay Packers and their fans, it is the finest hour," said Tony Walter of the *Press-Gazette*.[53]

Well, almost. The next stop was Dallas, who'd defeated them in the playoffs the last two seasons. A dark pall cast over Green Bay as the *Press-Gazette* set the mood on the Monday before the matchup. In the Sports section's lead story, headlined "Old Nemesis Awaits," reporter Pete Dougherty correctly diagnosed the Packers' losing ways against the Cowboys, whose offense had averaged 35 points a game in their last six meetings. And with good reason. Pro Bowler Michael Irvin was fifth in the league in receiving. And perennial All-Pro running back Emmitt Smith, who posted two 100-yard games in those prior playoff matchups, led the Cowboys' first-ranked running attack in the NFC. Both the pass and run game were made possible by an impenetrable offensive line, completing the trifecta.[54]

Favre nevertheless came within a touchdown of avenging their '90s nemesis, taking the lead in the third quarter before succumbing to the Dallas secondary.

Rolling right on first down, the Mississippi gunslinger threw it away but not far enough off and into the hands of cornerback Larry Brown. Two plays later, Smith punched in a 16-yard touchdown run to lock in the win. Favre failed to convert on two more possessions, coming within twelve points of the Super Bowl. Final: 38–27, Dallas.[55]

On ESPN's highlight reels that night, Chris Berman's disquieting words rang throughout Packer Nation. "Next Packer possession: The Mistake," he intoned, describing Favre's ill-fated pass. The ubiquitous SportsCenter replayed the lowlight over and over again, tormenting the Packers' faithful like an incubus having his way in a horrid nightmare. "The mistake…The mistake…The mistake."

But unlike in past years, the mood in Green Bay wasn't all misery.

"I think we've closed the gap considerably," said Ron Wolf. The Packers left Texas not demoralized but rejuvenated. The team suggested they were "only a home-field advantage away" from conquering the NFC, according to Dougherty.

"When they mention the [premier] teams in the NFC, we should be on that list," said Green Bay tight end Mark Chmura.[56]

Sports Illustrated predicted the Packers would meet the Kansas City Chiefs in Super Bowl XXXI the following year—and lose to them.[57] But before the Packers could make the Super Bowl, the team's leader and 1995 league MVP had to reveal, and overcome, some personal demons.[58]

On May 14, 1996, at a press conference in Green Bay, with long-time girlfriend Deanna Tynes at one side and his coach at the other, a humbled Favre announced that he had endured a long-running pain-killer addiction. "Voluntarily I am going to admit [myself] into an in-treatment facility," he said, his head down and hands shoved sheepishly into his pockets, "for however long it takes to get better, and my objective is to get better."[59]

Although a functioning alcoholic between weekends—for his first practice in April of 1992, he showed up "with the scent of alcohol adhered to his body," according to Jeff Pearlman in the Favre biography, *Gunslinger*[60]—Favre's painkiller revelation was news, though it made sense. It was baffling how the unrestrained gunslinger persevered through pain and injury when any drug-free quarterback would've left the field or even the sport itself. Plus, one addiction can easily morph into another.

For those who wanted to know when it all began, Favre offered not just the date but the exact play: "Green right H6 white corner fullback flat."

On November 15, 1992, his future teammate Reggie White, then of the Philadelphia Eagles, drove Favre into the turf and crushed his left shoulder early in the first half.

It was Favre's first "meeting" with White—and painkillers.

"They injected [the collarbone] and I was like, this feels great," Favre recalled in ESPN's *30 for 30* documentary on White. "It popped like popcorn every move I made, but it didn't hurt. So, I said, I could deal with it." Favre stayed in the game and in the second half mounted a comeback drive—again—to win 27–24. No wonder White was impressed.[61] Favre entered rehab at the Menninger Clinic in Topeka, Kansas, in the middle of May and left at the end of June.[62] But that would not be the end of his issues with addiction. Unbeknownst to fans at the time, he would go to rehab three times in total for either painkiller and/or alcohol abuse, including a stay in 1998 after his second trip to the Super Bowl. He revealed the information 20 years later in 2018 in an interview with *Sports Illustrated* columnist Peter King.[63]

Favre and the Packers had gotten inchingly close to the Super Bowl, but not without paying a steep price. Favre cleaned up his act, married his high school sweetheart, and began the march to Super Bowl XXXI. Starting the first game of the season, Favre was officially a family man and set to make a personal and professional comeback.

Across their long history, the Packers consistently shined before national audiences. If the 1983 *Monday Night Football* donnybrook against the Washington Redskins was the most memorable, then the Packers' 1996 win over the 49ers was the most consequential.

Going into the matchup, Green Bay was off to a strong 5–1 start. It was shaping up to be a banner year, but stiff divisional competition sat on the western horizon, where regional foe Minnesota—their only loss thus far—boasted the same record. For Favre, the Monday night game against San Francisco on October 14—"…a team that for more than a decade dominated the NFL…"[64]—was his "most physically demanding" game to-date, according to the *Press-Gazette*.[65] To say he worked hard would be an understatement. No. 4 threw for a whopping 395 yards in a team-record 61 passes that evening, grinding the 49ers defense to a pulp with 24 first downs. Appropriately, the game ended with an overtime field goal. But instead of Green Bay's opponent missing one, as had Washington's Mark Moseley in 1983, the Packers had control. Chris Jacke split the uprights with a 53-yarder, tied for the second longest in team history. The Green and Gold didn't merely luck out today; this time they won on their own accord. Final: 23–20, Packers.[66]

Cheers pushing 100-plus decibels at Lambeau Field set off a chain reaction of euphoria across the state.[67] "Spontaneous demonstrations" popped up on college campuses, including at the University of Wisconsin–Oshkosh and UW–Whitewater. The latter was left with $20,000 in damaged property. "Students emptied out of dorms and gathered in the middle of the campus," said alumnus Judd Gehl. "Next thing, the crowd of one-thousand plus were on its way to Main Street and the bar district," he added. "Well, not all of us—others went to the football field and tore down the goal posts."[68]

As the sports world turned its attention to Green Bay, stories about the team popped up in *Esquire,* the *New York Times, TIME* magazine, and just about every sports publication. Later, the NFL Films' *Packers: Super Bowl XXXI Champions* video would become standard fare in every Wisconsin living room; families bought multiple copies as gifts for loved ones and replacements for overplayed VHS tapes with snapped ribbons. (More than 70,000 copies would be sold in Green Bay alone).[69] Packermania was in full effect.

When the playoffs arrived, the 13–3 Packers were comfortably seeded first in the NFC, allowing them to rest during the wild card round. In the divisional playoffs, they made quick work of the 49ers, winning 35–14.[70]

Although they'd long for the chance to take on the Cowboys and slay their longtime demons, it was not to be. The upstart Carolina Panthers, in their second NFL season, fell to Dallas 26–17 the week before.

Despite temperatures 16 degrees warmer than that of the legendary Ice Bowl game, the thermometer still hovered at just above zero for the NFC championship 29 years later on January 12, 1997. Unforgiving wind gusts set the wind chill at minus-13.

The Packers slipped up in the first quarter and Carolina jumped out with a 7–0 lead, but Green Bay quickly got their bearings and finished the half ahead of Carolina 17–10. In the second half, Green Bay outscored Carolina 13–3. On paper, the Packers were impressive (479 total offensive yards, 22 first downs); in person, they were brilliant. In one spectacular sequence in the second half, under a collapsing pocket Favre went downfield and down the depth chart and hit Don Beebe for a gain of 29. A few minutes later, on the same possession, Favre escaped the NFL sack leader Kevin Greene when it appeared he had finished off Favre, but the gunslinger got it off in time, shoveling the pigskin to running back Dorsey Levens for an eight-yard gain. The drive ended in a Chris Jacke field goal, but the score and magical preceding plays were enough to dash Carolina's hopes. Winning 30–13, the Packers were NFC champions with a trip to Super Bowl XXXI. After 29 years, the spell had been broken: the Packers were returning to the game they won in its first incarnation. GM Ron Wolf considered it the best win of his career. Beating Carolina "was my magical moment," he said.[71]

A full week of festivities kicked off the next day, when Green Bay fans began migrating south to Super Bowl host city New Orleans. Bourbon Street was an apt cousin to College Avenue in Appleton or Washington Street in Green Bay, each of which boasted one of the highest concentration of bars in the Dairy State. The whiff of Creole cooking in the Big Easy was a change of pace from the ever-present waft of bratwurst and burgers at Lambeau Field's parking lot on gameday but no less celebratory. The French Quarter's party atmosphere was certainly something the Green Bay faithful could appreciate.

Some fans even made pilgrimages to Favre's hometown of Kiln, Mississippi, an hour drive from New Orleans. They downed Miller Lites and brandy old fashioneds at Favre's favorite watering hole, the Broke Spoke. Bartenders could allegedly pick out the Wisconsinites, but not by their accents or cheesehead hats. "Packers fans always return empty beer cans cold," one barkeep reportedly said.

Compared to the action-packed NFC championship, the Super Bowl was somewhat anticlimactic, as many of them are. As predicted, the

Packers topped the Patriots and by the exact spread 35–21. But the road to victory wasn't pretty. In this game neither defense nor offense took the spotlight, notwithstanding Favre's solid 107.9 passer rating and Reggie White's three sacks. Rather, special teams dominated the day. On the strength of a timely 99-yard touchdown return late in the 3rd quarter, Desmond Howard claimed the game's MVP, the first special teams player to do so. (Another bullseye free-agent acquisition by Wolf.) Howard piled up a record-tying 244 all-purpose yards in the game.[72]

The welcome home celebration was nearly as impressive as the Super Bowl victory. One hundred thousand fans lined a five-mile parade route from Austin Straubel Airport to Lambeau Field. Onlookers spilled into the freshly plowed streets, turning a 15-minute parade into a three hour-plus traffic jam. Still dressed for a Southern climate, players and coaches were without coats, and the bus without windows.

"Gonna be a short little parade, we'll go through town, we'll come back, 15 minutes you'll be fine," former fullback William Henderson recalled in the team's centennial documentary. "Three and a half hours later, we're still riding, still waving, borrowing jackets, mittens, coats, hand warmers, hot chocolate—anything to stay warm."

At Lambeau Field, 60,000 fans crowded in, some waiting for seven hours to see the team. The mid-winter sun had long since set and temperatures were dropping like the 10,000 pounds of confetti that rained down on Walnut Street earlier in the day. The wind chill sat at minus-10 by the time Harlan, Wolf, Holmgren, and a few players climbed the riser at midfield. Lifting the Lombardi Trophy high, each thanked the faithful.[73]

"We thank you once again for the support you've given this organization, from the time it started, through the good years and the bad years," Harlan said. "This trophy is for you."[74]

Chapter 11

Makeover

Going into the 1997 season, *Sports Illustrated* picked the Packers to win it all, as did just about everyone else.[1] A majority of sports publications surveyed by the *Press-Gazette* in August that year predicted the Packers to either go to or win the Super Bowl.[2] At the annual Welcome Back Luncheon that summer, Packers coach Mike Holmgren made comparisons to the 1972 undefeated Miami Dolphins squad, claiming that the team "has the mindset to go 19–0."[3] The Green and Gold were such overwhelming favorites it was hard for fans not to ask: Why not just skip the regular season altogether?

Shortly after the gun fell silent on the NFC Championship Game—having shrugged off the 49ers 23–10 in San Francisco on January 11, 1998—the Packers were anointed as 12.5-point Super Bowl favorites.[4] With a convincing championship win the year before, when Green Bay dusted off the New England Patriots 35–21 in the Big Easy, followed by strong performances during the 1997 regular season, going 13–3, the Packers were certainly on track for a repeat. So confident were the fans that they were thinking past this year's Super Bowl to a possible third championship three-peat. No other franchise had won three consecutive titles, as had the Packers back in the Great Depression and later in the 1960s.

For Green Bay fans the game was a heartbreaker, rendering the 1997 season a thorough disappointment on par with the 1989, 1982, or 1972 teams, when it felt like the franchise was on the cusp of something truly great. The club had improved dramatically throughout the '90s after a long epoch of mediocrity—and fan expectations tracked accordingly. (Area medical professionals even cautioned fans to temper their hopes to avoid bouts of depression, in case the Packers lost.)

To understand just how much of an underdog the Denver Broncos were in Super Bowl XXXII, you have to go beyond betting lines and predictions. In fact, you need to go back to the 1983 season, the last time an AFC team won the Super Bowl, when the Raiders upset the Redskins in Super Bowl XVIII. And during that 13-year span of NFC dominance, in which the AFC mostly failed to even compete in the big game, Elway and his Broncos were responsible for three losses.[5]

Even though the entire sports world seemed to rally around little Green Bay just a year earlier, football fans were now coalescing behind a new underdog. For Packers fans to hear folks who never watched an NFL game in their lives cheer on John Elway to win his first Super Bowl, it was enough for them to cough up a cold one into their Chili John's chili. The *New York Times* called the 37-year-old Elway, who had come tantalizingly close to winning a title but could never quite get over the hump, the "sentimental favorite."[6]

Apparently, the Packers were no longer America's "it" team.

The championship in San Diego came down to two fourth-quarter drives, an appropriate denouement for two quarterbacks known for their late-game heroics. The powerful tandem of Elway and running back Terrell Davis stormed 48 yards downfield, and Davis waltzed into the end zone on a one-yard handoff, putting the Broncos up a touchdown 31–24.

Now it was Favre's turn. After a strong return attempt by Antonio Freeman, who was cut down just shy of the Packers' 30, the three-time MVP-winning QB strutted onto the field for what would be his final march of the game.

"If anyone loves this role, it's this man," NBC's play-by-play announcer Dick Enberg told a national audience of 90 million.[7] As Favre took his time setting up, Enberg filled dead air recalling the gunslinger's nicknames: "They call him Country, from little Kiln, Mississippi, his dad Irv calls him Hammerhead…" What could be more American than a smalltown southern boy with a father for a high school coach marching his way to Super Bowl glory?

It was a reprieve from the previous week's news cycles, which were dominated by a national political scandal being cooked up as another Watergate: President Bill Clinton had been carrying on an affair with a White House intern 27 years his junior. The unethical if not inappropriate relationship between Clinton and Monica Lewinsky had shaken officialdom and captivated American audiences.[8] But for three hours, the NFL's top dueling gunslingers would take the spotlight and entertain both national and worldwide audiences.

As Green Bay's drive began with 1:39 remaining, Packers center (and Favre's best pal) Frank "Bag of Donuts" Winters slipped the pigskin into No. 4's waiting hands. In a quickly collapsing pocket, Favre carefully tossed a screen pass up the middle to running back Dorsey Levens, who broke out for a 22-yard gain.

With 23 seconds off the clock, Favre dropped back and repeated the play—though just missing an interception as defensive tackle Maa Tanuvasa tipped the ball toward defensive end Alfred Williams. Pro Bowler Levens thought fast and snatched the flapping pigskin, preventing a game-ending turnover—no gain. In 1987, Elway had Sammy Winder; today, it seemed Favre would have Levens.

Favre called timeout and cursed his rookie mistake while no doubt thanking the football gods for giving him another chance.

On second down, with no options downfield—the Broncos secondary was just as strong as its mighty offensive line—Favre found Levens again on a screen for a gain of 13 and a first down.

"The NFC on a 13-year run in the Super Bowl," Enberg reminded his audience between downs.

With just over a minute of play left on the clock, Favre hit Levens for the fourth time of the series, bringing the squad to the Denver 32. A touchdown and extra point would tie it—a field goal would do nothing. Favre could no doubt feel the screws tighten, but a cool Coach Holmgren—donning a pair of blue blockers from the sideline—calmed his quarterback, maintaining his rep as the least excitable head coach in the league. It seemed to work. For a second.

On second down, instead of spiking the ball or taking a timeout, Favre allowed 22 seconds to roll off the clock while fans screamed at him to call time. The situation recalled play-by-play announcer Jim Lampley's admonition five years earlier in Week 3 of the 1992 season, Favre's first game with the Packers: "You live and die with someone like Favre." The timing couldn't be worse; you'd hope the QB would have learned a lesson or two since his debut.

Next, Favre upped the tempo, firing a rocket up the middle into heavy traffic that bounced off wide receiver Antonio Freeman's numbers and tumbled to the turf. Third down.

Favre went up the middle again, this time to receiver Robert Brooks, also in double coverage, but with little chance against defenders who offered no daylight. Then it got worse: Brooks got pinched between two colliding Denver defenders as free safety Steve Atwater inadvertently speared defensive back Randy Hilliard covering the other side of the field. Atwater and Hillard fell limply to the ground. The crack of helmets could be heard coast to coast. Risking life and limb, Denver was leaving it all on the field. They wanted it more than Green Bay. All three players were ruled injured, and, per NFL rules, each team was docked a timeout, leaving Favre with none remaining. Freeman, Atwater, and Hilliard were pulled from the game due to the injuries. Fourth down; 32 seconds to go.

With a single bullet left in the chamber, Favre threw toward tight end Mark Chmura across the middle, seven yards down field—just enough for a first down—but couldn't get enough zip to avoid Denver linebacker John Mobley, who swatted the ball away.

Broncos win, 31–24. Game over—Elway gets his Super Bowl victory.[9]

Packer Nation had seemingly taken counseling sessions ahead of the loss; "We Had a Good Year" read the front page of the *Press-Gazette*.[10] "We're disappointed, but they're still champions," said one fan, referring to the Packers as a Little League dad would his Pee Wee players after a tough loss.[11]

Some fans remained optimistic. "The last step off the field this Super Bowl is the first step toward the next Super Bowl," wrote *Press-Gazette* cartoonist Joe Heller.[12]

Favre, too, was hopeful. "I'm 28, I think I'll be back to several Super Bowls," he said.

Back in the front office, shared revenue and salary cap rules instituted as part of the 1993 collective bargaining agreement had leveled the playing field among small and large market teams, helping the Packers immensely. But while the hundreds of millions from selling TV broadcasting rights was divvied equally among teams, propriety revenue generated by individual teams—ticket sales, club seats, concessions, pro shops, parking—was not. This led to some franchises with limited in-house revenue opportunities, including the Packers, who in turn suffered low cash reserves.

This revenue disparity was nothing new to Green Bay. Nor was the solution: a new stadium. New facilities meant more seating, refurbished and added luxury suites, and expensive amenities. This is to say nothing of raising franchise value exponentially—literally. The Dallas Cowboys' value has skyrocketed *70-fold* over Jerry Jones' ownership tenure beginning in 1989, when he bought the team for $140 million. Today, its value is pegged at around $10 billion. Jones opened a new stadium in 2009. (Imagine that: A socialist redistributive scheme—revenue sharing—that makes rich owners even richer?!)

Additional revenue from capital improvements would grow cash reserves, giving teams flexibility to offer big signing bonuses to top prospects. Although upfront bonuses, like all player compensation, counted against the salary cap, stocked reserves offered teams the ability to pay more and bigger bonuses up front. And because salary caps equalized payrolls among all NFL teams, their only advantage when luring players was the size of signing bonuses. This is why the stadium boom of the 1990s happened. Free agency and salary caps applied upward pressure on wages, while limits on player salaries incentivized teams to build up cash reserves so they could entice players with big bonuses. The only thing left was figuring out who would pay for all of it. The owners? They certainly stood to gain the most. But as in any monopoly, the producers had the upper hand. Indeed, the NFL is a sanctioned monopoly that had crushed its closest competitor, the upstart USFL, in the 1980s.[13]

If there is one thing rich people don't like to do it is spend their own money—especially when they don't need to. (How do you think they got rich in the first place?) Sports owners applied overwhelming pressure on cities that hosted teams by threatening to relocate their teams. These communities capitulated, handing over millions of dollars in taxpayer subsidies to finance stadium construction, a phenomenon that included other pro sports leagues like the National Basketball Association (29 new arenas since 1989) and Major League Baseball (25 new stadiums since 1989).[14]

The Packers didn't have a rich owner who could cut big checks for signing bonuses, but they did have legions of fans, who, in the wake of a euphoric Super Bowl victory in 1997, were looking for excuses to spend money on anything "Packers": shirts, posters, key chains, even pieces of paper. Which led team president Bob Harlan to hatch an unoriginal but tried-and-true idea.

It was time for another stock sale.

Harlan believed he could sell 400,000 shares of the team at $200 a pop and raise $80 million. Not bad for a product worth only the paper it was printed on. (Recall that shares paid no dividends and came with diluted voting rights.) This would give the organization an immediate cash infusion to compete with other teams. And the timing couldn't have been better.[15]

The team's roster was in rough shape. Players were aging and free agents were getting poached by other squads. What had helped the Packers in 1993 with the Reggie White signing—expansive free agency rules offering more teams opportunities to sign top talent—disadvantaged them in 1998, five years into this era. The NFL's labor market had destabilized, leading to skyrocketing salaries; players earned 38 percent more than in 1993 alone.[16]

Though the plan for a stock sale arose shortly after the Packer's Super Bowl XXXI win, it wasn't implemented until the following year because league owners had initially voted to deny a new stock sale for the Packers at the owners' spring 1997 meeting. It soon became obvious why: they didn't want extra competition in the free agency market. So, Harlan promised not to use proceeds for player salaries, only for capital projects such as a new stadium. But cash is fungible, and new revenue would simply free up money elsewhere on the books.

At the October 1997 meeting, the owners were still unwilling to approve a sale. The situation was getting dire, and at one point, Harlan told the team's general counsel, "[T]he stock thing might die." Soon after, Commissioner Paul Tagliabue overruled the owners, claiming that a stock sale fell under the Packers' grandfathered ownership clause, established decades earlier, that granted the right to proceed with a sale. (Why this obvious and simple explanation wasn't given earlier is unclear.)

The sale commenced in mid-November 1997 and continued through the spring of 1998. Initial interest was off the charts. Within 24 hours, the team website received 2 million hits. In the end, the sale missed projections wildly and reached only one-third of its original goal. The team sold 120,010 shares and raised $24 million.[17]

As a brilliant midsummer sun enveloped Lambeau Field, more than 18,000 shareholders and guests basked in its glow on July 8, 1998, for the first annual shareholder meeting at the stadium. The location was necessary to accommodate the influx of new stockholders. Existing ones showed up in numbers, too, with nearly 62 percent of *all* shareholders attending in person or by proxy. (A quorum of 50.1 percent had to be present to conduct business.)[18]

Among other team business, Harlan discussed recently announced plans to remodel stadium facilities, including a new press box, additional luxury seating, a pro shop, and eateries. Weeks earlier, he had revealed details of the proposal, namely that a national sports architectural firm had been retained.[19] The project was estimated to run $75 million.[20] It wasn't like Harlan was proposing a new half-billion-dollar stadium or threatening to move the team if fans wouldn't agree to a tax referendum to pay for it. The Packers were above all that. Indeed, a referendum or public subsidies to pay for new facilities was never broached. But Harlan's silence on the topic was deafening. With enormous bottom-line pressure from salaries and proposed construction costs, it was only a matter of time before the team president would have no choice but to go to the taxpayers for help.

Nevertheless, the club announced record profits and solid cash reserves. For fiscal year 1998, the team reported a $6.7 million profit, or 15 percent more than in 1997, and cash reserves peaked at $51.9 million, thanks largely to the stock sale. That was the good news. The bad news: The team was committed to $29 million in unamortized signing bonuses, and player salary expenses for the year were about two-thirds of operating expenses. (In 1998, player bonuses equaled the entire book value of team facilities!)

Thankfully, shared revenue from record TV contracts was ticking up—though it wasn't enough. Moreover, 15 clubs, or half the league, had recently built new stadiums or planned to before the decade was out. (Only two NFL stadiums were built between 1981 and 1994.)[21] All these new stadiums and facilities meant new additional revenue streams for those franchises. Once their new homes were complete, most of those clubs would "leapfrog" the Packers in proprietary revenue, as Green Bay team treasurer John Underwood admitted weeks earlier in an interview with the *Press-Gazette*.[22] And it would happen fast because construction elsewhere had been underwritten with tax subsidies, allowing new revenue to go toward player salaries immediately.

For the time being, Packers fans were uneasy but seemed to accept this new financial reality. "I think the salaries are out of line, but having said that, the players are worth whatever they can get," said one Green Bay resident.[23]

Those fans likely did not read the full finance report, nor did they read between the lines of Underwood's overall assessment of the financial

1919 Green Bay Packers. In front of Indian Packing Company, Green Bay, Wisconsin. (Public domain)

The original *Green Bay Press-Gazette* building at 315-317 Cherry Street in Green Bay, where Packers president Andrew Turnbull devised the idea of a stock sale to resurrect the team in 1922. (Courtesy of the Neville Public Museum of Brown County)

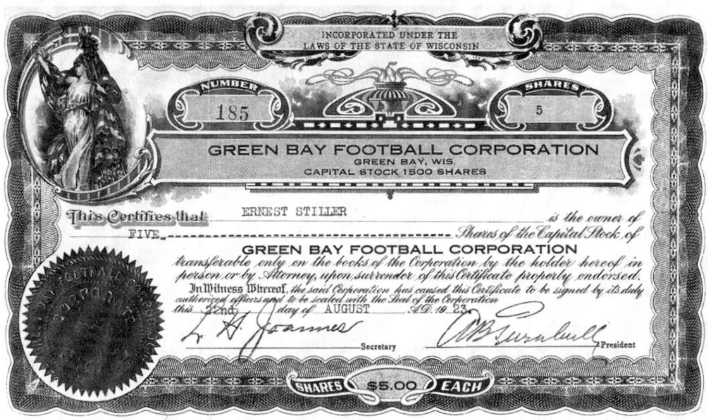
INCORPORATED UNDER THE LAWS OF THE STATE OF WISCONSIN

NUMBER 185 SHARES 5

GREEN BAY FOOTBALL CORPORATION
GREEN BAY, WIS.
CAPITAL STOCK 1500 SHARES

This Certifies that ERNEST STILLER is the owner of FIVE Shares of the Capital Stock of
GREEN BAY FOOTBALL CORPORATION
transferable only on the books of the Corporation by the holder hereof in person or by Attorney, upon surrender of this Certificate properly endorsed.
In Witness Whereof, the said Corporation has caused this Certificate to be signed by its duly authorized officers and to be sealed with the Seal of the Corporation this 22nd day of AUGUST A.D. 19 23.

Secretary President

SHARES $5.00 EACH

A stock certificate from the team's 1923 drive that sold for $5 and raised about $5,000; a certificate was auctioned off for $152,000 in 2025. (Courtesy of the Neville Public Museum of Brown County)

Lavvie Dilweg (1927–34), considered the best two-way end of the pre–Don Hutson era, is one of two members of the 1920s NFL All-Decade team not in the Hall of Fame. Dilweg practiced law and, after football, served in Congress (WI-8). (Sean Dilweg)

Fans want this Packers scout/business manager (1950–60) in the Pro Football Hall of Fame. Jack Vainisi drafted or signed 13 future Hall of Famers; this contribution is not yet recognized league-wide. (Sam Vainisi)

Curly Lambeau outside Rockwood Lodge in New Franken, Wisconsin. The practice facility was a money pit and burned to the ground in January 1950, shortly before Lambeau left the team. (Courtesy of the Neville Public Museum of Brown County)

Team cofounder George Calhoun (right) covered the Packers for the *Press-Gazette* while doubling as team publicist. State Fair Park, Milwaukee; November 1943. (Courtesy of the Neville Public Museum of Brown County)

1944 championship celebration in the locker room at the Polo Grounds in New York City. Curly Lambeau center. December 17, 1944. (The Tom Pigeon Collection)

Lee Remmel covered the Packers for the *Press-Gazette* (1945–74) and later directed the team's public relations (1974–2004). December 1960, Green Bay, Wisconsin. (Courtesy of the Neville Public Museum of Brown County)

Halfback Paul Hornung perfected the Packers sweep, head coach Vince Lombardi's signature offensive play that led the team to five NFL titles in the 1960s. (Malcom Emmons—Imagn Images)

Vince Lombardi being carried by Green Bay Packers players after defeating the Dallas Cowboys for the 1966 NFL season championship. (Getty Images/Bettmann)

During his tenure (1971–74), head coach Dan Devine (left) produced a losing record and no shortage of gaffes, including benching Packers great Ray Nitschke (right) for a hapless rookie in 1971. (© Green Bay Press-Gazette / USA TODAY NETWORK)

Fans descend on preseason practices every August. Here, the author (lower right) and family wait in line for autographs. Ashwaubenon, Wisconsin; August 1986. (Steve Nelson)

Green Bay Packers president Bob Harlan raises his fist in victory September 12, 2000, at the Stadium View Sports Bar in Ashwaubenon, Wisconsin, after Brown County voters approved the stadium sales tax referendum. (AP Photo/Mike Roemer)

QBs Brett Favre (1991–2008) and Aaron Rodgers' (2005–2022) tense and often frictious relationship as teammates would soften in later years. Here, Rodgers congratulates Favre on the occasion of his NFL Hall of Fame induction. (© Ken Blaze—Imagn Images)

Quarterback Jordan Love (left) and defensive lineman Micah Parsons (right) are the latest offense-defense duo to anchor a championship-caliber Packers squad. (Kevin Sabitus via AP)

Book co-dedicatee Steve Vander Loop in his season-ticket seats. The Packers are a publicly owned team that boasts 500,000-plus stockholders, including paper mill execs, teachers, lawyers, and yes, school janitors. (Mark Vander Loop)

Maria Nelson (author's wife) with longtime Packers PR director and book co-dedicatee Lee Remmel and wife, Noreen. Maria and Lee made fast friends when she interned for the Packers, remaining close until his passing in 2015. (Maria Nelson)

picture, accumulating expenses, and league competition. "We have to continue to deal with the challenge of revenue because we continue to plan to win," he said.[24] Fans would understand fully what Underwood meant in short order.

All good things come to an end, it is said. So too would a dominant era end for the Packers in the wake of the 1998 season. Reggie White would play his final game for Green Bay, winning his second career Defensive Player of the Year award in a masterful swan song of a season. While the team made it to the postseason for the sixth year in a row after amassing an 11–5 record, the Packers settled on a distant fifth seed, which got them a ticket to Mike Holmgren's old hometown for a wild card matchup with the 49ers. There in San Francisco, Holmgren faced his former apprentice, Steve Mariucci. Save for Holmgren himself, no other coach in the league knew Favre better than the "Mooch," his first quarterback coach with the Packers. "Brett's style, that gunslinger attitude, it's very high risk and high reward. He's going to take chances… Sometimes the other team is going to catch it," Mariucci told Packers.com in a 2007 retrospective.[25]

Favre was average at best in the matchup, throwing two touchdowns and two interceptions and getting sacked twice. San Francisco's Jerry Rice fumbled a reception that officials ruled complete. Without the aid of instant replay, which was eliminated after the 1991 season, the Packers had no recourse but to take it on the chin. On the last play of the game, 49ers quarterback Steve Young threaded a pass to young star receiver Terrell Owens for a go-ahead touchdown and the win. No tandem but a pair of future Hall of Famers could have connected on the play. San Francisco wins, 30–27.

"If this was the final game of the Mike Holmgren era in Green Bay, it's difficult to imagine a more stunning and painful ending," said Pete Dougherty of the *Press-Gazette*.[26] And so it was.

A week later, on January 8, Holmgren left the Packers and signed with the Seattle Seahawks as both their head coach and general manager.[27] Rumors abounded that Holmgren had bottom-lined operational control before exploring options elsewhere.[28] Harlan demurred—Wolf was not ready to leave. Perhaps Harlan knew better; though Holmgren would remain Seattle's coach through 2008, the Seahawks relieved him of general manager responsibilities in 2002.[29]

Three days later, Wolf hired former Packers defensive coordinator and recently fired Eagles head coach Ray Rhodes. "There's No Doubt: Rhodes Is the Man," read the lead in the *Press-Gazette* Sports section. To an outsider, it seemed a rash move, one made quickly and without consideration of any other coach.[30] And he did so despite a bumper crop of available talent, including Andy Reid, Dick Jauron, and Bill Belichick, among others.[31] Yet Wolf made clear Rhodes had been top of mind for at least a year. As the GM often said, "If you're not getting better, you're getting worse," a mantra that understudy and successor Ted Thompson would repeat ad nauseum through the years.[32] That wisdom applied to coaches, too. Well aware that Holmgren's stock was only going up and his wares were in high demand, Wolf knew it was simply a matter of time before Holmgren walked—especially if Wolf was unwilling to surrender his job to Holmgren (or anyone for that matter).

Rhodes knew the team well, having worked under Holmgren as defensive coordinator in 1992 and 1993, and was a star pupil of the San Francisco/West Coast offense, offering Wolf "the chance to continue with the offensive scheme and demands for excellence," said Dougherty. If there is one word to describe Wolf's personnel strategy, it is churn. In the revolving door that was the Packers, Wolf was always evaluating new players to replace old ones. ("Every two weeks you'd see what seemed like hundreds of guys working out," Hall of Fame safety LeRoy Butler, creator of the Lambeau Leap, recalled in 2019.) It only made sense he would apply the same strategy for coaches.[33]

Whether Wolf's move was rushed or well thought out over several years, his pick for coach would prove disastrous. Aside from Scooter McLean's dumpster fire 1–10–1 season in 1958, no single Packers campaign felt more ignominious than Rhodes' in 1999, even though the team went a respectable 8–8. It was an enormous comedown from two consecutive Super Bowl seasons just a couple years earlier, as well the worst finish since Lindy Infante's 4–12 in 1991. Like McLean, Rhodes was known as a "players' coach," which translated to lax discipline, lack of control over players, and nurturing a "country club atmosphere," said team historian Cliff Christl.[34]

Wolf dumped Rhodes within hours of the team's final game of the season. "Our players did not respond to his program," Wolf explained.[35] No kidding.

Wolf committed the first coach-hiring sin in picking Rhodes. His second came right on the heels of jettisoning Rhodes. The GM pivoted from that mistake by hiring Mike Sherman for the 2000 season on the strength of a single interview. "Bob, I've just been swept off my feet by this guy," Wolf told Harlan at the time. "If I had any guts, I'd hire him right now." He slept on it and made the offer to Sherman the following morning.[36]

It seemed odd that none of the 18,707 shareholders on July 8 thought to ask Harlan about a stadium tax. Plenty of time was afford the assembled to speak up during the Q and A:

> "Has any consideration been given to adding a stadium bar and restaurant?"
>
> "Who in the sales department was responsible for the stupid setup of shareholder sales stands?"
>
> "What is up with the grass on the field?"

By now "tax subsidy" and "sports stadium" were synonymous. Or it was rare the two were not uttered at the same press conference. As the '90s closed out, standard practice among pro sports owners was to grovel before taxpayers for subsidies to finance new stadiums. That question would soon be asked by the Packers.

In January 1999, all of Titletown was abuzz with media reports that Harlan would in fact go to the taxpayers for support. At first, he was coy, offering only official statements simply saying that the team was "exploring a number of options" to pay for stadium improvements and offering precious few details. That only fueled speculation. On February 2, 1999, the day Harlan's statement was released, the *Press-Gazette* ran a story on the prospect of a 0.5 percent county sales tax to fund stadium construction, including charts of how much more items would cost memorializing the era itself—compact disc (7.5 cents), Furby (15 cents), or computer ($7.50)—and statements from local legislators.[37]

For nearly an entire year Harlan, the Packers and local and state politicians would be peppered with questions about stadium financing. It couldn't have come at a worse time than the singular Ray Rhodes season and worst record in eight years at 8–8. But the Packers did have some highlights, namely a convincing and gratifying win over the Bears at Chicago in December. Fortuitously, Harlan picked the day after the victory to announce plans for a stadium referendum. "We are a fan-owned franchise. We welcome the opportunity to take the issue to the fans," he said on December 6, 1999. At the same time, team officials began lobbying Madison for support to augment or even supplant local funding[38] Those efforts soon proved futile.[39] Politicians were fatigued from a recent battle to pay for the Milwaukee Brewers' new stadium, an ordeal that led to recall elections and a shift in party control.

Some folks questioned not just the necessity of stadium improvements but whether the team would actually leave if funding did not materialize. Indeed, that was one of the best parts of a fan-owned team; the franchise could never leave town, and that included failed tax referenda. Former Green Bay Mayor Paul Jadin, who organized city support for the referendum, disagreed: "Unequivocally not true." As finances spiraled relative to the rest of the league, the NFL would intervene, claimed Jadin. "They would say, 'We can't allow this anymore. You will be forced to move.' It wouldn't have taken the Packers out of Wisconsin. Probably would have been a move to Milwaukee."[40] The mayor's assessment certainly aligns with the team's experience from the 1920s through the 1950s, when County Stadium was built in 1953.

So, the Packers had two strikes against them as they stepped into the political arena. First, the state legislature was snake-bit from the Brewer stadium imbroglio. The only help they could expect from Madison was enabling legislation for county voters to adopt a 0.5 percent sales tax for stadium improvements which proved eminently doable. Second, Harlan and the team had unwittingly pounded a message that had finally stuck: the Packers have enough money. The team consistently boasted record-breaking profits, with the recent stock offering having generated $24 million, and huge league-wide television contracts were making *all* NFL teams fabulously rich. The TV deals alone more than quadrupled within a decade from a four-year, $3.6 billion contract ($900 million per year) (1990–93) to an eight-year $17.6 billion deal ($2.2 billion per year) (1998–2001).[41] The untimely release of an NFL Players Association report on June 1, 2000, that revealed the Packers had the highest payroll for 1999 in the league didn't help matters.[42]

Nevertheless, fans seemed open to a referendum. "Immediately, voters said they would support the legislation," said Jadin, who was privy to Harlan's internal polls. "In other words, they're generically saying, 'Yeah, we want to help the Packers.'" Indeed, a public poll conducted of Brown County residents in early February 2000 showed strong support for a referendum, 62 percent to 34 percent.[43] "But that was before they understood what was in the bill," Jadin qualified.

Pro- and anti-stadium referendum forces organized quickly. Despite the Packers returning to the Super Bowl only two years prior, opposition began to build quickly. Why? "I think we were killed by the word 'tax;' people did not like that word,'" Harlan explained.[44] Messaging from one anti-referendum group, the Brown County Taxpayers Association, channeled voter antipathy to public financing of stadiums. "The nationwide scheme to build sports stadiums with public tax dollars is extortion… The citizens of Brown County are being duped…"[45] Ron Wolf was mystified by this sentiment. "I have no idea. I thought they were nuts," Wolf said.[46] (Keep in mind Titletown was only two years removed from its most recent Super Bowl run.)

On May 2, 2000, the Legislature approved enabling legislation for Brown County to adopt an additional 0.5 percent sales tax—subject to voter approval through a local, county referendum—for the stadium and by an overwhelmingly margin, 80–19 in the assembly, 28–5 in the senate.[47] Two weeks later, Governor Tommy Thompson signed the legislation into law.[48] The balance of funding would derive from season ticket user fees; those user fees and additional support from the team would total about $125 million. The total project cost was $295 million for the renovation and about $90 million to cover some operational and maintenance expenses.[49]

Despite massive bipartisan margins in the Legislature and earlier polls showing widespread support for a stadium, albeit in concept only, county residents were now evenly divided on the matter, 49 percent to 46 percent in favor of a sales tax (a statistical tie), according to a poll commissioned by the *Press-Gazette* on May 3.[50] Neither Jadin nor the Packers wavered. Key leaders backed the proposal, including the county's paper of record, the *Press-Gazette*, rekindling the age-old relationship that gave birth to the franchise 81 years ago and had nurtured it over the decades since. "The legacy of the Packers is in our hands. Please give your support so this unique story will continue for decades to come," wrote *Press-Gazette* publisher Bill Nusbaum in January 2000, and the newspaperman maintained the position throughout the campaign.[51] George Calhoun would have been proud.

On August 10, Jadin officially endorsed the referendum by announcing his support near the hallowed grounds of the original City Stadium on the east side. It was at that historical site where Curly took snaps under center, Johnny "Blood" McNally wowed capacity crowds with derring-do runs and hijinks, and Lavvie Dilweg gracefully caught impossible passes. Today, Jadin and Packers officials were imploring fans to vote "yes" on the referendum. "It's been 43 years since the Packers last played in this stadium," Jadin said. "Do you want a mayor in 2044 to have a press conference at Lambeau Field, saying, 'remember when we had professional football here?'"[52] Powerful words.

In the final weeks of the campaign, channeling the spirit of their forebearers in the last stadium referendum in 1956, Packers fans stormed the streets and corner shops of the city and surrounding communities to drum up support for the measure. One Shawano, Wisconsin, native and California resident even moved home to stump for the measure.[53] Team president Bob Harlan got in on the action, too. The weekend before the election he skipped the team flight to play Buffalo to instead stay home and campaign. Like an old country pol, he spent the weekend knocking on doors and glad-handing outside grocery and hardware stores. "On Saturday morning, I went to 15 restaurants and just walked table to table. I went to Sam's Club, Walmart for two hours. Then I went to De Pere and went door to door," Harlan recalled. "It was tough. People either hated me or loved me. No in between."[54]

Three polls in the waning weeks of the campaign showed the contest "too close to call," according to the *Press-Gazette*, but on Tuesday, September 12, 2000, Brown County voters came through and approved the referendum 53 percent to 47 percent.[55]

"Yet again, community comes to team's aid. One more miracle," read the *Press-Gazette*. It was a good thing they didn't wait another year to get the vote passed. "Think about it; September the 12, 2000," Harlan recounted later. Had the team not got the referendum on the September 2000 ballot in time, "We would have voted on September 11, 2001."[56]

Ron Wolf announced his retirement from the Packers and pro football on February 1, 2001.[57] The 62-year-old steered the Packers to two NFC championships and one Super Bowl win over nine seasons, making him the most successful general manager in team history after Lombardi.[58] Before his tenure in Green Bay, he compiled a 29-year career in personnel departments with the Raiders (1963–75; 1978–90), Buccaneers (1975–78) and Jets (1990–91).[59]

Wolf's departure was bittersweet on many levels. Between his announcement and parting on June 1, the team held a groundbreaking for the new stadium, which Wolf headlined. On May 19, under the banner of a brilliant blue Wisconsin spring sky, about 1,000 fans joined Wolf and others for a ceremony inside the bowl. To celebrate, 872 fans gathered in a semicircle on the field for a group embrace that extended from the south end zone to midfield. They couldn't coax an extra 28 fans to break the world record for the largest-ever hug—that would have to wait for a future renovation.

"You fans have been entrusted with an awesome responsibility," Wolf told the assemblage. "You must continue to keep the flame burning here in this…the mecca of professional football."[60] It was one of Wolf's last public appearances as a Packer.

With twisting cranes, buzzing saws, and churning concrete mixers in the background, the Mike Sherman period was already underway, though the new head coach had a long way to go to instill confidence in fans. The team finished 9–7 in 2000 and missed the playoffs for the second consecutive year.

With Wolf and Holmgren both gone, Harlan's trinity had now dissolved to a savior of one, though Favre had looked adrift since his mentor left. The connection between the two couldn't be over-emphasized. "[T]he greatest head coach I ever played for was Mike Holmgren," Favre said on the eve of his induction into the Pro Football Hall of Fame in 2016. "My only regret…is that we didn't play together longer." Holmgren shared the sentiment. "He was the son I never had," he told ESPN.com in 2016.[61] In 1999, Favre's first season without Holmgren, he had his lowest quarterback rating in six years, landing him below the league average. Despite throwing for more than 4,000 yards, Favre also tossed the second most interceptions in the NFL.[62] And those stats wouldn't improve much in 2000 if at all.

In the wake of Wolf's departure, Harlan made a rare strategic blunder, albeit a big one: he handed Sherman the position of general manager. The move was mind-boggling, given the organization's history. It hadn't worked for coaches Phil Bengtson, Dan Devine, Bart

Starr, or Forrest Gregg.[63] What made Harlan think it would work for Sherman? "I was concerned that if a new man came in from the outside, [Sherman] might have trouble getting along with him," Harlan told ESPNMilwaukee.com in 2012, or "the new man might want to come in and want to totally change the scouting staff… And so I decided to do something that I don't like to do—give one man both jobs."

In some respects, Harlan's decision smacked of the good ol' boys' club of the 1970s and '80s, when part-time presidents hung onto coaches or players too long because they didn't want to upend the status quo or hurt feelings. Frustratingly, Harlan had a front row seat for that debacle and should have known better.

On paper, Sherman was a solid choice for coach. "[Sherman] didn't hurt us on the field—we went 12–4, 12–4, 10–6, 10–6. [He] did a great job of coaching," Harlan said.[64] Sherman's win percentage (.578) was less than Holmgren's (.670), but he led the team into the playoffs four years in a row, from 2001 to 2004.[65] Had he taken over for Devine or Starr, Sherman would have been heralded a savior.

But he hadn't. Like Favre handing the offense to Rodgers, so too did Holmgren to Rhodes/Sherman. The difference was that Rodgers won a Super Bowl of his own, whereas neither Mike Sherman nor Ray Rhodes even came close.

On September 7, 2003, the Packers rededicated Lambeau Field following the first major remodel of the hallowed stadium since its opening in 1957. Much care went into construction, as expected. For Packers fans, it was akin to building an addition on to the Sistine Chapel—a sacred place where a great institution was worshipped. Meanwhile, Soldier Field down in Chicago got a $632 million face lift, which was panned by architectural critics, including their hometown paper. "Imagine a bloated enormous starship *Enterprise* crashing into the middle of Los Angeles Memorial Coliseum," wrote *Chicago Tribune*'s Blair Kamin. "That's what it looks like, like a giant spaceship just crashed into the lakefront."[66]

Where the Bears failed, the Packers succeeded—a tough pill to swallow for the Windy City, particularly as the Packers had won five of the last six games against them.

The new Lambeau was indeed a sight to behold, beginning with a 376,000-square-foot glass atrium that anchored the addition on the stadium's northeast corner. Outside the atrium stood two 14-foot-tall bronze statues, one of Curly Lambeau and the other of Vince Lombardi, the twin foundational pillars of the Packers.[67] Inside an east entrance for tailgaters stood a 50-foot-tall replica of the Lombardi Trophy, an impressive sight made more so on game day with the assistance of the stadium's ever-flowing beer taps.

The original bowl and field remained fully intact and unchanged, protecting their historic lineage. Outside, brick towers were fixed into the ground like sentries at the entrance to an inner sanctum. Neutral red brick and sandstone colors complimented the façade's forest green hue. Between the towers stood two-story brick posts, which secured the bowl like the elegant prongs of a ring's setting.

Not only did the remodeled stadium stun visually, but it embraced utility, as well. About 12,000 seats were added, bringing the total to 72,515.[68] Inside and around the Atrium included the Packers Pro Shop, a restaurant and bar, the relocated Packers Hall of Fame, and banquet facilities, all of which remained open year-round. Harlan's do-or-die referendum, amidst dwindling cash reserves and a team that was becoming uncompetitive in the free agency market, changed everything seemingly overnight.

In 2003, the Packers' reserves jumped from $35.6 million to $58 million. By 2004, the team was sitting on $84 million. "Without the redeveloped Lambeau, we would have run into financial oblivion," said treasurer John Underwood.[69] Today, the club's corporate reserves stand at more than a half-billion dollars.[70] As for the initial $295 million injection of taxpayer funding, it would end up leveraging $600 million in additional private investment through 2025. This included renovations in 2007 and 2011–13, the latter adding 6,700 new seats. Harlan proved a savant who could very well have saved the franchise or at least kept it competitive. Even more, the Packers contribute approximately $500 million in economic impact to the Greater Green Bay area each year. What Harlan said would happen back in 2000 came to pass: stable finances: check; competitive teams: check; world tourist destination: check.[71]

A head coach is about the here and now—winning games with the players they have. The general manager is about looking to the future, making personnel changes to position the club for continued success. The jobs involve two very different tasks that require two different skill sets—a combination that is historically rare to find in one person, particularly in today's metric-obsessed and salary-capped game. For the uber-successful Wolf, effective personnel management meant constant churn. "Even after we started winning... Ron always made a point of bringing in free agents," said Harlan.[72] It was a 24/7/365 job.

The sizeable challenges in being both coach and GM were evident in the Packers' drafts under Sherman, who made a series of bad choices and missed out on a number of opportunities. Aside from a few highlights in his first draft in 2002, namely signing explosive receiver Javon Walker and future Pro Bowl defensive end Aaron Kampman, his next two drafts were busts. Sherman nabbed only one player of significance in 2003, middle linebacker Nick Barnett. And 2004 was just as underwhelming. That year, the team held four of the first 87 picks and spent them on four forgettable players: cornerbacks Joey Thomas and Ahmad Carroll, each of whom played two and three seasons, respectively, and combined for four interceptions; defensive tackle Donnell Washington, who was kept on for two years but didn't play any games; and punter B.J. Sander, who lasted a single season.[73]

Rather than following in Wolf's footsteps, Sherman's drafting career resembled that of Dan Devine, whose infamous trade for quarterback John Hadl was a cautionary tale of wasted picks traded away for subpar talent. During Sherman's tenure, the Packers would surrender 20 draft picks and get only 11 players in return, few of whom made any real impact. In addition, Sherman's trades and acquisitions throughout the season were too often fruitless. In one of his first trades in 2002, he sent a pair of draft picks to New England for Terry Glenn, an inconsistent receiver with heavy-duty personal baggage. Glenn lasted just one season in Green Bay. Sherman then signed New Orleans defensive end Joe Johnson to a lucrative free-agent contract, but the former Pro Bowler was on the downside of his career and came with a history of injuries. He twice got hurt, playing just 11 games in two seasons for the Packers.[74]

The Green and Gold were adrift. Bob Harlan was still around, but he had promised all his general managers he would not interfere with their day-to-day jobs. It was increasingly clear that Mike Sherman was no Ron Wolf, and the Packers were suffering dearly because of Sherman's miscast role. How long would the team tolerate losing? How long until they finally learned you can't have it both ways—that you can't have the coach *and* general manager be the same person? As the front office did finally come to understand and accept this cardinal rule and act on it, matters improved. What happened next would be an easy call. Now the only question was: When?

Chapter 12

Redemption

Former Raiders cornerback Sam Seale famously recalled the oft-heard threat in the 1980s when coaches were trying to strike fear into the hearts of their players: "If we did something wrong or they got mad at us, the first thing they'd say: 'We're sending you to Green Bay.'" At the time, Titletown was considered the Siberia of the NFL, with Lambeau Field like a notorious gulag.[1]

Ron Wolf was the Raiders' personnel director at the time. Two years after Seale left the game as a player, however, Wolf hired his former player as a Packers scout in 1995. After two seasons scouting college talent in the Southwest, Seale went to work as the team's West Coast scout from 1997 to 2018,[2] racking up hundreds of thousands of miles on the road, zigzagging across the mountain west from Southern California to the Rockies and the Pacific Northwest to the Bay area—just like Curly Lambeau once did many decades earlier. In place of a Hollywood starlet riding shotgun, however, Seale had player reports and perhaps spent coffee cups and old burger wrappers on the floor of his car.

To say scouting was different in the '90s compared to the old days would be the mother of all understatements. "I get up at four o'clock in the morning and drive from San Diego to Salt Lake City, Utah," Seale said. "Now that's a drive."

But it was Seale's trips back to Green Bay that mattered most. Because on those occasions, he made the case for players he liked, including a particularly pivotal one that would define the franchise from 2008 to 2022. So it was in April 2005, in the cloistered draft war room above the Atrium at Lambeau Field, where Seale and his boss, newly hired general manager Ted Thompson, defended their plan to scoop up University of California quarterback Aaron Rodgers in the first round.

Rodgers, who began his collegiate career in 2002 at Butte Community College in Oroville, California, failed to attract attention from a Division I program out of high school.[3] That year, he led the Roadrunners to a conference championship and a national ranking. The next year, he transferred to his home state's flagship school, the University of California–Berkeley, where he led the Golden Bears to a winning record and a bowl appearance. The following season in 2004, Cal finished top five in the BCS rankings and Rodgers was ninth in the Heisman Trophy voting.[4] Scouts marveled at his meteoric rise.

Not surprisingly, Rodgers was expected to go early in the 2005 draft.

Most of the Packers draft room begged Thompson to fill glaring defensive needs with their opening pick, but few if any first-round caliber defensive players were left on the board. Thompson recalled and then acted on two important lessons he'd learned over the years: If you can take a good quarterback, grab him. And if your expert in the field tells you to take a guy, listen to him. Wolf preached the former; GM/coach Bart Starr botched the latter, famously ignoring his regional scout and passing on Joe Montana in the 1979 draft. Besides, though Brett Favre was still playing at a high level, the MVP quarterback was 35 years old and couldn't play forever.

Thompson shrugged off his staff's pleas. Would arguably the best quarterback in the draft still be there after 23 picks? Thompson was certainly taking a big chance by ignoring a pressing need on defense, but holding out and not trading up to get his man was even riskier. According to Packers historian Cliff Christl, "[I]f Rodgers did drop out of the top 10, somebody would trade up to get him. The chance of him falling to No. 24 was a long shot, at best." When the Packers turn came and Rodgers' name remained on the board, Thompson grabbed him. Fans attending the draft in New York who sympathized with Rodgers' torturously long wait gave the quarterback a standing ovation when the pick was announced.

In Green Bay, the response was decidedly different. Furious fans in the atrium below booed Thompson so loudly he could hear them in the draft room. The jury rendered its decision immediately: How dare Thompson try and replace their beloved Brett Favre!? The new GM was off to a rough start.[5]

From the beginning, it was obvious that Rodgers had a chip on his shoulder. Was it because he hadn't been picked earlier? Scouts didn't think he was good enough to go in the top 10? Or maybe he was still miffed at being overlooked by college recruiters in high school, or simply projecting something from childhood?

Rodgers himself intimated as much. "At times when you have some dysfunction or some separation in your family life, you have to kind of re-parent yourself and give yourself what you didn't get or wanted to hear more of when you were a kid, and I think for me, I just wanted to hear, 'I'm proud of you,'" Rodgers said in the 2024 documentary, *Aaron Rodgers: Enigma*. He hadn't talked to his parents in years.[6]

Rodgers' transition to the pros wasn't exactly helped along by Favre, who refused to mentor his backup over the three seasons they overlapped. "My contract doesn't say I have to get Aaron Rodgers ready to play," he said shortly after Rodgers was drafted.[7] When Rodgers eventually made his mark by winning games, breaking records, and ultimately winning a Super Bowl within three years of becoming the starter, Favre remarked in 2011, "He just kind of fell into a good situation."[8] (That sentiment would change in Favre's retirement.)

But something about the Rodgers selection unnerved Favre, who didn't hide his displeasure, either. It might've been the lesson he learned from his own predecessor, Don Majkowski, who left the Packers–Bengals game hurt in early 1992 and never returned under center after Favre replaced him. It would certainly explain, at least in part, why Favre persevered through so much pain—and eventually became addicted to painkillers.

The Packers went 4–12 the following season under Favre. "When Ted Thompson drafted Aaron [Rodgers], that was it," said Wisconsin sportscaster Bill Michaels in the Favre Netflix documentary *Untold*. "That was the beginning of the end."[9]

Favre's quarterback rating was fourth worst in the league in that 2005 season, with an NFL worst 29 interceptions and a miserable 70.9 QB rating. (Though consistent with his gunslinger persona, he threw a league best 607 attempts and thus a league high 372 completions.)[10] Was Favre's magic all a mirage?

Hardly, but the widely accepted image of Favre as a comeback impresario has its caveats. While he is credited with 30 fourth-quarter comebacks (defined as a coming back to win after trailing by a touchdown or less), he flubbed more than twice as many attempts, losing 72 of them. Favre did have 45 game-winning drives, however; a broader metric defined as possessions that put teams ahead for good whether they're behind or already ahead in the fourth quarter or overtime—nothing to sneeze at.[11]

Additionally, there was a difference between reality and perception. Favre admits as much: "Could have thrown more touchdowns. Could have thrown less interceptions. My interception rate was pretty low. It was that they came at a time when…it was, you know, everyone was watching." In his three MVP seasons (1995–97), he went 1–9 in comeback attempts, according to a 2018 Bleacher Report analysis.[12]

The memories of Favre grow dimmer by the day in Green Bay. But sports fans are selective about what they believe versus what they *want* to believe; remember the good times, forget the bad. Favre's triumphant fourth-quarter marches have seemingly absolved the gunslinger of his near-misses or the reckless unforced errors that broke hearts and ended seasons. So powerful are these moments—including his Super Bowl victory, 13 winning seasons, and 11 playoff appearances—they can forgive the hero of egregious mistakes made not just on the field, but in his personal life, as well. Fans forget or even explain away the misdeeds player-heroes commit that hurt people, ruin lives, and tarnish reputations. Packers like James Lofton, Paul Hornung, and Curly Lambeau come to mind; so, too, does Brett Favre after a 2016 Medicaid fraud case in Mississippi and sexual harassment allegations with the Jets in 2010.[13]

On New Year's Day 2006, Seahawks coach Mike Holmgren could have mistaken his Packers counterpart for a dead man walking. Head coach Mike Sherman, stalking the opposing sidelines with his Coke-bottle glasses and exhausted demeanor, seemed almost as if he were distracted by bigger problems than facing Holmgren's NFC-best squad.[14]

Holmgren knew something was afoot, and it wasn't just the worn, rumpled wrinkles on Sherman's face. Well versed in Favre-family dynamics, Holmgren took seriously Scott Favre's public comments a day earlier when he suggested that his little brother may not return to Green Bay in 2006: "'We want you back,' probably isn't going to be enough," Scott said. What would it take for the QB to stay? "The [coaches] have put Brett in a position where it's almost impossible to win," Scott continued. "If Mike Sherman comes back, I think there's got to be some changes, and I think there's going to be some coaches gone."[15]

What a mess. It's safe to say Holmgren sure didn't miss those days.

But player-personnel matters were no longer Sherman's problem; that honor fell to Thompson. Holmgren knew both men well; each had worked for him in Green Bay. Holmgren also must have known that his former vice president, Thompson, took direction from no one, especially from a cocksure gunslinger who created at least as many headaches as game-winning plays.

Despite Sherman's New Year's victory over the eventual NFC champions (Holmgren was resting six injured starters[16]), Thompson finished what Bob Harlan had started and fired Sherman the following day.

The ex-coach's last hurrah was not unlike the cruel fate Lindy Infante suffered 14 years earlier, when he defeated the rival Vikings in the final week of the 1991 season and was summarily dismissed from his duties right afterward. Nevertheless, each deserved their respective sentences. Both ended their seasons 4-12, fell well short of expectations, exhausted second chances, and had lost confidence from others within the organization.

Unlike Wolf, who moved quickly with his previous two head coaching hires, Thompson would take his time to find the person to lead the Packers into their next era. An undrafted Houston Oilers linebacker from the 1970s who persevered over a decade-long career as a backup, Thompson built a front-office career defined by the adage that achieving success is hard, but sustaining accomplishment is even harder. In a way, he was perfect for the general manager role. After Thompson's untimely passing in 2021 from an autonomic disorder, Wolf said of his mentee: "He wasn't drafted [by the Oilers]. He hung on. That toughness manifests itself now in what he's been able to accomplish."[17]

When Thompson returned to Green Bay in 2005 after a five-season tenure in Seattle, he was handed the franchise on a silver platter. The Packers had not one losing season in the previous 13, despite recent poor draft choices, and remained a solid club. Thompson would help lead the Green and Gold to eight consecutive playoff appearances from 2009 to 2016, overseeing arguably the best draft record among his NFL colleagues during that span, and selecting 18 future Pro Bowlers.[18]

For the third time in NFL history, a record 10 coaches would be replaced following the 2005 season.[19] Thompson had to act quickly if he wanted to snag a good one. Nevertheless, Thompson proceeded at his own pace as always, reviewing dozens of candidates and interviewing many of them.

The available pool included big names, no-names, and big names-to-be: Brad Childress, Gary Kubiak, Cam Cameron, Jim Fassel, Tim Lewis, Steve Mariucci, and Sean Payton. Favre's agent, Bus Cook, lobbied the team to include Mariucci, Favre's first Packers quarterbacks coach, among the final interviewees for the job, though to no avail.

One candidate who wasn't reported early on was a Holmgren successor, 49ers offensive coordinator Mike McCarthy, who served a stint as Packers quarterbacks coach in 1999 and had a good rapport with

Favre.[20] On day seven of the search, on January 8, 2006, McCarthy traveled to Green Bay to meet with Thompson and other team officials. He made an impression. A few days later, Thompson announced his decision. Mike McCarthy would be just the 14th head coach of the 87-year-old franchise.

It's possible that Thompson saw a little of himself in McCarthy, an underdog who confronted and overcame obstacles in life and came out on top. "His command presence—I think he's gone through some difficult things, he's been in charge of an offense on two different teams," Thompson said.

At his introductory press conference, McCarthy stood before the gathered media holding a Packers helmet to his waist like a champion high school debater would a tournament trophy. McCarthy seemed to look the part too: confident glare, coiffed black hair, and raised cheeks that betrayed his age—forty-two, the youngest among head coaches at the time—and genuine excitement for the moment.[21]

Yet Packer Nation was more interested in the potential drama between the new coach and the old quarterback. The will-he-or-will-he-not-return question with Favre was now at full tilt. Another wrinkle to the Wisconsin winter: Would it be Brett Favre "retirement season?" as the *Press-Gazette* characterized the ongoing soap opera.[22] For Packers fans and the incoming coach, the irascible gunslinger would never be far from mind. A retirement headline shared space next to the McCarthy announcement: "Favre is waiting, so act fast."[23]

McCarthy acclimated to Green Bay quickly, soon marrying a local woman and putting down roots with a family of seven, no doubt as his Pittsburgh-based, Irish American family expected. The new coach's childhood resembled that of a Green Bay native. "In the neighborhood I grew up in, the bar was packed at 8 in the morning," said McCarthy at his introductory press conference. "It was packed at 4 o'clock in the afternoon, and it was packed at midnight. That's just the way you grew up…it's just a no-nonsense approach. You know where you stand with people."[24]

Thompson nodded right along. McCarthy would fit in just fine.

After months of another will-he-or-won't-he roller-coaster ride, Favre decided to return for "at least" one more season on April 25, 2006. Perhaps reflecting on the absurdness of it all, the aging gunslinger added that "he never had said that he *wasn't* planning a return to the field" (my emphasis), as Packers.com characterized Favre's thinking.[25] But for how long Packer Nation wondered? In March he said that if he returned for the '06 season it would be his last. That call was subject to reversal too, and so he changed his mind in May, telling fans he was in for 2007, too.[26] The 2006 season proved as bumpy of a ride as Favre's tortured decision-making proclivities, with some near-wins in an otherwise respectable rebound season. The new head coach's team ended with an even record at 8–8. But it was the following season in 2007 that marked a remarkable turnaround—even by historic standards—ending in a 13–3 showing, the best finish in ten seasons and the first division title in three years. They would go all the way to the NFC championship but fall to an upstart New York Giants' squad in overtime.

Accolades were handed out all around. Thompson nabbed Executive of the Year honors from *The Sporting News*. *Sports Illustrated* named Favre Sportsman of the Year in recognition of the Packers' resurgence and playoff run (while also noting the continued talk of retirement for the 38-year-old quarterback, who remained a reliable source of copy).[27] The nation's sports magazine of record was seemingly on to something, despite local assurances that Favre was good for another year. "Favre will elect to come back again..." the *Press-Gazette* predicted on November 19, 2007.[28]

So confident of Favre's return in 2008 some local reporters called the Rodgers pick "dead money" two years hence. "He remains the highest-paid clipboard holder in Brown County..." *Appleton Post-Crescent* columnist Mike Woods teased, attempting, though no doubt failing, to get under Thompson's extra-thick skin.[29]

One absolutely certain retirement was that of Bob Harlan, who had reached the team's mandatory retirement age of 70. The era-shaping executive was closing out a 37-year career with the team.[30] Save for the two men honored in the form of statues outside Lambeau Field's north entrance, no other Packer had more of an impact on the franchise than Harlan. To be sure, Curly Lambeau and Vince Lombardi spent more time along the sideline and on the field, but the team's president, CEO, and chairman had a profound influence on the organization that resulted in three NFC championship appearances, two trips to the Super Bowl, and a Lombardi trophy. Since Harlan hired Ron Wolf in late 1991, the Packers have had the best regular season record in the NFL: 334–195–2 (through 2024). "Without the support of Bob and the executive committee—but more importantly Bob—I don't know if we would have done what we did," said Wolf.[31]

In short, along with Lambeau and Lombardi, Bob Harlan is the third leg upon which 13 Packers championship trophies stand.

On December 3, 2007, with the team 10–2 and well-positioned to make a deep playoff run, Harlan and the Packers announced that Northwestern University athletic director Mark Murphy would become the team's 11th president. It was an unusual choice. Unlike every other president before him, the 6'4", freckled redhead with a slight gap between his two front teeth and permanent smile had zero connection to the city, save his ignominious 1983 *Monday Night Football* defeat while playing safety for the Redskins.[32]

Before Northwestern University, Murphy served as athletic director of his alma mater, tiny Colgate University in upstate New York, from 1992 until 2003. To Harlan and the board, this was the only scratch on an otherwise sterling résumé. "Harlan and the executive committee strongly favor hiring someone already working in the front office of an NFL team who is versed in the league's increasingly complex and high-stakes revenue system…" according to the *Press-Gazette's* Pete Dougherty.[33] Such concerns came up before and even *after* the search committee recommended Murphy as president.

Perhaps not surprisingly, it wasn't Murphy's lack of NFL experience but local politics that drove disagreements and created schisms among board members over the future president. One third of the board was expected to vote "no" because they wanted a local candidate. Others got behind Murphy simply to increase their influence in the organization.[34] The good ol' boys must have resolved their differences quickly; two days after some board members predicted "fireworks" at the coming meeting, the committee voted unanimously for Murphy.[35]

Maybe it was more about Murphy's character and union experience, rather than Packers internal bickering, that won the day. "Mark Murphy talks like he's been in the Green Bay Packers' boardroom for the last decade," the *Press-Gazette* reported. The former NFL Players Association representative and later NFLPA vice president knew a thing or two about politics. During the '82 strike, Murphy adroitly built a relationship with his then-management counterpart Paul Tagliabue, who would go on to become league commissioner. Tagliabue most likely gave the current commissioner Roger Goodell a "good recommendation," according to the *Press-Gazette*'s Pete Dougherty in a contemporary article.[36] Also, there could've been behind-the-scenes lobbying for the hire.

That Murphy was able to build and maintain such a strong relationship with Tagliabue was remarkable. It takes a real talent to thread implacable anti-union league officials with a liberal firebrand like NFLPA executive director Ed Garvey, particularly at a time when labor-management relationships were at an all-time low. While still playing for Washington, Murphy was taking night classes at American University for a master's degree in business. He later took courses in law at Georgetown University, where he earned his law degree in 1988 and went to work at the US Department of Justice as a trial attorney between his playing and front-office days.[37] Murphy may have been an atypical candidate, but he sure wasn't unqualified.

With a new general manager in place, the Packers board was now in accord (at least publicly), all key front office slots filled, and the team's finances in impeccable order.[38] On the field, the Packers finished out the 2007 season 13–3 and landed the No. 2 seed in the NFC with a first-round bye. On January 12, 2008, they met up with the Seattle Seahawks at home and made quick work of Holmgren's squad, winning 42–20. (Holmgren would announce soon after that next season would be his last as a coach.)

Expecting to travel to Dallas to meet up with the top seed, the Packers instead found themselves playing host for the NFC Championship Game after the upstart Giants edged the Cowboys 21–17. Once again, the Packers would be denied a chance to take on the Cowboys for a championship.

Thermometers registered minus-1 degree at kickoff at Lambeau Field on the evening of January 20, 2008. Not quite as bad as the Ice Bowl's minus-13, but still plenty cold. While fans could make out a blade of grass or two atop Lombardi's busted heat grid back in 1967, the turf in 2008 appeared completely dead, like a barren moonscape surrounded by 70,000 screaming fans. The Packer faithful seemed to be exorcising Favre's retirement demons while hoping to prove Thompson wrong in believing that Rodgers was the team's future.

Once again No. 4 disproved his own comeback myth by all but ending the game on an interception. On the second play of overtime with the game tied 20–20, Favre underthrew a 16-yard out-route pass to Donald Driver that Giants cornerback Corey Webster easily picked off. Now in field goal range, the seven-point underdog Giants took over.[39] Three downs later, kicker Lawrence Tynes, who had missed his previous two attempts, lined up for a 47-yarder. Whereas Mark Moseley's kick veered right of the goal posts to give the Packers the dramatic win way back in 1983, Tynes put just enough English on the pigskin to curve in toward and through the uprights. Game over, 23–20, Giants.[40]

Green Bay was out of the playoffs, and Favre had just thrown his last pass as a Packer. Now the real quarterback controversy could begin.

On March 6, 2008, Brett Favre ambled into the team media room for his final press conference. "Seems just like yesterday we were here," he began as he settled into a chair behind a retro ribbon microphone. Whether he was referencing his very first meeting with the Wisconsin press corps as a Packer in February 1992 or the tortured retirement talk of the last several years was unclear. What was clear—at least at the moment—was that he was hanging it up.

"Well, I think we all know why I'm here," he continued in his disarming Southern drawl. "I am officially retiring from the NFL and the Green Bay Packers." That was about as far as he got before he had to compose himself. "I promised I wouldn't get emotional."[41]

Three league MVPs, nine Pro Bowl selections, two Super Bowl appearances, and one championship. NFL records he held at his (first) retirement included: most career attempted and completed passes; most touchdown passes; most passing yards (61,655 yards, or the distance from Green Bay to Appleton); and most consecutive starts.[42] Second only to the great Don Hutson, Favre would leave the Packers as the most decorated player in team history. And the winningest, with 160 victories.[43]

Almost as soon as he left the room, after giving a marathon 67-minute-long press conference, the rumor mill began churning out talk of a comeback and that the Packers would come crawling back to their old quarterback. But the Packers—and fans to an extent—were exhausted from the veritable cottage industry of retirement talk. No doubt the *Press-Gazette*, *Sports Illustrated,* and every other media and sports outlet had run out of retirement story angles. Even Favre was growing fatigued. "I'm mentally tired," he told ESPN.[44]

Ted Thompson, for his part, seemed anxious to move on. It had been almost three years since he drafted Rodgers, and he was no doubt ready to prove that his instincts were correct—and that seemingly everyone else's were wrong. More importantly, Rodgers was ready. He delivered an impressive performance when he relieved an injured Favre in the Dallas game on November 29, 2007, which convinced Thompson that Rodgers was the franchise's future.[45]

The month wasn't out before word got around that Favre was interested in returning. In April, Bus Cook began speaking with other teams about signing his client. On April 24, Favre hinted he might want to return to the NFL while he was a guest on the *Late Show with David Letterman*.[46] The Packers, however, were not interested. The team had moved on.

The renowned Major League Baseball executive Branch Rickey famously said, "It is better to trade a man a year too early than a year too late."[47] Sage advice. He also counseled trading such fading players to rivals.[48] But then again, Rickey never had Brett Favre. Thompson ultimately embraced the legendary general manager's first piece of advice but discounted the second. Favre may have been a monumental distraction, but the old gunslinger still could create major problems for his old team if he stuck around the NFC Central or even the conference.

Thompson had one of three options: reinstate Favre, trade him, or release him. The Packers GM resolved to hang onto Favre as long as possible so he could ensure the fading superstar wouldn't go to the Buccaneers or archrival Vikings, both of whom had showed strong interest in him.[49] (Minnesota in particular would've loved to stick it to Green Bay, and former Packers assistant Jon Gruden was then the head coach for Tampa Bay.) But Thompson was walking a fine line. He didn't want Favre hanging around the league and haunting the Packers, but he also didn't want his old starter at training camp threatening Rodgers' job. And yet that was exactly what Favre did.

Thompson had placed Favre on the reserve/retired list on April 24. On July 11, Favre asked the team to release him so he could play elsewhere which initiated a month-long back-and-forth between player and manager. With a league-imposed deadline to end the impasse set for Monday August 4, Favre boarded a plane for Green Bay from Hattiesburg, Mississippi, Sunday to report to training camp. Favre had called Thompson's bluff. Three days later, the Packers traded Favre to the New York Jets for a third-round draft pick.[50]

Favre lasted a single season in New York. It turned out Thompson's timing was impeccable. Eleven games into the 2008 season, Favre tore tendons in his throwing arm, though finished out the year. "The quarterback with a cannon arm suddenly found himself firing a popgun," Christl observed. The Jets ended the season 9–7 but missed the playoffs, while the Packers finished third in the NFC Central, at 6–10.

Favre retired again after the season, this time from health concerns. "There are several things that went into the decision but most importantly, the most important thing, was that physically, you know with my shoulder the last half of the year, it hampered the way I played," Favre said. "I'm 39, I had several options [to have surgery] and to let it heal. How that would affect me in terms of playing I had no idea and it wasn't something I was going to risk."[51]

And then it happened all over again.

Favre underwent arthroscopic surgery on his torn tendons and by early June, two months after the Jets released him, there was talk of another return, this time with the Vikings.[52] It seemed like a last gasp, however. "The Vikings are the only team to indicate interest in Favre…" the Associated Press reported on June 8.[53] The next day, Favre family members began buying up blocks of hotel rooms in Green Bay for the home game against the Vikings.[54] After a couple more bouts of second-guessing, Favre finally signed with Minnesota on August 18.[55]

It was too much for the Green Bay faithful: Favre signing with the hated Vikings. Fans burned his likeness in effigy and torched No. 4 jerseys and other Favre keepsakes.[56] It also broke his old bosses' hearts, the ones who made Brett Favre a legendary Hall of Fame quarterback.

"I couldn't handle that one. To wear that awful uniform. I couldn't handle that purple," Ron Wolf said.[57]

Bob Harlan deliberately skipped the Vikings game in Green Bay, missing just his second game at Lambeau since arriving in Green Bay in 1971. (Harlan would, however, lead the reconciliation effort that culminated in Favre's return visit to Lambeau Field in 2015 to retire his number.)

Nearly 30 million viewers tuned in to watch the game on Fox, one of the station's largest regular season audiences ever. Press interest was off the charts, too. "A media stakeout worthy of a hostage situation," the *Press-Gazette* described the big game.[58]

The Vikings were still the better team, downing the Green and Gold 38–26 and marking the first time in four seasons that Minnesota swept the lowly Pack. The red-hot Vikings would go on to make a strong playoff run, coming tantalizingly close to their first Super Bowl trip in 32 years before botching an overtime loss to the Saints (set up by another late fourth-quarter interception thrown by Favre).

The aging QB suffered injuries to his hamstring and ankle—the perpetrator of the latter, defensive end Bobby McCray, was fined $20,000 by the league[59]—in the NFC Championship Game and was unable to recover in the offseason. This led to a poor performance in the 2010 season, dropping the Vikings to last place in the NFC Central. His final game as a pro was about as bad as it could get. He threw an interception, got sacked, and was knocked out cold in the second quarter, forcing him to leave the game. The hit was so bad that he forgot what team he was playing against. (The Bears, naturally.) It was hardly the celebration the Vikings were hoping for on their 50th anniversary with dozens of decorated alumni on hand.

The late-career dalliance was over. Without bullets left in the chamber, the old gunslinger headed back to Mississippi for good.[60]

Out of the playoffs and permanently retired, Favre would have to settle for a couple bushels of apples from Thompson. While Favre and his Vikings had an ignominious 2010 season, the Packers squad that year was unlike any other in the franchise's long history. Rodgers was putting up numbers like a rock star. In the shadow of Favre's *dramatis personae* in gossip columns and sports talk radio, Rodgers threw for more than 4,000 yards and held a solid 93.8 passer rating in 2008. (Favre placed 21st in the NFL in passer rating with an underwhelming 3,472 passing yards and league-worst 22 interceptions.)[61] But the best was yet to come for this quickly maturing consistent and accurate field general. In 2009, Rodgers racked up 4,434 passing yards and finished out the year with a 103.2 rating earning a spot on the Pro Bowl team.

On the strength of Rodgers' passer rating of 101.2 in the 2010 season, the Green and Gold placed second in the NFC Central with a 10–6 record,[62] just good enough to earn the last Wild Card seed. It had been an impressive regular season run given the flurry of on and off the field tumult plaguing the team. Before the preseason, the league hit defensive end Johnny Jolly with an indefinite suspension following a second-degree felony drug charge. The explosive defender had earned a reputation for slapping down passes, leading all defensive linemen in 2009 with 10. His "nastiness and fire," according to the *Milwaukee Journal Sentinel*, lead the team in rushing defense for the 2009 season. In a word, he was indispensable.[63]

Moving into the regular season, the Packers were hobbled with devastating injuries that only grew as the year wore on. In Week 1, defensive end Justin Harrell, who was behind Jolly in the depth chart, and running back Ryan Grant were knocked out for the season. In October, standout middle linebacker Nick Barnett was injured, as was playmaking tight end Jermichael Finley, who had already posted two 100-plus-yard games early in the year. Treading water at 3–3, the Pack bounced back with a four-game winning streak. After dropping a game in Atlanta in Week 12, the team finished December and January with three wins and two losses—the latter two games decided by just eight points.[64]

The real roller-coaster ride was only just beginning as the Packers suited up for the postseason in Philadelphia on January 9, 2011, facing down the Eagles and former Green Bay assistant coach Andy Reid (who would eventually pile up more Super Bowl wins than any other in the Holmgren coaching tree).[65] The Packers squelched a late come-from-behind march by Eagles gunslinger and Comeback Player of the Year winner Michael Vick, downing the third-seed squad 21–16.

Despite missing key defenders Barnett, Harrell, and Jolly, Green Bay throttled an offensive powerhouse that had ranked No. 2 in the NFL in yards and third in points. Defensive end Ryan Pickett, filling in a defensive line devastated by injuries, wasn't boasting in a post-game interview when he said, "It's tough for teams to score on us, I don't care who they are." The explosive Vick was sacked three times and was held to just 33 rushing yards and a single touchdown, ending the game with a disappointing 79.9 passer rating—a far cry from Rodgers' blockbuster 122.5 rating on the strength of three touchdowns and efficient 18 for 27 passing for 180 yards.[66]

But it was the final defensive play of the game when the Packers defense truly shined. With no timeouts remaining, Vick had just stormed down the field on a crucial third down pass completion to wide receiver Riley Cooper, giving Philadelphia a first down inside the 30-yard line. Hurried and with the clock under 45 seconds, Vick surprised Dom Capers' defense by not spiking the ball and stopping the clock. He instead dropped back and, protected in the pocket, pumped once, spotted Cooper downfield along the left sideline, and then launched a rocket into the end zone. Not even a half-stride behind Cooper was the undersized, 5'11" cornerback Tramon Williams, who leapt with everything he had and pulled down an otherwise perfect bomb for an interception. Game over: Packers win, 21–16.[67]

With big momentum behind them, the Green and Gold marched down to Atlanta, where they made quick work of the top-seeded Falcons. The game was as close to perfect as you could get. Rodgers absolutely owned the Atlanta defense, racking up 366 passing yards, four touchdowns, and zero interceptions. Winning 48–21, Green Bay had scored the most points of any postseason matchup in the team's 91-year history.[68]

The defense was equal to the task, and defensive auteur Capers put on a clinic for the Falcons. Matt Ryan was sacked five times and intercepted twice. Save for a breakout first-quarter drive, the Atlanta quarterback was shut down at every turn until the fourth quarter, when the game was already lost. It was payback for a razor-thin 20–17 loss to the Dirty Birds in Week 12 of the regular season. Cheeseheads filled up the seats after Falcons season ticket holders thought twice about braving a mild mid-winter snowstorm. Packer backers travel well, and divisional round of the 2010-11 postseason was no exception.[69]

Despite strong performances, the Packers still had to win two more games to bag the ultimate prize. With a final stop in Chicago before the Super Bowl, the Green and Gold readied themselves for another Packers-Bears blockbuster—the best one ever, according to *Sports Illustrated* in 2025.[70] On the strength of a 14–0 lead going into half-time, Rodgers came out guns blazing. But middle linebacker and future Hall of Famer Brian Urlacher snagged the lone Rodgers interception and made a 39-yard run-back, getting tripped up by the quarterback himself in what at first appeared to be an easy pick-six. Chicago came within a touchdown of tying it up with 4:53 remaining in the fourth quarter, but rookie cornerback Sam Shields shut the door on a come-back attempt with under a minute to go when he picked off a pass from third stringer Caleb Hanie in for an injured Jay Cutler. Both of Shields' interceptions were inside the red zone.[71] Packers win the NFC Championship in a stunner 21–14. Next stop: Dallas.

Like Super Bowl XXXII in 1998, Super Bowl XLV was a nail-biter. But unlike that crushing loss to the Broncos, the Packers persevered and toppled the Steelers 31–25 thanks to their game-MVP quarterback, the once-maligned and now adored Aaron Rodgers.[72] The top player honors were well deserved. On the Packers' final set of downs in the fourth quarter with 3:47 left having burned nearly four minutes off the clock, Rodgers tossed two safe screen passes on first and second downs inside the 8-yard line. On third down on the 5-yard line, Rodgers found receiver Jordy Nelson fading into the corner of the end zone. Once again, Rodgers showed maturity and took extra care to ensure his toss had just enough zip to fall into the receiver's hands. Despite a perfect toss from Nelson's able field general, the veteran receiver's speed was off just enough to miss the pigskin by a finger length. But Rodgers—and the Packers—escaped the worst possible fate: short and intercepted. (How many times had Rodgers reviewed tape of Favre's sloppy interception that ended the 2007 season three years earlier?) Kicker Mason Crosby then chipped a 23-yarder to put the Packers ahead by six points, forcing Pittsburgh to go the length of the field for a touchdown, but Ben Roethlisberger and the Steelers ultimately came up short.[73]

"The Aaron Rodgers tale can't be told without referencing the beginning… The decision [to draft] Rodgers will never be questioned again," opined the *Press-Gazette*, the same newspaper that fomented angry mobs by calling for the general manager's head after drafting Rodgers.

"I told Ted Thompson back in 2005 he wouldn't be sorry with this pick. I told him that in '08, that I was going to repay their trust and get us this opportunity," Rodgers said. Did he ever. After notching 10 wins in the regular season, Rodgers plowed through a postseason in which the Packers were the undisputed underdog in each playoff game.[74] He finished off that spectacular run by becoming just the third quarterback in Super Bowl history to throw for more than 300 yards and three touchdowns with no interceptions.[75]

The cherry on top: they won in the Cowboys' home stadium. Ron Wolf even made the trip.[76] It must have been satisfying to exorcise the demons that had haunted him for a decade across a slew of heartbreaking losses that ended playoff runs. He no doubt slept well on that trip—in whichever city he decided to stay.

Chapter 13

Reckoning

Four days after Aaron Rodgers and the Packers returned home with the Lombardi Trophy held high, Wisconsin was plunged into political chaos.

On February 11, 2011, Republican governor Scott Walker told a private clique of GOP lawmakers that he was about to "drop the bomb." The metaphorical ordnance was legislation that would effectively eliminate public sector unions, save for police and fire. It was a big deal.[1] One out of every four voters were in a union household;[2] even more lived in Green Bay, with its rich organizing tradition in the paper mills and trades and among municipal workers and teachers. Politically, unions were the bane of the Republican Party's existence because the former underwrote Democratic campaigns and supplied reliable voting blocs.

Walker was right—the result would be nothing short of explosive.

Seemingly overnight, siblings stopped talking to each other, upcoming Easter get-togethers were canceled, neighbors said things to one another they'd live to regret. Whereas Packers fans had joined together in total euphoria just days early, now they were at each other's throats. On Valentine's Day, 2011, pro-union protesters descended on the state Capitol with crowds eventually reaching 100,000.[3] Activists filled the Capitol Square and spilled down adjoining State Street. Behind the mass along the western horizon, a low-setting winter sun shrouded the anxious crowd of teachers, plumbers, professors, and firefighters.

All of this in one week.

The Democratic Party soon initiated recall elections in the state senate with the first round of elections slated for August. (Presaging the future of national political division, Republicans were accused of running "fake" candidates in Democratic primaries to drain resources and momentum.) It proved a pyrrhic victory. Democrats flipped the upper chamber after a second round of recall elections in the spring of 2012 but lost their majority again after the fall elections.[4]

Wisconsinites would eventually simmer down, families would reunite, neighbors would make up, and Packers fans of all political stripes would cheer on the Green and Gold as they did before. Madison, Wisconsin's John Nichols, senior editor of *The Nation* and at the time de facto spokesperson for the Act 10 protests (so named after Walker's bill that effectively ended public sector unions), explained this phenomenon of community or family above politics.

"No matter what their partisanship or ideology, they unite around this sense that they can make something on their own that is stronger than what other states construct with greater resources, wider connections, and more seeming power," Nichols said. "The Packers are a touchstone in this regard: the community-owned team from a small town."[5]

The Packers had an undeniable way of uniting factions and bringing together disparate groups with otherwise unbridgeable differences. Despite major disturbances in the political realm, Packers football persevered and its followers invariably multiplied. Generational traditions and talismans continued to be handed down: season tickets, game-day customs, keepsakes, and family heirlooms. Packers games remain forever sold out, with TV viewership numbers off the charts. In 2023, three of the four most-watched NFL games in the country included Green Bay.[6] Nationally, the Packers drew an average 22 million TV viewers per game in 2024.[7] The Packers–Lions matchup on December 5, 2024, broke streaming records with 17.2 million viewers on Amazon Prime.[8] In the Green Bay–Fox Valley market, during some seasons, more than 80 percent of television sets have been tuned in to games—the highest percentage of any team in the league.[9]

In short, the Packers are a religion, and its worldwide fan diaspora is a family. Few things can bind a community as strongly as Packers football can in Green Bay. Yes, civic associations remain, though without nearly the same strength and vitality as decades ago. Robert Putnam's watershed 2000 civic study, *Bowling Alone,* remains true as ever today. People are active, just not as a group or community. More bowlers; fewer leagues. And where civic engagement has increased, it hasn't in a healthy way. Voter participation is up relative to 2000, but we are more divided while campaigns are beyond toxic and sometimes violent.[10] In a day and age when we hang by our fingertips, a binding cohesive like the Packers prevents us from following off the precipice and into an abyss. The rest of the country—and world—could use a few more like it.

On the field following their latest Super Bowl victory, the Packers would continue to post one winning season after another. In fact, 2011 would be their best record in the modern era, at 15–1. The team won 13 games in a row, averaging an astonishing 35 points per game. Rodgers nabbed MVP honors with a career-best and team-record 4,463 passing yards and 45 touchdowns.[11]

Ron Wolf consistently stated quarterbacks are the most important position in the game. "Wolf's most notable stamp on modern scouting are his views on quarterbacks," according to Fox Sports. "While there is only room for one starter, you can never acquire too many." That's a legacy he left for his successors and a lesson they learned well. Rodgers, a Thompson pick, went late in the first round; Jordan Love was 26th overall in 2020 and was picked by GM Brian Gutekunst (2018 to present) another Wolf understudy.

Like Favre and later Jordan Love, Rodgers was an undervalued QB at first. Skipped over by college scouts and going later than expected in the NFL draft, Rodgers would soon rise to the top of his game. On nearly every statistic, he eclipsed his predecessor including completion percentage (65.2 versus 62.0); passing yards per game (252.8 versus 237.9); and rushing touchdowns (35 versus 14). He owns Favre on career quarterback rating—102.7 compared to the latter's 86.0—and that of every other NFL quarterback in history. His nearest competitor Steve Young (1985 to 1999) holds a rating six points lower than Rodgers.[12]

Rodgers led Green Bay four more times to the NFC championship, each time coming up short including two heartbreakers against Seattle and Tampa Bay (2014 and 2020 respectively) in which the Packers lost by less than a touchdown. His highlight reel dominates his predecessors in theatrics, heroics and metrics. The *Milwaukee Journal Sentinel* counts four Rodgers comebacks as the franchise's all-time best. His sheer athletic ability makes a 1980s Soviet gymnast or hockey center seem like rank amateurs.

The 2018 season's fourth-quarter, 17-point comeback against the Bears ties a team record—also owned by Rodgers—and is considered one of the most memorable Titletown–Windy City rivalry moments.

It was life imitating art—except more dramatic. Like Johnny Moxon's second-half comeback in *Varsity Blues* or Paul Crewe (Burt Reynolds) in *The Longest Yard*, Rodgers' feat was as much drama as athletic genius. "It's one of those things where you go, 'Just when I think I've seen it all and the guy can't get any better…'" Brett Favre said following Rodgers' performance. Taken down hard by defensive end Roy Robertson-Harris for a loss of nine in the second quarter, Rodgers left the game unsure of his return. "That's about as bad a sight as any Packer fan can see," intoned NBC's Al Michaels as Rodgers lie crumpled up near the 30-yard line. But six minutes into the second half he returned to play and led his team down field to the Chicago 23, where kicker Mason Crosby split the uprights to get the Green and Gold on the board 20–3. After a three-and-out by the Bears, Rodgers exacted revenge on Robertson-Harris and the Bears with a methodical, hypnotical eight-play touchdown run that included six short passes combining for 85 yards.

One possession later, a five-play touchdown run added another seven points to the board, bringing it to 23–17 Chicago. It was a grind. "He is surviving out there, just surviving," said color commentator Cris Collinsworth. "I don't think I'll forget this game for a long, long time." For the team's final possession, Rodgers connected with Randall Cobb over the middle who raced 75 yards for the go-ahead touchdown. A rejuvenated defense rose to the occasion and stymied a frustrated Chicago pass offense, knocking down six tosses and capping off the ill-fated drive with a Nick Perry sack, the fourth sack of the evening for a hapless Bears QB Mitchell Trubisky. Packers, 24–23.[13]

And then there was off the field.

Few quarterbacks supported 49ers quarterback Colin Kaepernick more in the wake of the controversy about kneeling during the national anthem than Rodgers, who forthrightly defended his contemporary's constitutional right to protest. Racial injustice is "real," Rodgers said in 2017. "I don't understand what it's like to be in that situation. What it is to be pulled over, or profiled, or any number of issues that have happened..." The following year, Rogers chose Legal Action of Wisconsin for the Packers social justice donation. LAW offers free or low-cost legal services for the indigent who cannot access the legal system, many of whom are people of color.[14]

Mike McCarthy, who was still just getting started in his tenure, would hold on for eight more years until December 2018, a stint longer than any other coach in Packers history save for Curly Lambeau. He claimed two of the franchise's best regular seasons: in 2007 with a 13–3 record, and the 15–1 masterpiece in 2011. But once he missed the playoffs in 2017 and was on track to miss them again in 2018, the team let him go. The Packers were fully committed, organization-wide, to excellence. Losing was no longer tolerated, regardless of the coach's connection to the team.

General Manager Ted Thompson retired in 2017 due to a worsening neurological disorder, possibly another victim of a concussion-laden career of an NFL linebacker. He passed away four years later, on January 20, 2021, at age 68. The team's iconic GM was widely mourned; encomiums poured in from around Packer Nation and the NFL writ large. Thompson was one of the most important general managers in Packers history, next to Ron Wolf and Vince Lombardi. Under him the team went to the NFC Championship Game four times and won the Super Bowl once. Nineteen of the 22 starters on the 2011 Super Bowl squad were acquired by Thompson.[15] Thompson knew only success compiling an NFC-best regular season .603 record as GM piling up 125 regular season victories.[16] He also reassured folks that the Packers had finally separated the two-headed coach-general manager hydra including the armchair executive committee who had long since removed themselves from football operations. Without Thompson's steady, confident leadership, the Harlan era might very well have ended with its namesake's retirement. It didn't, thankfully, and Packer Nation has Thompson to thank.

Brett Favre made the Hall of Fame in the first round of balloting in 2016, but his personal and post-Packers career revealed a side to him that most fans didn't know. The 2010 controversy over unsolicited lewd texts and photos that he sent to the New York Jets' Game Day host Jenn Sterger would follow him—and rightfully so. His actions ended the victim's career in pro sports. Sterger was summarily dismissed by the Jets after the humiliation went public—despite no fault or even role on her part—and hasn't worked in the NFL since.[17] "My life was ruined and he went into the Hall of Fame," Sterger said.

In May 2022, Favre was implicated in a federal welfare fraud scandal involving boosters from the University of Southern Mississippi, where he was accused of funneling funding for Temporary Assistance for Needy Families (TANF) toward a volleyball gymnasium—which of course had nothing to do with feeding and clothing the state's poor. The scam consumed $5 million in program funding. Additionally, the deal netted the uber-rich former NFL star a cool $1.1 million for giving "speeches" that he never gave. It was considered the biggest public fraud case in Mississippi state history.[18]

Despite returning his million-dollar "honorarium," Favre denied any wrongdoing. Talk died down in 2024 after Favre publicly disclosed to a congressional committee on state welfare program failures that he had been diagnosed with Parkinson's disease.[19] He avoided any further legal consequences. Fortunately, his Parkinson's has so far been manageable with a medical regiment that controls symptoms.[20] (There is no cure for the neurological disorder.)

Back in Green Bay, Favre's stints with the Jets and Vikings had driven a wedge between fans and their former quarterback; the sexual harassment allegations made matters worse. Nevertheless, Bob Harlan took it upon himself to clear the air and reconcile differences. Like just about everything he has touched in life, he succeeded swimmingly and brought home the old gunslinger with a jersey retirement celebration fit for football royalty.

On Thanksgiving Day, 2015, Lambeau fans left their Rodgers jerseys at home (along with any scorched No. 4 jerseys or singed Favre football cards) to welcome back their prodigal son after five years in the football wilderness. During halftime in a rain-mist game against the Chicago Bears, Favre stood patiently at the end of the locker room tunnel just out of sight, like a rock star about to take the stage for one final time, as PA announcer Bill Jartz set up Number 4's last walk-out introduction.

"At quarterback, from Southern Mississippi, Number fooourrr, Brettt Favrrre," Jartz boomed.

The crowd lost their minds, cheering on and on.

Atop a dais at midfield, Mark Murphy welcomed the old quarterback, who returned the olive branch by embracing the Packers president and his former boss. Old teammates gathered around, a balding group with wrinkled brows and a few with not-so-discreet paunches hidden under their jerseys, grinning and clapping with approval. This was as much their honor as his, Favre told the assembled.

The platform was just big enough to include the most important people in Favre's football life: his wife, Deanna; Bob Harlan; and Ron Wolf.

"Ladies and gentlemen, please direct your attention to the north end zone and join me as we count down," Murphy said. "5, 4, 3, 2, 1!" Across the stadium's mezzanine were the names of the storied franchise's true legends: Tony Canadeo, Don Hutson, Bart Starr, Ray Nitschke, and Reggie White. A curtain that blended into the forest green paneling lifted to reveal the latest addition: "Brett Favre 4."

The crowd roared with approval as a mix of tears and raindrops collected on Favre's cheeks. His remarks were few, but from the heart.

"It is Thanksgiving. And we have so much to be thankful for, and as I think back to our time here in Green Bay I certainly thank God for the opportunity to play a game I loved so much and play it for such a long time and then the best place to play football in, in the world," Favre said, his echoing cadence reminiscent of another sports idol who considered himself the "luckiest man alive."

The game resumed and Favre's old team ultimately fell to the Bears 17–13,[21] calling to mind a similar game at the start of his career. Legends Gale Sayers and Dick Butkus might have taken extra delight in this Bears win, perhaps making up for their own jersey retirement ceremony on a cold, rainy Halloween night 21 years earlier in 1994, when Favre's Packers delivered a devastating 33–6 smackdown.[22]

Like so much in life, nothing is given, only won. Union leaders of yore—including several former Packers presidents—fought hard for good pay and benefits, a robust pension, and free agency. Today, the current generation has campaigned for concussion awareness and prevention including Brett Favre who produced *Shocked: A Hidden Factor in the Sports Concussion Crisis* (2018) and stars in the documentary *Concussed: The American Dream* (2024). Favre who says he may have suffered more than a thousand concussions during his football career, has become a key spokesman for concussion awareness and advocate for reforming policies at all levels of play.[23]

But advocates like Favre have a long way to go. Medical experts who have produced copious studies proving the hazards of repetitive head injuries fear NFL officials have not done enough. Wisconsin native and Packers fan Dr. Ann McKee conducted a study of 111 brains of deceased NFL players, diagnosing chronic traumatic encephalopathy (CTE) the resulting condition from concussion in all but *one* of the specimens. Six years after McKee's groundbreaking study on CTE was released in 2017, McKee on the occasion of a follow up study in 2023 asserted, "The NFL hasn't done anything substantial to prevent CTE or diagnose CTE. The risk is still there. The risk is high…"[24]

The Packers may be hard to beat on the field, but they can come in handy for the NFL off it. The nonprofit franchise provides occasional cover from critics who lambast the league as a $20-plus-billion professional sports empire that puts profits ahead of players (workers) and fans (customers). Among the NFL's many accused misdeeds: not taking CTE seriously enough; opening the door for private equity to claim stakes in franchises; and charging astronomical prices for tickets. The average ticket cost $120 in 2023.[25] On the secondary market, the figure was threefold, at $377. In 2025, the average Super Bowl ticket ran more than a used car at $8,076.[26]

To be clear, despite being the league's only publicly owned franchise, Green Bay is not entirely an outlier. In 2022, *Business Insider* ranked the Packers the fourth costliest team to watch based on a "fan cost index" at $719 for a family of four, which includes game tickets, parking, and concessions.[27] That figure more than doubled over a three-year period, landing at $1,659 in 2025, according to *Statista*.[28] That said, Green Bay—like all other NFL teams—faces enormous peer pressure to ratchet up prices under the shared revenue formula, in which ticket revenue is split about two to one with the league.[29] Curiously, though, tickets comprise a small percentage of the shared revenue fund, suggesting an opportunity to engage fans more fairly without draining the treasury. Though with scalpers tripling the team's per-ticket revenue, it seems unlikely the league would lower prices any further.

The goal of the NFL—like any for-profit enterprise—is to make as much money as possible. And teams are quite good at it. All NFL owners are billionaires (save the more than 500,000 stockholders who own the Packers). The richest, the Broncos' Rob Walton, is worth $118 billion, making him the 11th wealthiest person in America;[30] the piker of the bunch is the Bengals' Mike Brown, at just $1 billion.[31]

Safe to say that ownership's wealth is going in only one direction.

Fortune magazine predicts the next generation of NFL owners will be younger (the current average age is 75 years, even older than the sclerotic United States Senate), richer, and more apt to treat their investment like a corporation—not a sports team focused on winning.[32] Brown, the son of Cincinnati's cofounder Paul Brown, has opposed rule changes to improve team profitability; he was reportedly the lone "no" vote among owners in a 2024 decision to allow private equity investments in franchises.[33] The nonprofit Packers—who voted to allow private equity into the NFL—are otherwise in a company of one.

Pro football franchises have been good investments of late; there's a reason NFL families like the Maras, who've owned the Giants for more than a century[34] don't sell. Recently assessed franchise values have reached stratospheric levels. The average NFL team value has more than doubled in the last five years, from about $3.2 billion to $7.0 billion.[35] Seven of the last ten franchise sales transactions beat the S&P 500 percentagewise. Since the most recent expansion team, the Houston Texans, joined the league in 1999, the club's value outgained the S&P 500 threefold during that timeframe. What's the secret? "The escalation in football team values is largely the result of the league's massive and growing media deals," according to *CNBC*. The current broadcast contract across all networks and platforms is nearly $10 billion per year, an 85 percent increase over the previous deal.[36]

That's a lot of wealth generated from an income-redistribution scheme without precedent in any other sector of the American economy. In that sense, the NFL is more like the economy of a Scandinavian country with profit-sharing and income redistribution programs for 32 team owners. The result: billionaire owners have become bigger billionaires. The fortunes of players have also risen, albeit not as much. Minimum player salaries have doubled in the last six years. The average NFL salary in 2025 is $3.2 million, a 14 percent increase over the prior year.[37] At the highest end of the salary spectrum, the league's top-paid player in 2025—Cowboys quarterback Dak Prescott, averaging $60 million per year—made $15 million more than the NFL's highest paid in 2020, Chiefs QB Patrick Mahomes ($45 million). That's a 33 percent increase over five seasons.[38]

Benefits have grown along with salary wins at the bargaining table. In the current 2020 collective bargaining agreement (CBA), player fines have been lowered, neutral arbitration for disciplinary cases have been established, full-gear padded practices have been reduced, and added helmet protections were made in a weak nod to CTE concerns. This builds on the prior 2011

CBA, which established a $620 million legacy fund to augment pensions for retired players and minimum "cash-spends," a profit-sharing formula of sorts that raises player salaries when owners make more money.[39]

However, players are at a marked disadvantage at the bargaining table. The average tenure of ownership is 38 years, while the average player is in the league for only three years. As wide receiver Torrey Smith, who retired after eight years in the league, put it in an article in *Forbes* regarding the 2020 adopted CBA, "Dudes only care about themselves and the moment." Unsurprisingly, many players seeking short-term gains opposed the CBA. The contract was ratified by a slim margin of 60 votes out of about 2,000.[40]

Since the 1987 collective bargaining agreement, which set the stage for the 1993 CBA that codified generous free agency rules, player salaries have trended upward, once more proving that, on balance, unions pay more than similar or, in the case of pro sports, earlier non-union jobs. Before the NFLPA formed, most players held offseason jobs to make ends meet. This pro-labor mindset prevails in union towns like Green Bay. Indeed, the city's local unions showed unflagging support for their NFL union brothers and walked picket lines with them in 1982 and 1987. Packers history is synonymous with the NFL's union history; two NFLPA presidents were former Packers, while team President and CEO Mark Murphy (2008–25) was also active in the NFLPA as the union's vice president in the 1980s alongside the late NFLPA executive director and Burlington, Wisconsin, native Ed Garvey.[41]

It's worth noting that the Packers and their small-market, community-owned model did far more than just survive those long-ago eras predating labor-management equalization measures—they thrived as winners. There were championships aplenty in the 1930s and 1960s. Ranked by winning percentage, the Packers top two starkly different eras: 1921–1945 (ranked No. 2) and 1992–2024 (ranked No. 1).[42] It'd be inaccurate to conclude that shared revenue had no part in the Packers' success; the breathtaking size and scale of league economics makes it impossible for the small-market Packers to keep up with the Chicagos, New Yorks, and San Franciscos without an equitable slice of the pie. But more important is the simple fact that the team has endured for over a century *despite* all the NFL rule changes, governance structures, and league finance formulas. And that is the true measure of the team's success.

But a new twist in player contracts could have serious implications on small-market teams, particularly the Packers, who have no financial savior sitting in the owner's box. Guaranteed contracts are becoming the norm, and increasingly the "unofficial standard," according to The Athletic. To be clear, it is a long overdue benefit for workers/players in a business/sport prone to career ending injuries, an economic injustice of the first order when the combined value of all firms/teams hovers around a quarter of a *trillion* dollars. But here is the rub. The NFL's archaic "Funding Rule" requires teams to put the full contract—minus the current year payout—in escrow. Most owners are unable or simply unwilling to part with that kind of cash. But the unspoken agreement to avoid nine-figure guaranteed contracts was broken in 2022 when Browns owner Jimmy Haslam fronted $169 million to fully guarantee quarterback Deshaun Watson's $230 million deal. Fellow owners may have frowned upon the truck stop magnate's betrayal, but the union praised Haslam's move. (The NFLPA had filed a grievance in 2022 alleging collusion among owners on this matter.)

Eliminating the "Funding Rule" presents a win-win opportunity for owners and players alike. Owners wouldn't have to part with their hard-earned money—at least not right away—and agents and players would face one less excuse from owners not to guarantee contracts. But should the rule persist and expensive guaranteed contracts become the norm, the Packers with no Uncle Money Bags owner could put the Green and Gold at a marked disadvantage. On the other hand, the club's $500 million-plus reserves makes any near-term threat unlikely.[43]

Thanks to the solid foundation laid by Harlan, the Packers continue to thrive. Mike McCarthy's successor, Matt LaFleur, the youngest coach to helm the Green and Gold since Curly Lambeau, took over in 2019 and is the second winningest coach in team history save for Vince Lombardi (.675).[44] President Mark Murphy has proven to be one of the more effective executives in team history, both on and off the field. In addition to an impressive 174–106–2 record from 2008 to 2024, he oversaw a $600-plus million capital campaign. This included several construction projects, namely the addition of 7,000 seats and the Titletown district development west of the stadium, which is anchored by a venture capital company in partnership with Microsoft.[45] (Microsoft President Brad Smith is an Appleton, Wisconsin, native and, despite growing up in the 1970s, is an ardent Packers fan.)

Perhaps the most respected modern-day legacy of the Packers is that they've started only three primary quarterbacks in all but 21 games since Week 4 of the 1992 season: Brett Favre (1992–2008), Aaron Rodgers (2008–22), and Jordan Love (2023–present). By way of comparison, the Bears have started 37 over the same period.[46]

In between Mahomes' and Prescott's record-breaking contract signings, the Packers' Love tied for the highest-paid player in league history in 2024 when he inked a four-year $220 million contract.[47] It also made him the highest-paid player to wear the Green and Gold. Ever.

Love missed the eye of most college scouts and settled at a lesser-known football program in the Mountain West because of a late growth spurt. As a sophomore for Utah State in 2018, the late bloomer turned heads and made two-thirds of his passes, threw 32 touchdowns, and was intercepted just 6 times, leading the Aggies to a 11–2 season and bowl win.[48] He played three seasons for Utah State, compiling 8,600 passing yards and 60 touchdowns. Despite his truncated college career, Love holds the school record for total offensive yards at 9,003.[49]

The eye that didn't miss Love was that of legendary Packers scout Sam Seale, who flagged the rising star prior to the 2020 NFL draft. General Manager Brian Gutekunst, successor to the great Ted Thompson since 2018, certainly agreed with Seale and okayed the move, following Ron Wolf's old adage, "If there's a good quarterback on the board, take him!" But unlike Thompson in 2005, Gutekunst didn't chance fate and traded up to nab Love with the 26th selection overall.[50]

Into his third starting season, the California native maintains an above-average passer rating. Going into the 2025 season, Love was rated a top-10 quarterback despite concerns over injuries and inconsistency.[51] Then again, it took both of Love's predecessors more than two years to earn their spot in the pantheon of Packers greats. Favre took his squad to the NFC championship in his fourth season and won the Super Bowl in his fifth. Rodgers moved even faster than Favre and brought home the Lombardi Trophy in his third season as starting QB.

Love passed his first rite of initiation by defeating the Bears in Week 1 of 2023. As a bonus, he repeated the feat at the end of the season, downing Chicago 17–9 before a home crowd. It was also a must-win that put 9–8 Green Bay in the playoffs, where they advanced to the Divisional round after beating Dallas 48–32 in the wild card round. Love and the Packers came within a touchdown of reaching the NFC Championship Game the following week before succumbing to the 49ers 21–24 in San Francisco—familiar postseason terrain for underdog Green and Gold squads. Where Rodgers came up short a year earlier, Love had exceeded expectations. A good omen to be sure.

Packers fans may not care much about the political or economic phenomena of their own franchise. For many, it's a reprieve from the former and an equalizer for the latter—though the stadium's luxury boxes are an ever-present reminder of income inequality even in Green Bay, Wisconsin. Those suites at Lambeau Field begin at $60,000 per season, roughly equivalent to the average Green Bay household income in 2023.[52]

Football games suspend reality from life's often troubling authenticities. For Packers fans, that might be a grinding job on a screaming paper machine; having to deal with a crummy boss or an unruly class of students; or, even darker, perhaps an alcoholic, neglectful parent. Of the more than 3,000 counties in the United States, Brown County's neighboring county, Outgamie, is the "drunkest" in the nation.[53]

Meanwhile, wall-to-wall, yearlong coverage in the sports sections of the *Press-Gazette*, *Journal Sentinel*, and Appleton's *Post-Crescent* (plus on the five o'clock and ten o'clock news) feeds the never-ending Packers craze. Look no further than the always busy Packers Pro Shop, which consistently enjoys top sales among its peers (the Packers are currently sixth in team jersey sales league-wide).[54]

But for the NFL's 31 other teams, fans must stomach disconnected billionaire owners who share nothing in common with the hoi polloi. And it's spreading. The contagion infected Europe's Premier League in 2005, when Tampa Bay Buccaneers owner Malcolm Glazer bought Manchester United in a highly leveraged, hostile takeover.[55] The heretofore debt-free soccer team became Glazer's cash cow, generating $1.6 *billion* in debt-interest and fees, enriching his fortune even more, all the while draining the team of resources for player acquisition and development.[56] Said one fan, "They've suffocated the soul of the club… They are leeches." NFL fans could relate.

Any number of historical events have caused Americans to wander from their moorings in pursuit of "a more perfect union." Shortly before the United States' entry into World War I, and the founding of Packers soon thereafter, an ethos formed that would later be called the American Way of Life, "a distinct vision that encompassed everything that American society stood for—democracy, capitalism, prosperity, opportunity, individual liberty…" according to renown American history professor Andrew Preston. Such tradition articulated the most important component parts of the American experiment: "…individualistic, but also social, traditional but also progressive, faith-based, but also tolerant…."[57]

That's the Packers way.

And it's why the Packers are who we aspire to be as a country. And, yes, like politicians who say one thing and do another, or bad bosses who put profits ahead of their workers, all other NFL teams represent who we are, too. But the Green and Gold remind fans that who we *can* be isn't just aspirational, but real. It's all in Green Bay, Wisconsin, where everyone has a fair shot at the American Dream, from lousy Uecker seats to luxury boxes.

Epilogue

As I finish this book, the Packers are on the cusp of yet another resurgence this time with Jordan Love on offense, Micah Parsons on defense (the second coming of Reggie White), and Brian Gutekunst in the front office. It is uncanny how much Parsons reminds me of White. To be honest, I haven't enjoyed watching defense that much since The Minister dominated defense on the Packers squad and league for that matter. And how Love has so easily slotted into the role of his generation's Brett Favre or Aaron Rodgers and Gutekunst, Ron Wolf or Ted Thompson. It's safe to say the Packers as both a franchise and a football operation are an institution. I marvel at how long they have sustained a winning tradition ever since Ron Wolf arrived in Titletown in 1991. His defining role in Packers history cannot be overstated. He is the reason why they are the Green Bay Packers and not the Milwaukee Packers. (Or that UWGB does not have a basketball program that rivals that of Duke.) Perhaps I am drawn to Packers history—and enough so to write a full-arc narrative—because its modern evolution tracks my life. In the 1980s I was growing up; in the '90s, I was coming of age—just like the Packers. Soon we'd both be the adults in the room.

When I was seven years old, I was lucky to get a Packers preseason ticket; by the 1990s, getting into a game was impossible, at least for me. My dad and I have a tradition that whenever we go to a game and find our seats, we always say, "Hey, great seats!" as a salute to a fellow Wisconsinite, the late Bob Uecker. And like the old Brewers radio broadcaster, we seemed to always get the worst seats. Once, at a Bucks game, we sat in the top row right under the American flag. It seemed the entire arena pledged allegiance to my extended family.

If the social contract—making the world a better place for the next generation—covers Packers tickets, I've done right by my kids. While their first game would be Aaron Rodgers' last, Week 17 of the 2022 season, they didn't go away completely disappointed. My wife used to work for the team, and a gracious former coworker hooked her up with field passes. I cannot describe how a seven-year-old Thomas Nelson would have handled such manna from heaven in 1983. To be on the same field as Bart Starr, Lynn Dickey, James Lofton, and the rest of the squad for the *Monday Night Football* game; I would have lost my mind.

Unlike the thrilling 1983 Redskins–Packers *Monday Night Football* matchup, this game would end in a disappointing loss. With 3:37 left in the fourth quarter, facing a fierce Lions blitz, Rodgers seemed to be channeling Brett Favre's poor late-career decision-making and let rip an ill-advised deep throw down the right sideline. Rather than taking a sack and keeping the ball, Rodgers' toss was picked off with ease, setting up the loss. Detroit went on to the wild-card playoff game and the Nelsons went home. Parked on the opposite side of the stadium it was a long walk back to the car. After standing (no one sits) for three hours in 10-degree weather, Maria, the kids, and I were ready to leave. We probably won't go back for a while, since the kids will expect field passes.

The second dedication to this book—in addition to Steve Vander Loop—is a name familiar to most Packers fans: Lee Remmel.

If the Packers are a great American story, then the former public relations executive and team historian was a major supporting actor. Lee may not have been visible in every scene—but he was there. "Remmel was an eyewitness to Packers history like few others," wrote Cliff Christl on Remmel's Packers Hall of Fame page.[1]

The Shawano native penned his first newspaper story as a freshman in high school for the city's weekly at the tail end of the Great Depression in 1939. He made his way to the big city shortly after graduating, becoming a beat reporter in 1944 for the *Press-Gazette*, and moving on to the sports page two years later. After 30 years with the *Press-Gazette*, he became the Packers' public relations representative, which was really an extension of his newspaper job writing booster columns.

Lee was a successor to the paper's earlier Packers reporter and team cofounder George Calhoun, with whom he shared space in the press room in his early years, and for the most part conducted himself in that tradition. "People who were not Packers fans, Lee would have converted them," said former *Press-Gazette* writer Ginnie Erdmann.[2]

Later in his career as public relations director, Remmel befriended an intern named Maria Heim, a 20-year-old sports communications and public relations major out of Marquette University; only fitting, given the school's relationship with the team in the early years. In 1927, Lambeau brought aboard Marquette end and law school graduate Lavvie Dilweg to anchor Curly's pass offense and defend the team in court in the Willard Bent lawsuit. In 2005, Remmel mentored Maria to carry forth the great George Calhoun tradition.[3] The internship program was a one-year deal but in that time Lee and Maria became fast friends. She would remain by his side well after leaving the team in 2006, driving him to all home games and sitting with him in his namesake press box until he couldn't travel anymore in 2012.

The story of the Packers goes much further than the gridiron or Game Day. In any other NFL city, the Packers would play second fiddle to any number of attractions. Broadway in New York; the Sunset Strip in Los Angeles; heck, the Space Needle in Seattle. Not Green Bay. It's a reason why the team has been definitional in the lives of so many—not just players, coaches, board members, or interns. Steve Vander Loop and Lee Remmel being just two. But to me, they epitomize a quintessential fan. The elementary school/mission church janitor and season ticket holder; the small-town boy who worked his way to the top and one day would be inducted into its hall of fame. For our family each sparked a lifelong love for the team; for my wife, it was Lee, and for me, Steve.

I fondly recall sitting with Steve at his nursing home in Appleton watching preseason games in 2011, 28 years after our first game together. His condition had been worsening over the summer, and he wasn't ambulatory and didn't speak much. Still, being in the same room as him took me back to the ol' days. At Lambeau, Steve would admonish my dad and I and anyone in our section for that matter for attempting to leave the game early—regardless how far ahead or behind the Packers were in the score. It was a matter of respect; and the tickets didn't come cheap, especially on a janitorial salary. So, at the nursing home the month before he passed away, when I stood up to leave to get back to work, Steve scolded me, "SIT DOWN!" I'm glad he did.

Acknowledgments

In addition to total inspirations Lee Remmel and Steve Vander Loop, I have to thank my dad for nurturing my interest in the game and my wife, Maria, for making sure the TV is always tuned to the Packers when I'm distracted by work and projects (books, not outside chores). The ritual of watching the game together with family and friends began with our church group. Beginning around the time the Wolf–Holmgren–Favre years took hold, a few church family friends would gather on game day, rotating among houses. Each would bring a dish and plenty of pregame football fodder. We'd go outside and toss around a pigskin at halftime. Commentators like Terry Bradshaw drove my mom nuts, and we all had to leave the room when he came on; plus we could all stand to get a little exercise between puppy chow and Green Bay chili. (One Packer Party friend, Ed Albrent, read every line, checked every stat in this book.) The tradition ended a few years ago, unfortunately, but a new one took root with Maria's family for Sunday lunch or dinner.

Eternally grateful to my agent John Meils of DeFiore and Company for believing in this project from the beginning. Let's hope this sucker sells! Much thanks to Triumph Books for taking on the project and to my editors Danny Cooper and Michelle Bruton for their brilliant insights and edits. (John also wore the editor hat for a time.) Larry Tye for his continued friendship and inspiration. Friends like Jerald Podair,

Hilary Hinzmann, and Karl Weber, who played integral parts in past projects, too.

My assistant Anne Van and Outagamie County department heads and employees who work so hard to make our county a safe, prosperous and healthy place to call home: thank you.

I appreciate the generous time afforded me for interviews and help with research: Ed Albrent, Jeff Ash, Matthew Bent, Rosemary Bieker, Ken Calewerts, Paul Coffman, Judge John Des Jardins, Sean Dilweg, Judd Gehl, Mayor Eric Genrich, Jim Genrich, Bob Harlan, Mike Harlan, Mary Jane Herber, Paul Jadin, John Nichols, Thomas Olejnecizk, Jerry Parins, Tom Pigeon, Carol Jean Temp, Ron Wolf, and Judge Donald R. Zuidmulder.

And finally, to my wife, Maria, and my Mare Mare and Georgie, who are my sunrise and sunset—four legged kids Charley and Barb aren't too far off. (Rest in peace, sweet Lucy.) I am blessed with such a loving family and the biggest accomplishment of this and all other book projects is having enough time for (almost) every Pop Warner, basketball and volleyball game, scout meeting and campout, church choir, theater play, and D and D adventure. Love you very much.

A Note on Sources

Where possible, primary sources are used as opposed to secondary material. The primacy of research is in the following order: (1) firsthand accounts; (2) other primary source material; (3) subject matter experts; and (4) secondary sources. I relied extensively on material from *Green Bay Press-Gazette* and *Milwaukee Journal Sentinel* reporters, particularly Pete Dougherty, Cliff Christl, Lee Remmel, and Art Daley. George Calhoun, cofounder of the team, wrote most news accounts for the *Press-Gazette* of his era, so those stories were checked against other sources where possible. Longtime Brown County Library historian, Mary Jane Herber, who has worked with numerous Packers authors, provided invaluable guidance, as did former *Press-Gazette* editor and reporter Jeff Ash, Lambeau Field docent Tom Pigeon, and active shareholder Ed Albrent.

While the legion of Packers books provided important perspective and color, some works contained numerous errors and factual inaccuracies. Those authors were not used as much, and some were entirely discounted. Any oversights or mistakes in this work are mine entirely.

Sources

News Outlets (print and online)

Ad Meter (USA Today)
Akron Beacon-Journal
Appleton Post-Crescent
Associated Press
BizTimes
Bleacher Report
Buffalo Evening News
Business Insider
CapTimes
CBS News
Chicago Tribune
Chippewa Herald
Clarion-Ledger (Jackson, Miss.)
Dallas Morning News
Deadspin
Door County Pulse
ESPN
Forbes
Fortune
Green Bay Press-Gazette
Guardian UK
IBIS World
Las Vegas Sun
Los Angeles Times
Madison.com
Milwaukee Journal (1882–1995)

Milwaukee Journal Sentinel
Milwaukee Record
Milwaukee Sentinel (1837–1995)
National Affairs
New York Daily News
New York Times
Packers News (USA Today)
PBS
PBS Wisconsin
People
Pew Research
PFSN (Pro Football Network)
Politico
Press-Times (Green Bay, Wis.)
Racine County Eye
Reuters
SaturdayDownSouth.com
Slate
Smithsonian Magazine
Sports Illustrated
The Athletic
The Atlanta Journal-Constitution
The Brink
The Repository (Canton, Ohio)
The Spokesman-Review (Spokane, Wash.)
TIME
TMZ
Today
University of Tennessee Sports
UPI
US News and World Report
USA Today
VolsWire (USA Today)
Washington Post
WSN
Yahoo! Sports

Government

Advisory Council on Historic Preservation (achp.gov)
Brown County, Wisconsin (browncountywi.gov)
City of Green Bay (greenbaywi.gov)

Harry S. Truman Library (trumanlibrary.gov)
John F. Kennedy Presidential Library
Menominee Indian Tribe of Wisconsin (menominee-nsn.gov)
National Park Service (NPS.gov)
National Weather Service (weather.gov)
The Federal Reserve (federalreservehistory.org)
US Department of Commerce (Census.gov)
US Department of Defense (defense.gov)
US Department of Labor—Bureau of Labor Statistics (bls.gov)
US Senate (Senate.gov)
UW-Eau Claire Office of Research and Sponsored Programs, CERCA
UW-Green Bay Archives (facebook.com/uwgbarchives)
UW-Madison Libraries (library.wisc.edu)
Wisconsin Historical Society (Wisconsinhistory.org)
Wisconsin Legislature (docs.legis.wisconsin.gov)

Websites

Browns.com
California Community Colleges (ccco.edu)
CFBHall.com
ChicagoBears.com
Chiefs.com
FootballStadiumDigest.com
Fordham.edu
GoColgateRaiders.com
Heritage Auctions (sports.ha.com)
History.com
Hradil Auction Company (hradilauctions.hibid.com)
LAColiseum.com
MLB.com
NCAA.com
NFL.com
NFLPA.com
Nielsen.com
Packers.com (Cliff Christl, Lee Remmel)
Packerseverywhere.com
PackersHistory.net
PackersTalk.com
Packerswire.com
Predictem.com
ProFootballHoF.com

Raiders.com
Rawhide Youth Services (Rawhide.org)
SportsPro.com
Statista.com
TheStadiumView.com
TotalPackers.com
TVObscurities.com
VegasInsider.com
WeatherUnderground.com

Journals

Brookings
Law Justia
MU Law Faculty Blog (MULaw.edu)
UCLA Entertainment Law Review
Villanova Sports and Ent. Law Journal

Sports Compendiums

ESPN.com
NFL.com
Packerstats.com
Pro Football Reference
Sabr.org
StatHead.com

Interviews with Author

Jeff Ash
Matthew Bent
Rosemary Bieker
Ken Calewarts
Paul Coffman
John Des Jardins
Sean Dilweg
Judd Gehl
Eric Genrich
Bob Harlan
Mary Jane Herber
Paul Jadin
John Nichols
Thomas Olejniczak

Jerry Parins
Tom Pigeon
Ron Wolf

Presentations

"Drafting a Legacy: Jack Vainisi." Panel discussion, Heritage Hill, Allouez, Wis. April 25, 2025

"Frozen in Time: The Ice Bowl." Panel discussion, Heritage Hill, Allouez, Wis., April 24, 2025

Broadcast

ABC (Monday Night Football)
ABC Sports
Baltimore Football History
CBS Sports
CNBC
ESPN
Fox 6 Milwaukee
Fox Sports
MPR/AP
NBC Sports
NFL Films
Spectrum News
WBAY
WHBY
WTMJ

Documentaries

"30 for 30": The Minister of Defense. Directed by Courtland Bragg and Ken Rodgers. ESPN, 2023.

1967 NFL Championship Ice Bowl highlights. Directed by Bob Ryan. NFL Films, [undated]

Brett Favre's Dangerous Game. NFL Films. 2016

Legacy: 100 Seasons of the Green Bay Packers. Executive Producer: Green Bay Packers, Inc., Mark Murphy, president. Green Bay Packers, Inc., 2019

Untold: The Fall of Favre. Directed by Rebecca Gitlitz. Netflix, 2025

Vince Lombardi: A Football Life. NFL Films, 2015.

We Wuz Robbed: 1965 Conference Playoff at Green Bay. Baltimore Football History, 2025

Bibliography

Beech, Mark. *The People's Team*. Mariner, 2019
Carlson, Chuck. *Tales from the Green Bay Packers Sideline*. Sports Publishing, 2011
Christl, Cliff. *Greatest Story in Sports (Vols. 1–4)*. Green Bay Packers, Inc., 2021
Crepeau, Richard. *NFL Football: A History of America's New National Pastime*. University of Illinois Press, 2020
D'Amato Gary and Cliff Christl. *Mudbaths and Bloodbaths*. Trails, 2005
Eisenberg, John. *That First Season*. Mariner Books, 2010
Eisenberg, John. *The League*. Basic, 2019
Gullickson, Denis and Carl Hanson. *Before They Were the Packers*. Big Earth Publishing, 2004
Halas, George. *Halas: An Autobiography*. Taylor Trade, 1981
Hall, Sylvia. *Farewell to the Homeland*. Brown County Historical Society, 1995
Hersh, Seymour. *The Target is Destroyed*. Random House, 1986
Leonhardt, Kris. *Lambeau: The Boy Behind Green Bay Football*. Maxwell and McHale, 2024
Maraniss, David. *When Proud Still Mattered*. Simon and Schuster, 1997
Nelson, Thomas M. *One Day Stronger*. Rivertowns Books, 2021
Pearlman, Jeff. *Football for a Buck*. Mariner, 2018
Pearlman, Jeff. *Gunslinger*. HMH, 2016
Swain, Glenn. *Packers vs. Bears*. Charles Publishing, 1996
Torinus, John. *The Packer Legend, An Inside Look*. Laranmark Press, 1982
Walter, Tony. *Baptism by Football*. M and M Global Solutions, 2017
Willis, Chris. *The Man Who Built the NFL*. Scarecrow, 2010
Zimmerman, David. *Lambeau: The Man Behind the Mystique*. Eagle Books, 2003

Endnotes

Introduction

1. That year Soviet military officers had been "fired for failing to respond to US Navy overflights" near or in Soviet airspace. A couple of days after the commercial flight was shot down, General Charles L. Donnelly, commander of the 5th Airforce, had ordered F-15s to intercept Soviet MIGs only to decide later not to engage after a dog fight. Donnelly: "I don't think I'll start World War III this afternoon." Brian Morra, "The near nuclear war," *Air and Space Forces*, December 2, 2022, https://www.airandspaceforces.com/article/the-near-nuclear-war-of-1983/; See Seymour Hersh, *The Target is Destroyed* (Random House, 1986)
2. Rob Reischel, "Game to Remember," *Forbes*, December 8, 2019, https://www.forbes.com/sites/robreischel/2019/12/07/game-to-remember-green-bay-packers-48-washington-redskins-47/
3. Chuck Salituro, "Packers get a victory," *Milwaukee Journal Sentinel*, October 18, 1983, https://archive.jsonline.com/sports/packers/223053621.html/
4. Ibid.
5. "Find Your Nearest Packers Bar," Packerseverywhere.com, https://www.packerseverywhere.com/find-a-bar; "Green Bay Packers ticket waitlist; what you need to know," *Fox 6 Milwaukee*, February 9, 2023, https://www.fox6now.com/news/green-bay-packers-ticket-waitlist
6. "Green Bay Packers shareholders," Packers.com, https://www.packers.com/community/shareholders
7. Mike Lucas, "The Least and Most Popular NFL Teams on Social Media 2024," *WSN*, December 20, 2022, https://www.wsn.com/nfl/least-most-popular-nfl-teams-facebook/
8. Mike Ozanian, "The world's 50 most valuable," *Forbes*, September 8, 2023, https://www.forbes.com/sites/mikeozanian/2023/09/08/the-worlds-50-most-valuable-sports-teams-2023/

9. Devon Thorsby, "Why Green Bay, Wisconsin," *US News*, May 16, 2023, https://realestate.usnews.com/real-estate/articles/why-green-bay-wisconsin-is-the-best-place-to-live-in-2023-2024

Chapter 1. Beginnings

1. Cliff Christl, "The greatest story," Packers.com, July 27, 2017, https://www.packers.com/news/the-greatest-story-in-sports-19053957; Cliff Christl, *The Greatest Story in Sports*, 93
2. Christl, 43; Kendra Meinert, "Hagemeister to host," *Green Bay Press-Gazette*, November 10, 2015, https://www.greenbaypressgazette.com/story/sports/nfl/packers/2015/11/10/hagemeister-host-football-history-event/75470258/; Denis Gullickson and Carl Hanson, *Before They Were the Packers* (Big Earth Publishing, 2004), 4; Mark Beech, *The People's Team* (Mariner, 2019), 7
3. WM. C. Hunt, Fourteenth Census of the United States: 1920, https://www2.census.gov/library/publications/decennial/1920/bulletins/demographics/population-wi-number-of-inhabitants.pdf
4. Racine, Wisconsin was the closest city in their first NFL season. "Regular Season Schedule—1921," Packers.com, http://packers.com/schedule/1921/
5. "Population history of Akron from 1900 to 1990," https://physics.bu.edu/~redner/projects/population/cities/akron.html
6. Christl, 63
7. Tony Walter, *Baptism by Football* (M and M Global Solutions, 2017), 8
8. Christl, 13
9. AP, "George Calhoun Dies; Ex UB Gridder Named the Packers," *Buffalo Evening News*, December 6, 1963.
10. Documentary film: *Legacy, 1919–1929, "Humble Beginnings,"* YouTube, posted April 18, 2022
11. John Torinus, *The Packer Legend: An Inside Look* (Laranmark Press, 1982), 21, 25
12. Torinus, 27
13. Jeff Ash, interview by author, Green Bay, Wisconsin, September 30, 2024
14. It would seem unlikely that any instrument measuring rainwater would be that precise in the early 1920s. However, multiple sources reported this account including Christl.
15. Christl, 92
16. *Legacy, 1919–1929, "Humble Beginnings"*
17. *Legacy, 1919–1929, "Humble Beginnings"*; Tom Pigeon, interview with author, Allouez, Wisconsin, October 23, 2024
18. Christl, 92
19. Christl, 93
20. George Calhoun, "Lambeau scores touchdown," *Green Bay Press-Gazette*, December 1, 1922, 14

21. Christl, 93
22. Calhoun, 13
23. "Nicolet, Jean 1598–1642," Wisconsin Historical Society, https://www.wisconsinhistory.org/Records/Article/CS1665
24. "The fur trade era: 1650s to 1750s," Wisconsin Historical Society, https://www.wisconsinhistory.org/Records/Article/CS3585
25. "Green Bay, Wisconsin," Advisory Council on Historic Preservation, https://www.achp.gov/preserve-america/community/green-bay-wisconsin; "Green Bay, Wisconsin—A brief history," Wisconsin Historical Society, https://www.wisconsinhistory.org/Records/Article/CS2400; "Survey of historic sites and buildings," National Park Service, Marcy 22, 2005, https://www.nps.gov/parkhistory/online_books/explorers/sitee33.htm; "History of Brown County," Brown County, Wisconsin (government), https://www.browncountywi.gov/government/history-of-brown-county/
26. "Belgium" was a made-up construct that combined two distinct people—the Walloons and Flemish—under one ethnicity. Ken Calewarts, interview with author, September 30, 2024
27. Sylvia Hall, *Farewell to the Homeland*, 16. As much of a bargain as the price seemed, someone was making big money. Years earlier the Treaty of the Cedars between the Wisconsin territory and the Menominee Nation was signed in present-day Little Chute, Wisconsin. Among other provisions, the compact conveyed four million acres of Menominee land in northeast Wisconsin to the US government for *17 cents* per acre. "Menominee Indian Tribe of Wisconsin," September 3, 1836 Treaty," https://www.menominee-nsn.gov/CulturePages/Treaty1836; "Treaty of the Cedars," Wisconsin Historical Society, https://wisconsinhistory.org/Records/Article/CS13768
28. IBIS World, "Wisconsin industry trends," 2024, https://www.ibisworld.com/united-states/economic-profiles/wisconsin/#BuildingSection (Note: rankings updated annually)
29. U.S. Bureau of Labor Statistics, "Occupational employment and wage statistics," https://www.bls.gov/oes/2023/may/oes_wi.htm#47-0000
30. Christl, 18–19
31. Kris Leonhardt, *Lambeau: The Boy Behind Green Bay Football* (Maxwell and McHale, 2024), 24
32. "Curly Lambeau fractures," *Green Bay Press-Gazette*, September 30, 1915, https://greenbaypressgazette.newspapers.com/image/188008524/
33. Kris Leonhardt, "Lambeau: watching from the sidelines," *Press Times*, May 3, 2024, 8 https://gamma.creativecirclecdn.com/mmc/files/20240903-152912-21a-the-press-times-050324.pdf
34. Christl, 20
35. Christl, *Greatest Story*, 22–23; Leonhardt, *Lambeau*, 33–34. Lambeau saw no action in World War I because he was too young to be drafted (under 21)

until September of 1918 when the draft age was lowered to 18. Nevertheless, he was not called up largely because the war would conclude two months later.

36. Christl, 23
37. Ibid.
38. Leonhardt, *Lambeau,* 35
39. "1918 Curly Lambeau Signed, Handwritten Letter and Envelope," *Heritage Auctions,* August 28, 2016, Dallas, Texas, 2025, https://sports.ha.com/itm/football-collectibles/others/1918-curly-lambeau-signed-handwritten-letter-and-envelope-early-exemplar-from-only-season-at-notre-dame/a/7160-80501.s
40. Leonhardt, 41
41. Christl, 25
42. Christl, 24–26
43. Christl, 26; Leonhardt 41; David Zimmerman, *Lambeau,* 43

Chapter 2. Pigskin Pioneers

1. George Calhoun, "Packers wallop Menominee," *Green Bay Press-Gazette,* September 15, 1919
2. *Legacy, 1919–1929, "Humble Beginnings"*
3. Justin Skiba, "Football's 'Father of the Forward Pass' born in Sturgeon Bay," *Door County Pulse,* February 5, 2016, https://doorcountypulse.com/footballs-father-of-the-forward-pass-born-in-sturgeon-bay/
4. *Legacy, 1919–1929, "Humble Beginnings"*
5. George Calhoun, "Packers defeat," *Green Bay Press-Gazette,* October 24, 1921, https://greenbaypressgazette.newspapers.com/image/186409861/
6. *Legacy, 1919–1929, "Humble Beginnings"*
7. Glenn Swain, *Packers vs. Bears,* (Charles Publishing), 10
8. Kris Leonhardt, *Lambeau,* 45
9. Ibid., 48–49
10. John Eisenberg, *The League* (Basic, 2019), 1, 7
11. Christl, "Selling snake oil," Packers.com, October 29, 2015, https://www.packers.com/news/selling-snake-oil-football-in-green-bay-in-1919-16181553
12. Ibid., 47
13. *Legacy, 1919–1929, "Humble Beginnings"*
14. Christl, 57
15. Cliff Christl, "What was Acme," Packers.com, November 20, 2014, https://www.packers.com/news/what-was-acme-packing-s-role-in-forming-packers-14285346; Des Jardins, interview with author, Buchanan, Wisconsin, September 13, 2024
16. *Legacy, 1919–1929, "Humble Beginnings"*
17. Christl, *Greatest Story,* 51
18. AP, "NFL Week 16," *New York Times,* December 31, 2001, https://www.nytimes.com/2001/12/31/sports/nfl-week-16-favre-rescues-packers-again

.html; Marcus Riley, "Brett Favre's greatest game," *WTMJ*, March 16, 2021, https://www.tmj4.com/longform/brett-favre-greatest-game-dad-died-oral-history; John Clayton, "Sunday, October 21," *ESPN.com*, https://www.espn.com/nfl/columns/clayton_john/1267284.html; JR Radcliffe, "Packers bizarre," *Milwaukee Journal Sentinel*, December 26, 2019, https://www.jsonline.com/story/sports/nfl/packers/2019/12/26/packers-season-finale-20-years-ago-featured-frenetic-tiebreaker-battle/2665742001/

19. George Calhoun, "Packers defeat," *Green Bay Press-Gazette*, October 24, 1921, https://greenbaypressgazette.newspapers.com/image/186409861/
20. *Legacy, 1919–1929, "Humble Beginnings"*
21. The Chicago Bears were called the Staleys in the 1920 and 1921 seasons.
22. Ibid.
23. Christl, *The Greatest Story*, 75–76
24. George Halas, *Halas: An Autobiography* (Taylor Trade, 1981), 320
25. *Legacy, 1919–1929, "Humble Beginnings"*
26. Gary D'Amato and Cliff Christl, *Mudbaths and Bloodbaths*, (Trails, 2005), 26
27. *Legacy, 1919–1929, "Humble Beginnings"*
28. Chuck Carlson, *Tales from the Green Bay Packers Sideline* (Sports Publishing), 2011), 122; "Racine remembers: the game that brought professional football to Racine," *Racine County Eye*, December 9, 2016, https://racinecountyeye.com/2016/12/09/game-professional-football-racine/
29. See footnote 37 for sources of the rendering of the Packers expulsion and controversy.
30. Walter, 18–19; The Acme company did not own the Packers per se, rather the owners of the company held title to a franchise. Cliff Christl, "The Acme Packers were short-lived," Packers.com, March 23, 2017, https://www.packers.com/news/the-acme-packers-were-short-lived-18677091
31. Christl, *Greatest Story in Sports*, 82
32. Walter, 15
33. Beech, 55
34. Halas, 92
35. Christl, 85; Chris Willis, *The Man Who Built the NFL* (Scarecrow, 2010), 148
36. *Legacy, 1919–1929, "Humble Beginnings"*
37. Rendering of the Packers expulsion and controversy based on following sources: Christl, 82–86; Walter, 15; John Eisenberg, *The League*, 86–87; Zimmerman, 61–62; David Haugh, "Halas helped save," *Chicago Tribune*, August 23, 2021, https://www.chicagotribune.com/2011/01/18/halas-helped-save-packers/; Christl, "Pro football gave," Packers.com, June 23, 2016, https://www.packers.com/news/pro-football-gave-packers-the-boot-17286375
38. Calhoun, "Cal's comments," *Green Bay Press-Gazette*, January 12, 1922
39. Walter, 54
40. Ibid., 53

41. Christl, *Greatest Story*, 52
42. Christl, 94
43. Jeff Ash, interview with author, Green Bay, Wisconsin, September 30, 2004
44. Christl, 95–96
45. Cliff Christl, "Selling snake oil football in Green Bay in 1919," Packers.com, October 29, 2015, https://www.packers.com/news/selling-snake-oil-football-in-green-bay-in-1919-16181553
46. Christl, *Greatest Story*, 96
47. Christl, 99
48. *Legacy, 1919–1929, "Humble Beginnings"*
49. Ibid.
50. The Packers had three more stops on their East Coast trip and wouldn't return to Green Bay until December 9.
51. "Green Bay blasts Giants' title hopes," *New York Times*, November 25, 1929
52. Christl, 114
53. Ibid., 115–116

Chapter 3. An Unlucky Fall

1. Documentary film: *Legacy, 1930–1939, "Picking Up the Pieces,"* YouTube, posted April 18, 2022; National Register of Historic Places, "Fox Theatre," Green Bay, Brown County, Wisconsin. Reference Number: 256, https://www.wisconsinhistory.org/Records/NationalRegister/NR1723
2. Cliff Christl, "Joseph 'Red' Dunn," Packers.com, https://www.packers.com/history/hof/joseph-red-dunn
3. Like most players, Darling was a two-way player and filled the center position on offense. Christl, "Bernard 'Boob' Darling," Packers.com, https://www.packers.com/history/hof/bernard-darling
4. "Packers win national football crown," *Green Bay Press-Gazette,* December 15, 1930, 14 https://greenbaypressgazette.newspapers.com/image/186530387/
5. Oliver Kuechle, "Packers tie Spartans," *Milwaukee Journal*, December 15, 1930, https://archive.jsonline.com/sports/packers/259171161.html
6. "City to burn red fire for 'grid' heroes," *Green Bay Press-Gazette*, December 15, 1930, 1, https://greenbaypressgazette.newspapers.com/image/186530149/
7. David Lawrence, "Stocks unfair," *Green Bay Press-Gazette*, December 15, 1930, 1, https://greenbaypressgazette.newspapers.com/image/186530387/
8. Thomas M. Nelson, *One Day Stronger* (Rivertowns Books, 2021), Chapter 2
9. "The Railroads of Wisconsin, 1827–1937," Wisconsin Historical Society, https://content.wisconsinhistory.org/digital/collection/tp/id/70032
10. "Depression and unemployment," Wisconsin Historical Society, https://www.wisconsinhistory.org/Records/Article/CS426

11. Carissa Dowden, "Queen cow and the Eau Claire rule," UWEC Office of Research and Sponsored Programs, CERCA, May 2019, https://minds.wisconsin.edu/handle/1793/80259
12. Christl, *Greatest Story*, 128
13. *Legacy, 1930–1939, "Picking Up the Pieces"*
14. Alfred Stantasiere II, "Yankees Mag: The House that Lombardi Loved," MLB.com, September 14, 2022, https://www.mlb.com/news/yankees-mag-the-house-that-lombardi-loved. Perhaps a more historically accurate analogy would be Hewlett-Packard, the first Silicon Valley company, in what would become one of the nation's largest industry locale.
15. It was not uncommon for football teams to share monikers with their city's baseball teams, e.g., New York Yankees (1926–29), Boston Braves (1932), Pittsburgh Pirates (1933–39), and Brooklyn (1930–43).
16. "Brooklyn team," *Green Bay Press-Gazette*, September 15, 1931, 17, https://greenbaypressgazette.newspapers.com/image/186370037/; "Packers wallop," *Green Bay Press-Gazette*, September 21, 1931, 11, https://greenbaypressgazette.newspapers.com/image/186374586/
17. Matthew Bent, interview by author, Menasha, Wisconsin, January 9, 2025
18. "Eight injured," *Green Bay Press-Gazette*, September 21, 1931, 17, https://greenbaypressgazette.newspapers.com/image/186374734/; *Bent v. Jonet*, Wisconsin Supreme Court, January 9, 1934, https://www.courtlistener.com/opinion/8233482/bent-v-jonet/. Grandson Matthew Bennett claims his grandfather suffered an upper-back injury, a second-hand account. Court documents record a second lumbar/lower back injury. Bent interview.
19. "Capacity crowd," *Green Bay Press-Gazette*, September 22, 1931, 13 https://greenbaypressgazette.newspapers.com/image/186375201/
20. Arthur Bystrom, "Packers subdue," *Green Bay Press-Gazette*, September 28, 1931, 14, https://greenbaypressgazette.newspapers.com/image/186379608/
21. Christ, *Greatest Story*, 130
22. J. Gordon Hylton, "Lavvie Dilweg ('27): MU Law's contribution to the NFL," *MU Law Faculty Blog*, November 9, 2009, https://law.marquette.edu/facultyblog/2009/11/lavvie-dilweg-27-mu-laws-contribution-to-the-nfl-and-to-congress/
23. "Six criminal cases," *Green Bay Press-Gazette*, January 14, 1933, 11, https://greenbaypressgazette.newspapers.com/image/189072713/
24. Richard Crepeau, *NFL Football: A History of America's New National Pastime*, (University of Illinois Press, 2020), 21
25. "Act to create section 331.045 of the statutes, relating to personal injury actions," Wisconsin Session Laws, 1931. Published June 16, 1931, https://docs.legis.wisconsin.gov/1931/related/acts/242.pdf
26. "Bent wins," *Green Bay Press-Gazette*, March 1, 1933, 13, https://greenbaypressgazette.newspapers.com/image/188842494/

27. Gene Chamberlain, "Red Grange barnstorming tour," *Chicago Bears on SI*, January 30, 2024. https://www.si.com/nfl/bears/news/red-grange-barnstorming-tour-labeled-pivotal-to-league; *C.C. PYLE, PROMOTER OF SPORTS EVENTS; Red Grange's Manager Dies—Organized Transcontinental "Bunion Derbies" MADE FOOTBALL FORTUNE Had Caused Suzanne Lenglen, Richards and Other Tennis Stars to Turn Pro Signed Grange in 1925 Formed Own League.* (1939, February 4). TimesMachine. https://timesmachine.nytimes.com/timesmachine/1939/02/04/102396247.html?pageNumber=15
28. "Packer broadcast," *Green Bay Press-Gazette*, December 23, 1932, 2 https://greenbaypressgazette.newspapers.com/image/187549751/; Christl, *Greatest Story*, 138
29. Christl, 138
30. Cliff Christl, "Ward Cuff on Curly Lambeau," Packers.com, June 21, 2018, https://www.packers.com/news/ward-cuff-on-curly-lambeau-a-miserable-guy
31. Cliff Christl, "Curly Lambeau: Loved, hated equally," *Milwaukee Journal Sentinel*, October 17, 1998, https://archive.jsonline.com/sports/packers/209873171.html
32. Cliff Christl, "Packers' three-month road trip," Packers.com, March 16, 2017, https://www.packers.com/news/packers-three-month-road-trip-led-to-lambeau-s-first-divorce-18656773
33. *Legacy, 1930–1939, "Picking Up the Pieces"*
34. "Green Bay Football," *Green Bay Press-Gazette*, August 16, 1933, 11 https://greenbaypressgazette.newspapers.com/image/187539070/
35. "Jonet's role worthy of Packers' HOF," Packers.com, July 21, 2011, https://www.packers.com/news/jonet-s-role-worthy-of-packers-hof-5181296
36. "Green Bay Football"
37. Swain, 59
38. "Another Packer season," *Green Bay Press-Gazette*, September 16, 1933, 6 https://greenbaypressgazette.newspapers.com/image/188795017/
39. *Tribune* quote cited from: "Bad bleachers and near bankruptcy," Packershistory.net, https://www.packershistory.net/1934packers
40. Tyler Maas, "The short, scandalous story," *Milwaukee Record*, October 21, 2021, https://milwaukeerecord.com/sports/the-short-scandalous-story-of-milwaukees-nfl-team/; "Packers will get," *Green Bay Press-Gazette*, June 12, 1931, 17, https://greenbaypressgazette.newspapers.com/image/186983221/
41. Cliff Christl, "The truth and myth about 'The Hungry Five,'" Packers.com, May 26, 2016, https://www.packers.com/news/the-truth-and-myth-about-the-hungry-five-17191426; Jonet conducted the day-to-day financial business for over a year while the team was in receivership. Mathys was on the executive committee but absent from the re-organizing meeting on December 14, 1934, due to an illness. "Will raise $10,000," *Green Bay Press-Gazette*, December 15, 1934, 1 https://greenbaypressgazette.newspapers.com/image/187412033/

42. Christl, *Greatest Story*, 133–4
43. "UWGB Archives and Area Research Center," Facebook.com/uwgbarchives, August 24, 2019, https://www.facebook.com/uwgbarchives/posts/one-of-our-recent-donations-depicts-a-prominent-and-early-green-bay-business-joa/2857095457652828/
44. "Pro football to continue in Green Bay," *Green Bay Press-Gazette*, January 30, 1935, 11, https://greenbaypressgazette.newspapers.com/image/187407657/

Chapter 4. Going Hollywood

1. Beech, 168
2. Cliff Christl, "Packers' three-month road trip," Packers.com, March 16, 2017 https://www.packers.com/news/packers-three-month-road-trip-led-to-lambeau-s-first-divorce-18656773
3. "Mrs. Lambeau files a suit," *Green Bay Press-Gazette*, May 18, 1934, 21 https://greenbaypressgazette.newspapers.com/image/187801545/
4. "1934 Marguerite Van Kessel Lambeau Handwritten Letter Sent to Curly Lambeau to End Marriage..." *Heritage Auctions*. October 18, 2018. Dallas, Texas, https://sports.ha.com/itm/football-collectibles/others/1934-marguerite-van-kessel-lambeau-handwritten-letter-sent-to-curly-lambeau-to-end-marriage/a/50006-50602.s
5. "Mrs. E.L. Lambeau wins divorce suit," *Green Bay Press-Gazette*, May 23, 1934, 9, https://greenbaypressgazette.newspapers.com/image/187804321/
6. Christl, "Packers' three-month road trip"; The *Press-Gazette* reported on the sales team's out-of-state trips. Various stories, *Green Bay Press-Gazette,* 1940–59.
7. Copeland took the name Susan Lambeau when she married Curly.
8. Christl, "Curly Lambeau: Loved, hated equally," *Milwaukee Journal Sentinel*, October 17, 1998, https://archive.jsonline.com/sports/packers/209873171.html; David Fleming, "How the Green Bay Packers averted financial ruin," ESPN.com, April 1, 2020, https://www.espn.com/nfl/story/_/id/9669836/mysterious-fire-1950-saved-green-bay-packers-espn-magazine
9. Frank Litsky, "Don Hutson, Star Pass-Catcher, Dies at 84," *New York Times*, June 27, 1997, https://www.nytimes.com/1997/06/27/sports/don-hutson-star-pass-catcher-dies-at-84.html
10. Beech, 137
11. Ibid., 291
12. Beech, 137; Tom Pigeon, interview with the author, Allouez, Wisconsin, October 23, 2024
13. Dan Pompei, "NFL 100: At No.13, Packers' Don Hutson," The Athletic, July 17, 2023, https://www.nytimes.com/athletic/2780970/2021/08/27/nfl-100-at-no-13-packers-don-hutson-defined-poetry-in-motion-as-the-first-great-wide-receiver/

14. Four of Hutson's eleven seasons were played during World War II when 600 NFL players were serving in the war and athletic caliber of the league was comparatively low. Some clubs were so desperate for players that they hired "anyone who could run around the field twice" which was the case for George Halas's Bears. Fred Bowen, "Pandemic has disrupted," *Washington Post*, December 2, 2020, https://www.washingtonpost.com/lifestyle/kidspost/pandemic-has-disrupted-football-but-world-war-ii-shook-up-the-league-even-more/2020/12/02/08e7bba6-2ad2-11eb-92b7-6ef17b3fe3b4_story.html. Quality of play could have been a factor in Hutson's record-haul. In his four WWII seasons (1941–44) Hutson claimed more NFL receiving/rushing records (25) than he did in his seven non-war years (22). "Don Hutson," Pro Football Reference, https://www.pro-football-reference.com/players/H/HutsDo00.htm
15. Documentary film: *Legacy, 1940–1949, "Last Hurrah"*; Cliff Christl, "Don Hutson," Packers.com, https://www.packers.com/history/hof/don-hutson
16. David Maraniss, *When Proud Still Mattered*, (Simon and Schuster, 1997), 197
17. Cliff Christl, "All-time great Don Hutson earned the laurels," Packers.com, May 18, 2023, https://www.packers.com/news/all-time-great-don-hutson-earned-the-laurels
18. Pigeon interview
19. "Evolution of the NFL player," NFL.com, https://operations.nfl.com/inside-football-ops/players-legends/evolution-of-the-nfl-player/; Bob Oates, "Don Hutson: After helping invent the forward pass," *Los Angeles Times*, April 30, 1989, https://www.latimes.com/archives/la-xpm-1989-04-30-sp-3081-story.html
20. David Whitley, "Hutson was first modern receiver," ESPN.com, https://www.espn.com/sportscentury/features/00014269.html
21. Litsky; Cliff Christl, "All-time great Don Hutson earned the laurels," Packers.com, May 18, 2023, https://www.packers.com/news/all-time-great-don-hutson-earned-the-laurels; "The 1940s and the amazing Don Hutson," ProFootballHoF.com, https://www.profootballhof.com/football-history/the-1940s-and-amazing-don-hutson/; Christopher Smith, "25 interesting facts," SaturdayDownSouth.com, April 11, 2015, https://www.saturdaydownsouth.com/news/college-football/25-facts-about-alabama-legend-don-hutson/
22. Smith
23. Bud Lea, "Last of the Legends," *Milwaukee Journal Sentinel*, July 16, 1997, https://archive.jsonline.com/sports/packers/206355991.html
24. "Pass through time," Profootballhof.com, July 31, 2018, https://www.profootballhof.com/blogs/2018/07/blogs-stories-from-the-pro-football-hall-of-fame-archives-passing-through-time-a-1930s-rule-change/
25. Christl, *Greatest Story*, 152; Cliff Christl, "Larry Craig," Packers.com, https://www.packers.com/history/hof/larry-craig

26. Ken Kranz, "Curly Lambeau: Packers found," ESPN.com, June 1, 2013 https://www.espn.com/nfl/story/_/page/greatestcoach10/greatest-coaches-nfl-history-curly-lambeau
27. Christl, "Packers three-month"; Cliff Christl, "Bob Kahler," Packers.com, March 12, 2020, https://www.packers.com/news/bob-kahler-curly-lambeau-was-demanding-vocal
28. "Packers 1936 schedule," Packers.com, www.packers.com/schedule/1936/
29. Oliver E. Kuechle, "Dec. 13, 1936: Packers win first NFL title game," *Milwaukee Journal Sentinel*, December 14, 1926, https://archive.jsonline.com/sports/packers/164339896.html
30. George Calhoun, "Packers drilling in New York," *Green Bay Press-Gazette*, December 10, 1936, 15–16; "1936-NFL team stats," ProFootballReference.com, https://www.pro-football-reference.com/years/1936/opp.htm
31. Calhoun, "Packers drilling"
32. Video: "Memorable Moments: Packers win 1936 NFL Championship game," Packers.com, https://www.packers.com/video/memorable-moments-packers-win-1936-nfl-championship-game; "Play-by-Play," *Green Bay Press-Gazette*, December 14, 1936, 14, https://greenbaypressgazette.newspapers.com/image/187430916/; Hutson's touchdown score is recorded as a 50-yard play in the contemporary account, 48 yards in the box score and Packers.com highlight reel.
33. George Calhoun, "Packers again reign," *Green Bay Press-Gazette*, December 14, 1936, 13, https://greenbaypressgazette.newspapers.com/image/187430873/
34. "Great aerial attack is praised," *Green Bay Press-Gazette*, December 14, 1936, 13, https://greenbaypressgazette.newspapers.com/image/187430873/
35. John Walter, "10,000 fans greet Packers," *Green Bay Press-Gazette*, December 15, 1936, https://greenbaypressgazette.newspapers.com/image/187431212/; "Welcome Packers back," *Green Bay Press-Gazette*, December 14, 1936, 11, https://greenbaypressgazette.newspapers.com/image/187430556/
36. Christl, *Greatest Story*, 168–9
37. Dick Flatley, "Move Green Bay franchise?" *Green Bay Press-Gazette*, December 11, 1939 https://greenbaypressgazette.newspapers.com/image/187565454/
38. "About David who socked Goliath," *Green Bay Press-Gazette*, December 14, 1939, 6 https://greenbaypressgazette.newspapers.com/image/187565587/
39. "Wants Packers out," *Green Bay Press-Gazette*, December 6, 1939, 13, https://greenbaypressgazette.newspapers.com/image/187565159/
40. John Walter, "Packers crush New York," *Green Bay Press-Gazette*, December 11, 1936, 1, https://greenbaypressgazette.newspapers.com/image/187565454/
41. Stoney McGlynn, "Bays crush Giants in title game," *Milwaukee Journal Sentinel*, December 10, 1939, https://archive.jsonline.com/sports/packers/373175711.html

42. John Walter, "Packers are cheered," *Green Bay Press-Gazette*, December 15, 1939, 19 https://greenbaypressgazette.newspapers.com/image/187565688/
43. Ibid., 20
44. John Walter, "Looking up in the realm of sports," *Green Bay Press-Gazette*, January 20, 1940, 11 https://greenbaypressgazette.newspapers.com/image/187856079/
45. While no evidence exists that indicates Lambeau tried avoiding conscription in World War I, correspondence with then girlfriend Marguerite Van Kessel betrayed serious concerns about getting drafted. "Curly Lambeau Signed, Handwritten Letter," *Hradil Auction Company*. April, 20, 2023, Sealy, Texas, https://hradilauctions.hibid.com/lot/154019625
46. Cliff Christl, "Packers' Smiley Johnson gave his life," Packers.com, December 29, 2016, https://www.packers.com/news/packers-smiley-johnson-gave-his-life-for-his-country-18356337
47. Dan Pompei, "NFL 100: At No. 13, Packers' Don Hutson," The Athletic, July 17, 2023, https://www.nytimes.com/athletic/2780970/2021/08/27/nfl-100-at-no-13-packers-don-hutson-defined-poetry-in-motion-as-the-first-great-wide-receiver/
48. "Packers, world grid," *Green Bay Press-Gazette*, December 19, 1944, 15, https://greenbaypressgazette.newspapers.com/image/187805554/
49. Various headlines, *Green Bay Press-Gazette*, December 18, 1944, 1 https://greenbaypressgazette.newspapers.com/image/187804326/
50. Cliff Christl, "Don Hutson," Packers.com, https://www.packers.com/history/hof/don-hutson
51. "Lambeau divorce granted," *Green Bay Press-Gazette*, March 26, 1940, 6 https://greenbaypressgazette.newspapers.com/image/187581110/; "Lambeau divorce is set for April term," *Green Bay Press-Gazette*, March 18, 1940, 21 https://greenbaypressgazette.newspapers.com/image/187580947/
52. Martin Hendricks, "Rockwood Lodge had turbulent existence," *Milwaukee Journal Sentinel*, August 18, 2016, https://www.jsonline.com/story/sports/nfl/packers/2016/08/18/rockwood-lodge-had-turbulent-existence/88904044/; Christl, *Greatest Story*, 211–219
53. Torinus, 60
54. Christl, *Greatest Story*, 254–5; Beech, 187; Torinus, 63
55. "Reorganization of Packers,'" *Green Bay Press-Gazette*, January 13, 1950, 13 https://greenbaypressgazette.newspapers.com/image/186318230/
56. Christl, 255
57. Ibid., 246–247
58. Art Daley, "Pro grid peace," *Green Bay Press-Gazette*, December 10, 1949, 11 https://greenbaypressgazette.newspapers.com/image/186317380/
59. Christl, 256–9

Chapter 5. A New Home

1. "1949 in Review," Packershistory.net, https://www.packershistory.net/1949packers
2. Lee Remmel, "Coaching changes a fact of NFL life," Packers.com, January 10, 2006, https://www.packers.com/news/coaching-changes-a-fact-of-nfl-life-2451644
3. According to then-Packers historian Lee Remmel, "details … remain murky" about this time period between November 1949 and January of 1950, though no evidence suggests the board leaned on Curly to sign the contract and stay. Remmel
4. Christl, 260
5. "Ronzani becomes head coach," *Milwaukee Sentinel*, February 6, 1950
6. Office of the President. "Statement by the president on the Hydrogen bomb," News release, January 31, 1950, https://www.trumanlibrary.gov/library/public-papers/26/statement-president-hydrogen-bomb
7. US Senate, "McCarthy and Army-McCarthy Hearings," https://www.senate.gov/about/powers-procedures/investigations/mccarthy-and-army-mccarthy-hearings.htm
8. "The American Experience: Eisenhower and McCarthy," PBS.org, https://www.pbs.org/wgbh/americanexperience/features/eisenhower-politics/
9. The Federal Reserve marks years 1929 to 1941 as the Great Depression. Gary Richardson, *The Federal Reserve*, "The Great Depression: 1929–1941," November 22, 2013, https://www.federalreservehistory.org/essays/great-depression; "Championship seasons," Packers.com, https://www.packers.com/history/championship-seasons
10. Christl, 265–6, 269–70; "Packers stock plans," *Green Bay Press-Gazette*, February 28, 1950, 17
11. "Voluntary subscriptions," *Green Bay Press-Gazette*, April 12, 1950; "Applause for coach," *Press-Gazette*, April 12, 1950, https://greenbaypressgazette.newspapers.com/image/186372479/; Christl, 269
12. Cliff Christl, "Emil R. Fischer," Packers.com, https://www.packers.com/history/hof/emil-r-fischer
13. Christl, *Greatest Story*, 269
14. "25" referred to the stock price: $25 per share.
15. Christl, 268–271
16. Christl, 272; Art Daley, "Workers boom," *Green Bay Press-Gazette*, May 23, 1950, https://greenbaypressgazette.newspapers.com/image/186320490/
17. Christl, 280–1
18. Christl, 279–81; "Shaugnessy, Father of Modern-T, dies," *Press-Gazette*, May 16, 1970, https://greenbaypressgazette.newspapers.com/image/189089245/; Lee Remmel, "Packers 'Deserved to win,'" *Press-Gazette*, October 2, 1950, https://greenbaypressgazette.newspapers.com/image/187652905/

19. Michael Lombardi, "Drafting a Legacy" (Panel discussion, Heritage Hill, Allouez, Wisconsin, April 25, 2025)
20. Dr. Sam Vainisi, "Drafting a Legacy" (Panel discussion, Heritage Hill, Allouez, Wis. April 25, 2025)
21. Jeff Alexander, "Countdown 2 the Draft," WBAY, July 10, 2024, https://www.wbay.com/2024/07/10/countdown-2-draft-jack-vainisi-architect-dynasty/
22. Christl, 279
23. Cliff Christl, "Jack Vainisi," Packers.com, https://www.packers.com/history/hof/jack-vainisi
24. Christl, *Greatest Story*, 284–5
25. "Packers players from Marquette," *Green Bay Packer History*, https://packerstats.com/playersByCollege.php?cid=122
26. Art Daley, "Lisle Blackbourn," *Press-Gazette*, January 7, 1954, https://greenbaypressgazette.newspapers.com/image/188883128/
27. A sample of all-time best NFL coaches rankings that feature Brown among the Top 10 include: Shawna Seed, "Paul Brown: New ways to win," ESPN.com, June 6, 2013, https://www.espn.com/nfl/feature/index/_/page/greatest-coaches; Bryan DeArdo, "Top 10 NFL coaches of all time," CBS Sports, January 11, 2024, https://www.cbssports.com/nfl/news/top-10-nfl-coaches-of-all-time-bill-belichicks-place-among-the-greatest-in-league-history/; "Ranking the winningest coaches," NBC Sports Boston, December 13, 2024, https://www.nbcsportsboston.com/nfl/bill-belichick-andy-reid-winningest-nfl-coaches-history/673952/
28. Lee Remmel, "Packers get four," *Green Bay Press-Gazette*, July 26, 1957, 13
29. "NFL Standings, 1956 season," NFL.com, https://www.nfl.com/standings/league/1956/reg
30. Beech, 204
31. Marc Edelman, "The House That Taxpayers Built: Exploring the Rise in Publicly Funded Baseball Stadiums from 1953 Through the Present," 16; Jeffrey S. Moorad, *Villanova Sports and Ent. Law Journal.* 257 (2009), https://digitalcommons.law.villanova.edu/mslj/vol16/iss2/2. By deduction, neither Wrigley nor Polo Grounds were publicly financed in any way, to wit, "Sixty years ago, Cleveland Municipal Stadium was the only publicly funded Major League Baseball ("MLB") stadium in the United States."
32. Cliff Christl, "Andrew B. Turnbull," Packers.com, https://www.packers.com/history/hof/andrew-b-turnbull
33. *Legacy, "Two Extremes"*
34. "Board Ok's," *Press-Gazette*, August 23, 1955, 17, https://greenbaypressgazette.newspapers.com/image/188909988/
35. "Stadium study group," *Press-Gazette*, January 11, 1956, 4 http://greenbaypressgazette.newspapers.com/image/188294643/

36. James Bartlet, "New stadium needed," *Green Bay Press-Gazette*, March 13, 1956, 3 https://greenbaypressgazette.newspapers.com/image/188988250/; "Group asks," *Green Bay-Press-Gazette*, February 3, 1956, 1 https://greenbaypressgazette.newspapers.com/image/188889459/; "Proceedings of the Council," *Green Bay Press-Gazette*, March 3, 1956, 22, https://greenbaypressgazette.newspapers.com/image/188987579/
37. Beech, 306
38. Steven Potter, "Wisconsin's role in the Civil War origins of absentee balloting," PBSWisconsin.com, October 30, 2024, https://pbswisconsin.org/news-item/wisconsins-role-in-the-civil-war-origins-of-absentee-voting/; Ballots are printed three weeks before local and state elections.
39. "Group asks"
40. *Legacy, "Two Extremes"*
41. James Bartelt, "New stadium will cost," *Green Bay Press-Gazette*, March 14, 1956, 9 https://greenbaypressgazette.newspapers.com/image/188988384/
42. Art Daley, "Packers to 'play,'" *Green Bay Press-Gazette*, March 8, 1956, 35 https://greenbaypressgazette.newspapers.com/image/188987945
43. Art Daley, "Packers' Day," *Green Bay Press-Gazette*, March 27, 1956, 17, https://greenbaypressgazette.newspapers.com/image/188989560/
44. Christl, *Greatest Story*, 306
45. "1956 Tornado Outbreak Overview," National Weather Service, https://www.weather.gov/grr/1956TornadoOutbreakOverview
46. "Wisconsin tornadoes," National Weather Service, https://www.weather.gov/grb/wisc_tornadoes
47. "Facsimile ballot," *Green Bay Press-Gazette*, March 26, 1956, 26 https://greenbaypressgazette.newspapers.com/image/188989499/
48. Document: "Historic Preservation Analysis, Smart Growth Plan," City of Green Bay, 2022, 13–4, https://www.greenbaywi.gov/DocumentCenter/View/1275/Historic-Preservation-PDF
49. Jeff Bollier, "Proposal would repeal," *Green Bay Press-Gazette*, January 24, 2024, https://www.greenbaypressgazette.com/story/news/local/2024/01/24/green-bay-considers-repeal-of-decades-old-liquor-license-restrictions/72317160007/
50. Art Daley, "Build new stadium," *Green Bay Press-Gazette*, February 2, 1956, https://greenbaypressgazette.newspapers.com/image/188888580/
51. Kendra Meinert, "NBC's 'Today' show," *Green Bay Press-Gazette*, November 29, 2024, https://www.greenbaypressgazette.com/story/sports/nfl/packers/fans/2024/11/29/green-bay-packers-season-ticket-waiting-list-featured-on-nbcs-today-show/76654736007/
52. Art Daley, "Civic pride," *Green Bay Press-Gazette*, March 14, 1956, 25, https://greenbaypressgazette.newspapers.com/image/188988422/
53. Christl, *Greatest Story*, 308
54. Website: The Stadium View, https://www.thestadiumview.com/history

55. "Stadium dedicated," *Green Bay Press-Gazette*, September 30, 1957, 1–2, https://greenbaypressgazette.newspapers.com/image/187725356/
56. "Nixon praises," *Green Bay Press-Gazette*, September 30, 1957, 1

Chapter 6. The Pope

1. "Vince Lombardi: Simply the best," ESPN.com, June 11, 2013, https://www.espn.com/nfl/story/_/page/greatestcoach1/greatest-coaches-nfl-history-vince-lombardi; Mark Wogenrich, "Remember the Lambert trophy?" SI.com, February 4, 2025, https://www.si.com/college/pennstate/football/remember-the-lambert-trophy-penn-state-wins-3rd-straight-01jk9cd4j3wv
2. Theodore Roosevelt quotes: "Theodore Roosevelt," Goodreads.com, https://www.goodreads.com/author/quotes/44567.Theodore_Roosevelt; Lombardi quote: "In his own words," ESPN.com, September 1, https://www.espn.com/classic/quotesbmartin000806.html [Source did not publish year.]
3. Art Daley, "Bengtson, Cochran," *Green Bay Press-Gazette*, February 4, 1959, 21, https://greenbaypressgazette.newspapers.com/image/188840677
4. *Legacy, "Lombardi Reigns"*
5. Maraniss, *When Pride Still Mattered*, 22, 436
6. Jerry Kramer, "Winning wasn't everything," *New York Times*, January 24, 1997, https://archive.nytimes.com/www.nytimes.com/ref/opinion/06opclassic.html?pagewanted=print
7. Cliff Christl, "Jerry Kramer," Packers.com, https://www.packers.com/history/hof/jerry-kramer
8. "Jesuit educational philosophy," Fordham.edu, Fordham University, https://www.fordham.edu/about/living-the-mission/teaching-and-scholarship/jesuit-educational-philosophy/
9. Maraniss, 244–5
10. John Eisenberg, *That First Season* (Mariner Books, 2010), 83
11. Ibid., 84
12. Beech, 216; Maraniss, 193–5
13. Christl, *Greatest Story*, 229–330
14. "Impact of television," NFL.com, https://operations.nfl.com/gameday/technology/impact-of-television/; Robert S. Lyons, *On Any Given Sunday* (Temple University Press, 2009) 246; Christl, *Greatest Story*, 330
15. "1959 Regular season schedule," Packers.com, https://www.packers.com/schedule/1959/; Art Daley, "Packers' Ringo," *Press-Gazette*, December 23, 1959, 18, https://greenbaypressgazette.newspapers.com/image/188870078/
16. "1960 NFL Standings and Team Stats," Pro Football Reference, https://www.pro-football-reference.com/years/1960/index.htm
17. "Pack title rivals," *Green Bay Press-Gazette*, December 17, 1960, 13, https://greenbaypressgazette.newspapers.com/image/187775434/

18. Daley, "Packers win title," *Green Bay Press-Gazette*, December 18, 1960, https://greenbaypressgazette.newspapers.com/image/187776196/; Green Bay Packers, Inc. *Legacy: "1960–69: Lombardi Reigns,"* YouTube, April 18, 2022
19. Art Daley, "Packers win title," *Green Bay Press-Gazette*, December 18, 1960, 1 https://greenbaypressgazette.newspapers.com/image/187776196/
20. Maraniss, 260
21. Art Daley, "Packers miss world," *Green Bay Press-Gazette*, December 27, 1960, 1 https://greenbaypressgazette.newspapers.com/image/187786271/; Historic Packer Games, "1960 Championship Game," YouTube, January 17, 2021, https://www.youtube.com/watch?v=F-criX5Wnko
22. Cliff Christl, "Art Daley," Packers.com, https://www.packers.com/history/hof/art-daley
23. Christl, *Greatest Story*, 395
24. Cliff Christl, "The Packers history story," Packers.com, December 24, 2020, https://www.packers.com/news/this-packers-history-story-is-a-holiday-heart-warmer; Christl, *Greatest Story*, 399; "Green Bay 'Titletown, USA,'" *Press-Gazette*, December 6, 1961, 47, https://greenbaypressgazette.newspapers.com/image/189334411/; Peter Bukowski, "Green Bay, Wisconsin: The crown," Bleacher Report, June 6, 2018, https://bleacherreport.com/articles/26211-crown-of-titletown-not-up-for-debate; Josh Bourne, "The Packers own 'Titletown,'" *Fair Winds Partners*, August 16, 2011, https://fairwindspartners.com/the-packers-own-titletown-just-not-titletown-com/
25. *Legacy, "Lombardi Reigns"*
26. John Torinus, "Cobb points," *Green Bay Press-Gazette*, December 10, 1961, 43, https://greenbaypressgazette.newspapers.com/image/189335528/
27. Martin Hendricks, "Lombardi places call to Kennedy," *Milwaukee Journal Sentinel*, October 5, 2011, https://archive.jsonline.com/packerinsider/lombardi-goes-to-top-131186848.html; Josh Katzowitz, "Remember when," CBS Sports, November 22, 2013, https://www.cbssports.com/nfl/news/remember-when-john-f-kennedy-vince-lombardi-were-friends/
28. BJ Hollars, "Wisconsin for Kennedy," Wisconsin Historical Society, https://www.wisconsinhistory.org/Records/Article/CS17145; Papers of John F. Kennedy, Pre-Presidential Papers, Presidential Campaign Files, 1960, Campaigns by State: Pre-Convention Political Files, 1960, Wisconsin: Primary: Results; Christl, *Greatest Story*, 397–8, 401; Maraniss, 290; Lombardi letter to Kenneth O'Donnell, special assistant to the president, March 16, 1962, Papers of John F. Kennedy, Presidential Papers, President's Office Files, (JFKPOF) 1962: LO (JFKPOF-011-005,))
29. Christl, *Greatest Story*, 403–4; "HAP-PY," *Green Bay Press-Gazette*, January 1, 1962, 2, https://greenbaypressgazette.newspapers.com/image/189338300/
30. Maraniss, 294

31. Giants founder Tim Mara had died in 1959, and son Wellington took over that same year.
32. AP, PICTURE: "Coach at the Vatican," *Green Bay Press-Gazette*, February 9, 1962, https://greenbaypressgazette.newspapers.com/image/189336462/
33. "Meet four men," NFLPA.com, https://nflpa.com/posts/meet-the-four-men-who-broke-the-nfl-s-color-line; Cliff Christl, "Bob Mann," Packers.com, https://www.packers.com/history/hof/bob-mann
34. Johnny Smith, "Vince Lombardi would be proud," *Slate*, September 30, 2017, https://slate.com/culture/2017/09/vince-lombardi-hated-protests-but-he-fought-for-racial-justice.html
35. *Legacy, "Great Losses"*
36. Beech, 8
37. Andy Thompson, "Outagamie County judge," *Post Crescent*, May 20, 2018, https://www.postcrescent.com/story/news/2018/05/20/appleton-des-jardins-treasures-grandfathers-ties-1919-packers-green-bay/587997002/
38. Cliff Christl, "Who was Packers' first," Packers.com, January 28, 2016, https://www.packers.com/news/who-was-packers-first-african-american-player-16759587; Christl, *Greatest Story*, 273–4
39. Lee Remmel, "Letters to Lee," Packers.com, May 20, 2007, https://www.packers.com/news/letters-to-lee-remmel-2440025
40. Cliff Christl, "Bob Mann," Packers.com, https://www.packers.com/history/hof/bob-mann
41. Christl, *Greatest Story*, 493
42. Maraniss, 343–344
43. "Jesuit Educational Philosophy," Fordham.edu, Fordham University, https://www.fordham.edu/about/living-the-mission/teaching-and-scholarship/jesuit-educational-philosophy/
44. Maraniss, 241
45. Cliff Christl, "Herb Adderley," Packers.com, https://www.packers.com/history/hof/herb-adderley; Warren Gerds, (Panel discussion, Heritage Hill, Allouez, Wisconsin, April 24, 2025)
46. Christl, *Greatest Story*, 493
47. Cliff Christl, "The greatest of Bart Starr," Packers.com, August 25, 2016, https://www.packers.com/news/the-greatness-of-bart-starr-17556876
48. Beech, 259
49. Beech, 261; Eisenberg, 229; Martin Hendricks, "McHan once held," *Milwaukee Journal Sentinel*, March 18, 2015, https://archive.jsonline.com/sports/packers/mchan-once-held-the-packers-starting-job-over-starr-b99459968z1-296680551.html/
50. Maraniss, 230

51. "Bart Starr," ProFootballHoF.com, https://www.profootballhof.com/news/2019/05/bart-starr-1934-2019/; Cliff Christl, "Bart Starr," Packers.com, https://www.packers.com/history/hof/bart-starr
52. "Brett Starr," UPI, July 13, 1988, https://www.upi.com/Archives/1988/07/13/Bret-Starr-the-24-year-old-son-of-former-Green-Bay/4166584769600/; "Our story," Rawhide Youth Services, https://rawhide.org/about/our-story/
53. Cliff Christl, "An oral history," Packers.com, April 16, 2025, https://www.packers.com/news/an-oral-history-best-of-vince-lombardis-drafts-1961; Michael Lombardi, (Panel Talk, Heritage Hill, Allouez, Wisconsin, April 25, 2025)
54. Cliff Christl, "Bart Starr," Packers.com, https://www.packers.com/history/hof/bart-starr
55. Christl, *Greatest Story*, 409
56. "1962 NFL Leaders and leaderboards," Pro Football Reference, https://www.pro-football-reference.com/years/1962/leaders.htm; "Hall of famer Bart Starr passes away," Packers.com, May 26, 2019, https://www.packers.com/news/hall-of-famer-bart-starr-passes-away
57. Cliff Christl, "Jim Taylor," Packers.com, https://www.packers.com/history/hof/jim-taylor
58. Cliff Christl, "Willie Wood," Packers.com, https://www.packers.com/history/hof/willie-wood
59. "The news magazine." *TIME* did not credit stories to specific reporters.
60. "Sport: Vinnie, Vidi, Vici," *TIME,* December 21, 1962, https://time.com/archive/6873263/sport-vinnie-vidi-vici/
61. Bud Lea, "Packers still champs," Packersnews.com, February 21, 2018, https://www.packersnews.com/story/sports/nfl/packers/2017/12/28/dec-30-1962-packers-still-champs-ray-nitschke-leads-way-title-8-13/986238001/
62. Cliff Christl, "Ray Nitschke," Packers.com, https://www.packers.com/history/hof/ray-nitschke; "Selection process FAQ," Profootballhof.com, https://www.profootballhof.com/hall-of-famers/selection-process-faq/
63. QB rating is based on a contemporary formula which is based on completion percentage, yards per attempt, touchdowns per attempt, and interceptions per attempt.
64. Art Daley, "Title-seeking Packers," *Green Bay Press-Gazette*, December 16, 1962, 25 https://greenbaypressgazette.newspapers.com/image/188970915/; Box score: Packers at Giants, Pro Football Reference, December 30, 1962 https://www.pro-football-reference.com/boxscores/196212300nyg.htm; Bud Lea, "Packers still champs," *Milwaukee Journal Sentinel*, December 31, 1962, https://archive.jsonline.com/sports/packers/215008381.html; Bob Berghaus, "Excerpt: 1962 Packers-Giants title game," *Milwaukee Journal Sentinel*, January 11, 2012, https://archive.jsonline.com/sports/packers/137137208.html; Bob Berghaus, *The First America's Team*, (Clerisy Press, 2011), 11, 15; Bob Knaus, "Crowd at

airport," *Press-Gazette*, December 31, 1962, 1–2 https://greenbaypressgazette.newspapers.com/image/188974121/;

65. *Legacy "Lombardi Reigns"*; "Vince Lombardi: Class of 1971,": ProFootballHofF.com, https://www.profootballhof.com/players/vince-lombardi/; John Eisenberg, "How Tim Mara," *New York Daily News*, December 12, 2018, https://www.nydailynews.com/2018/10/27/how-tim-mara-went-from-paper-boy-to-bookmaker-to-becoming-the-patriarch-of-footballs-first-family-in-new-book-on-nfls-beginnings/
66. Cliff Christl, "Yes, Curly Lambeau fathered," Packers.com, November 22, 2018, https://www.packers.com/news/yes-curly-lambeau-fathered-a-second-son
67. Christl, *Greatest Story*, 437
68. J. Gordon Hylton, "Regulating the Yankees," Faculty Blog, MU Law School, January 11, 2011, https://law.marquette.edu/facultyblog/2011/01/regulating-the-yankees-baseball-and-antitrust-in-1939/
69. Greg Wyshynski, "The ten best player-inspired," *Yahoo Sports*, Augst 19, 2010, https://ca.sports.yahoo.com/blogs/nhl-puck-daddy/10-best-player-inspired-nhl-rules-changes—nhl.html; Anthony Cotton, "NBA creates," *Washington Post*, September 21, 1987, https://www.washingtonpost.com/archive/sports/1987/09/21/nba-creates-an-illegal-offense-call/7cbd3cb1-9f67-4a11-bb0d-bcc991b74982/
70. Paul Hornung, *Golden Boy* (Simon and Schuster, 2004), 1, 17
71. "Shocking moments in NFL history," *ESPN Page 2*, https://www.espn.com/page2/s/list/football/shocking/moments.html
72. Cliff Christl, "Would Paul Hornung," Packers.com, September 12, 2024, https://www.packers.com/news/cliff-notes-would-paul-hornung-have-made-a-difference-in-1963
73. Cliff Christl, "Yes, that was Paul Hornung," Packers.com, June 1, 2023, https://www.packers.com/news/yes-that-was-paul-hornung-on-packers-sideline-in-ice-bowl
74. Earl 'Curly' Lambeau, Profootballhof.com, https://www.profootballhof.com/players/earl-curly-lambeau/
75. Art Daley, "Packers extend," *Press-Gazette*, November 4, 1965, 21, https://greenbaypressgazette.newspapers.com/image/189346272/
76. Art Daley, "Record coaching turnover," *Press-Gazette*, January 23, 1966, 23 https://greenbaypressgazette.newspapers.com/image/189277911/
77. Ron Speer, "Hecker named," *Press-Gazette*, January 26, 1966, 21 https://greenbaypressgazette.newspapers.com/image/189278269/
78. "Mike Holmgren—Coaching tree," Pro Football History, https://pro-football-history.com/coach/187/mike-holmgren-bio; "Vince Lombardi—Coaching tree," Pro Football History, https://pro-football-history.com/coach/238/vince-lombardi-bio
79. Art Daley, "Scuttle Bays," *Green Bay Press-Gazette*, November 1, 1965, 13 https://greenbaypressgazette.newspapers.com/image/189343652/

80. Lee Remmel, "Bears great," *Green Bay Press-Gazette*, November 1, 1965, 13 https://greenbaypressgazette.newspapers.com/image/189343652/
81. Jon Kendle, "Evolution of the Game: Goal Posts," Profootballhof.com, October 16, 2018, https://www.profootballhof.com/blogs/2018/10/blogs-stories-from-the-pro-football-hall-of-fame-archives-evolution-of-the-game-goal-posts/
82. "We wuz robbed," February 25, 2025, by Baltimore Football History, YouTube, 4:30, https://www.youtube.com/watch?v=adj2ESuxs48
83. 1965 – The NFL adds a Sixth Official, Profootballhof.com, https://www.profootballhof.com/football-history/football-history/1960-19791/1965/; "1965 Colts at Packers Playoff Game," June 4, 2020, by Comrade Dobler, YouTube, 25:00 https://www.youtube.com/watch?v=BdQ7pKYNvdE; Art Daley, "Chandler's FG," *Green Bay Press-Gazette*, December 27, 1965, 13, https://greenbaypressgazette.newspapers.com/image/189325162
84. Cliff Christl, "Paul Hornung," Packers.com, https://www.packers.com/history/hof/paul-hornung; "1965 Browns and Packers," January 17, 2021, by Historic Packer Games, YouTube, 24:20 https://www.youtube.com/watch?v=keAIguvWSmY; "Here are all 94 plays," *Green Bay Press-Gazette*, January 3, 1966, 17, https://greenbaypressgazette.newspapers.com/image/189276219/
85. Art Daley, "Packers capture," *Green Bay Press-Gazette*, January 3, 1966, 13 https://greenbaypressgazette.newspapers.com/image/189276215/
86. Bryan DeArdo, "Why is it called," *CBS Sports*, February 1, 2025, cbssports.com/nfl/news/why-is-it-called-the-super-bowl-how-name-of-nfls-signature-game-was-birthed-by-childs-toy-lamar-hunts-wit/; "Lamar Hunt, Sr.," Chiefs.com, https://www.chiefs.com/team/ownership/lamarhuntsr
87. Christl, *Greatest Story*, 463–5
88. "1965 NFL Standings and Team Stats," Pro Football Reference, https://www.pro-football-reference.com/years/1965/index.htm#all_team_stats
89. "Green Bay Packers—Dallas Cowboys 1966 NFL Championship," December 31, 2021, by Way Past Junk, YouTube, 22:56 https://www.youtube.com/watch?v=D6pEKd87g7M; "NFL passer rating calculator," Pro Football Reference, https://www.pro-football-reference.com/about/qb-rating.htm; 1966 NFL opposition and defensive statistics," Pro Football Reference, https://www.pro-football-reference.com/years/1966/opp.htm; Art Daley, "Super Team?" *Green Bay Press-Gazette*, January 3, 1967, 20, https://greenbaypressgazette.newspapers.com/image/189390868/; "The fine print," *Green Bay Press-Gazette*, January 3, 1967, 21, https://greenbaypressgazette.newspapers.com/image/189390875/; "The official play by play," *Green Bay Press-Gazette*, January 3, 1967, 25, https://www.newspapers.com/image/189390895/
90. "Today's weather," *Green Bay Press-Gazette*, January 1, 1967, 1, https://greenbaypressgazette.newspapers.com/image/189390293/; Len Wagner, "Nearly 15,000," *Green Bay Press-Gazette*, January 3, 1967, 1, https://greenbaypressgazette.newspapers.com/image/189390740/

91. "Hosts first Super Bowl," LAcoliseum.com, https://www.lacoliseum.com/timeline/coliseum-hosts-first-super-bowl/
92. Emily Mae Czachor, "How much were Super Bowl," *CBS News*, February 9, 2025, https://www.cbsnews.com/news/how-much-super-bowl-tickets-2025/
93. "Super Bowl LIX," AP, February 11, 2025, https://www.nfl.com/news/super-bowl-lix-averages-record-audience-of-127-7-million-viewers
94. Rick Suter, "How much does a Super Bowl," *Ad Meter*, January 9, 2025, https://admeter.usatoday.com/story/sports/ad-meter/2025/01/09/super-bowl-commercial-costs-since-1967/77584990007/
95. Passer ratings had been calculated since the 1960 season but was not an official NFL statistic until 1973.
96. Cliff Christl, "Max McGee," Packers.com, https://www.packers.com/history/hof/max-mcgee
97. Christl, *Greatest Story*, 465
98. Chuck Johnson, "First of three straight," *Milwaukee Journal*, January 3, 1966, https://archive.jsonline.com/sports/packers/227912991.html/
99. Bud Lea, "Ice Bowl: The day," *Milwaukee Journal Sentinel*, January 10, 2015, https://archive.jsonline.com/sports/packers/ice-bowl-the-day-vince-lombardis-electric-blanket-failed-b99422098z1-288171931.html
100. "1967 NFL Championship Ice Bowl highlights," December 31, 2017, by TomG1555, YouTube, 24:41, https://www.youtube.com/watch?v=Hq1VUu05ZBQ&ab_channel=TomG1555
101. Maraniss, 413
102. Andy Hutchins, "Vince Lombardi didn't like the 'Frozen Tundra,'" *SBNation.com*, December 26, 2010, https://www.sbnation.com/nfl/2010/12/26/1897069/vince-lombardi-frozen-tundra-lambeau-field-origin-steve-sabol
103. Beech, 250
104. "1967 Ice Bowl," YouTube, December 25, 2023, NFL Two Shoes, https://www.youtube.com/watch?v=ce-cEm8-97U&ab_channel=NFLTwo-Shoes
105. Rob Schultz, "50 years later," *CapTimes*, December 31, 2017, https://captimes.com/sports/football/professional/50-years-later-ice-bowl-memories-live-on/
106. NFL Films (@NFLfilms) Dec. 27, 2017, "Actor Willem Dafoe," https://x.com/NFLFilms/status/946063401792475136?lang=en
107. Warren Gerds, "Drafting a Legacy" (Panel discussion, Heritage Hill, Allouez, Wisconsin, April 25, 2024)
108. "The Ice Bowl," ProFootballHofF.com, https://www.profootballhof.com/football-history/the-ice-bowl/
109. NFL Films, "Vince Lombardi: A Football Life," YouTube, March 10, 2015, https://www.youtube.com/watch?v=FhNn7ENixBY&ab_channel=NFLFilms
110. Frank Luksa, "A ch-ch-chilling recollection," *ESPN.com*, January 16, 2008, https://www.espn.com/nfl/playoffs07/columns/story?columnist=luksa_frank&id=3198023

111. "49ers at Packers," Pro Football Reference, https://www.pro-football-reference.com/boxscores/196612040gnb.htm; https://greenbaypressgazette.newspapers.com/image/187713060/
112. This rule was changed in 2005 to allow pushing while still making the more egregious infractions like carrying or pulling the ball carrier illegal. Sam Farmer, "How did it get," *Los Angeles Times,* December 30, 2002 https://www.latimes.com/sports/story/2022-12-30/pushing-the-pile-nfl-rule-officiating
113. Cliff Christl, "Memories of an Ice Bowl," Packers.com, January 7, 2015, https://www.packers.com/news/memories-of-an-ice-bowl-witness-14735822
114. Robert Jay, "Nielsen Top 10, December 26, 1966-January 8, 1967," TV Obscurities, March 30, 2009, https://www.tvobscurities.com/2009/03/nielsen-top-ten-december-26th-1966-sunday-january-8th-1967/
115. Beech, 250
116. Christl, *Greatest Story*, 488; Barry Horn, "Too cold to bleed," *Dallas Morning News*, December 20, 2017, https://www.dallasnews.com/sports/cowboys/2017/12/21/too-cold-to-bleed-why-the-ice-bowl-still-resonates-50-years-later/
117. Lee Remmel, "Odds mean nothing," *Press-Gazette*, January 14, 1968, 1
118. "John Madden," Raiders.com, https://www.raiders.com/history/john-madden; "Bill Walsh," ProFootballHof.com, http://profootballhof.com/players/bill-walsh/
119. "Al Davis," Pro Football Hall of Fame, https://www.profootballhof.com/players/al-davis/
120. Dave Devenport, "Wild receptions," *Green Bay Press-Gazette*, January 15, 1968, 1, https://greenbaypressgazette.newspapers.com/image/187718511/; Len Wagner, "Retirement?" *Green Bay Press-Gazette*, January 15, 1968, B-1, https://greenbaypressgazette.newspapers.com/image/187718665/

Chapter 7. The Sorry '70s

1. Tom Rosentiel, "Polling wars: Hawks vs. doves," *Pew Research*, November 23, 2009, https://www.pewresearch.org/2009/11/23/polling-wars-hawks-vs-doves/
2. Matthew Twombly, "A timeline of 1968," *Smithsonian magazine*, January 2018, https://www.smithsonianmag.com/history/timeline-seismic-180967503/
3. "1968 Green Bay Packers—Rosters, stats, schedule, draftees," Pro Football Reference, https://www.pro-football-reference.com/teams/gnb/1968.htm; "Bart Starr," Pro Football Reference, https://www.pro-football-reference.com/players/S/StarBa00.htm; "1968 Green Bay Packers—Roster and Players," Pro Football Reference, https://www.pro-football-reference.com/teams/gnb/1968_roster.htm; Beech, 259
4. "1967 NFL opposition and defensive statistics," Pro Football Reference, https://www.pro-football-reference.com/years/1967/opp.htm
5. The NFL and AFL had not yet merged.

6. Cliff Christl, "A look at Lombardi's messy exit," Packers.com, May 27, 2021, https://www.packers.com/news/a-look-at-vince-lombardi-s-gm-decisions-and-messy-exit
7. Len Wagner, "Packers lose," *Green Bay Press-Gazette*, February 6, 1969, https://greenbaypressgazette.newspapers.com/image/189182822/
8. Mike Puma, "Leader of men," *ESPN Classic*, September 13 [year missing from source], https://www.espn.com/classic/Lombardi_Vince.html
9. Dave Anderson, "Cardinal celebrates funeral mass," *New York Times*, September 8, 1970, https://www.nytimes.com/1970/09/08/archives/cardinal-celebrates-funeral-mass-for-lombardi.html; Cliff Christl, *Greatest Story*, 511; *Legacy*, "*Great Losses*"; David Maraniss, 496
10. "Vince Lombardi: Class of 1971," ProFootballHoF.com, https://www.profootballhof.com/players/vince-lombardi#statistics
11. Christl, 510
12. "1968 Green Bay Packers Roster and Players," Pro Football Reference, https://www.pro-football-reference.com/teams/gnb/1968_roster.htm
13. Maraniss, 434–5
14. "1970 Team standings and stats," Pro Football Reference, https://www.pro-football-reference.com/years/1970/index.htm
15. Christl, 520
16. *Legacy, "Great Losses"*
17. "Jim Carter," Pro Football Reference, https://www.pro-football-reference.com/players/C/CartJi00.htm
18. Christl, *Greatest Story*, 520
19. Christl, 513; Cliff Christl, "Don Shula was once," Packers.com, May 7, 2020, https://www.packers.com/news/don-shula-was-once-eager-to-coach-the-packers; "Don Shula: Class of 1997," Pro Football Hall of Fame, https://www.profootballhof.com/players/don-shula
20. Christl, *Greatest Story*, 522–524
21. "Russ Bogda," Pro Football Reference, https://www.pro-football-reference.com/executives/BogdRu0.htm; "Dominic Olejniczak," Pro Football Reference, https://www.pro-football-reference.com/executives/OlejDo0.htm; "Robert Parins," Pro Football Reference, https://www.pro-football-reference.com/executives/PariRo0.htm
22. Cliff Christl, "Packers own best," Packers.com, January 2, 2025, https://www.packers.com/news/packers-own-best-nfl-record-for-past-33-seasons
23. *Legacy, "Great Losses"*; Christl, *Greatest Story*, 527, 530
24. Matt Mattare, "Notre Dame Football 101," Bleacher Report, June 7, 2018, https://bleacherreport.com/articles/722038-notre-dame-football-101-devine-turbulence
25. Alex Kennedy, "NFL scores history," *PFSN*, October 6, 2024, https://www.profootballnetwork.com/nfl-scores-history-highest-lowest-scoring-game-common-scores-more/

26. Leonard Koppett, "Giants thwart Packers," *New York Times*, September 20, 1971, https://www.nytimes.com/1971/09/20/archives/giants-thwart-packers-rally-to-win-4240-files-intercepts-to-save.html; Christl, *Greatest Story*, 530
27. "US troops withdraw," History.com, May 28, 2025, https://www.history.com/this-day-in-history/march-29/u-s-withdraws-from-vietnam
28. Emily Kaplan, "That '70s Strike," SI.com, July 31, 2014, https://www.si.com/nfl/2014/07/31/1974-nfl-players-strike-hall-of-fame-game-canton; "1970s: The NFLPA becomes a real union," NFLPA.com, https://nflpa.com/about/history/1970s-nflpa-becomes-real-union
29. Christl, *Greatest Story*, 546–7; *Legacy "Great Losses"*
30. "1970s: The NFLPA"
31. George M. Thomas, "Fifty years ago striking NFL," *Akron Beacon-Journal*, August 1, 2024, https://www.beaconjournal.com/story/sports/nfl/2024/08/01/fifty-years-ago-striking-nfl-players-picketed-the-hall-of-fame-game/74584916007/; Kaplan 2014
32. *Legacy "Great Losses"*; Mike Kupper, "Packers trade," *Milwaukee Journal*, October 23, 1974, https://archive.jsonline.com/sports/packers/195472911.html/
33. "Rams franchise," Pro Football Reference, https://www.pro-football-reference.com/teams/ram/index.htm
34. Larry Mayer, "Former Chicago Bears executive," ChicagoBears.com, April 19, 2024, https://www.chicagobears.com/news/former-chicago-bears-executive-bill-tobin-passes-away; Cliff Christl, "Packers' first director of pro-scouting," Packers.com, April 22, 2024, https://www.packers.com/news/packers-first director-of-pro-scouting-bill-tobin-dies-at-83
35. Paul Srubas, "Newspaper marks 150 years," *Press-Gazette*, September 30, 2016, https://www.greenbaypressgazette.com/story/news/2016/09/30/newspaper-marks-150-years-witness-history/91342404/
36. "Journalist Cliff Christl," *Milwaukee Journal Sentinel*, February 8, 2014, https://archive.jsonline.com/sports/journalist-cliff-christl-takes-job-as-packers-historian-b99200491z1-244578431.html/; Christl, *Greatest Story*, 544; *Legacy, "Great Losses"*
37. Martin Hendricks, "Q and A: Packers team historian," Packersnews.com, November 21, 2018, https://www.packersnews.com/story/sports/nfl/packers/2018/11/21/packers-team-historian-cliff-christl-natural-fit-job/2083180002/
38. Jeff Ash, interview with author, Green Bay, September 30, 2024
39. Christl, 554
40. Dominic Gentile, *The Packers Tapes* (Prairie Oak Press, 1995), 115
41. Christl, 555
42. Cliff Christl, "Who shot Dan Devine's dog?" Packers.com, September 18, 2014, https://www.packers.com/news/who-shot-dan-devine-s-dog-13796408
43. Christl, *Greatest Story*, 555; *Legacy, "Great Losses"*
44. Ash interview

45. Cliff Christl, "Bart Starr named," *Green Bay Press-Gazette*, December 24, 1974, 21, https://greenbaypressgazette.newspapers.com/image/188922764
46. "Advertisement: Prayer of Saint Francis," *Green Bay Press-Gazette*, December 24, 1974, 20, https://greenbaypressgazette.newspapers.com/image/188922698/
47. Christl, *Greatest Story*, 557
48. Rob Demovsky, "Bart Starr was the boss," ESPN.com, May 27, 2019, https://www.espn.com/blog/green-bay-packers/post/_/id/47215/bart-starr-was-the-boss-but-he-was-such-a-gentleman
49. Richard Ryman, "Bart Starr tributes," *Green Bay Press-Gazette*, May 26, 2019, https://www.greenbaypressgazette.com/story/news/2019/05/26/bart-starr-tributes-reflect-kind-humble-icon-who-exuded-class-packers-icon-quarterback-coach/1244918001/
50. Jason Wilde, "'He set the bar so high,'" Madison.com, May 27, 2019, https://madison.com/sports/football/professional/article_7c64dfbc-964d-559f-89e4-ad45044cf456.html; "Legendary Packers QB Starr dies," *Reuters*, May 26, 2019, https://sports.yahoo.com/legendary-packers-qb-starr-dies-85-172915175—nfl.html
51. Christl, *Greatest Story*, 559, 562
52. Ibid., 562–3
53. *Legacy, "Great Losses"*
54. Dale Hofmann, "Packers acquire Lynn Dickey," *Milwaukee Journal Sentinel*, April 3, 1976, https://archive.jsonline.com/sports/packers/197693651.html/
55. "Lynn Dickey," Pro Football Reference, https://www.pro-football-reference.com/players/D/DickLy00.htm
56. Jason Wilde, "Starr, Favre, Rodgers…" ESPN.com, August 18, 2016, https://www.espn.com/blog/nflnation/post/_/id/210598/starr-favre-rodgers-dickey-injuries-circumstances-conspired-against-packers-other-talented-qb
57. *Legacy, "Great Losses"*
58. "1976 NFL opposition and defensive stats," Pro Football Reference, https://www.pro-football-reference.com/years/1976/opp.htm
59. Cliff Christl, "Players angry," *Green Bay Press-Gazette*, November 14, 1977, https://greenbaypressgazette.newspapers.com/image/189332048/
60. *Legacy, "Great Losses"*; Christl, *Greatest Story*, 569
61. "Lynn Dickey," Pro Football Reference. https://www.pro-football-reference.com/players/D/DickLy00.htm
62. *Legacy, "Great Losses"*; Christl, *Greatest Story*, 573–5

Chapter 8. Darkest Before Dawn

1. Cliff Christl, *Greatest Story*, 579
2. Frank Deford, "Troubled Times in Titletown," *Sports Illustrated*, May 5, 1987, https://vault.si.com/vault/1987/05/25/troubled-times-in-title-town

3. Christl, 586
4. "Packers in the pro-football Hall of Fame," Packers.com, https://www.packers.com/history/hall-of-famers
5. Christl, 579–580; Rick Gosselin, "Bookend All-American," UPI, September 26, 1980, https://www.upi.com/Archives/1980/09/26/Bookend-All-America-defensive-tackles-Bruce-Clark-and-Matt-Millen/9814338788800/
6. Bill Gosse, "Facing problems," *Green Bay Press-Gazette*, April 30, 2016, https://www.greenbaypressgazette.com/story/sports/2016/04/30/facing-problems-can-make-us-stronger/83405654/
7. JR Radcliffe, "Seven other times," *Milwaukee Journal Sentinel*, April 26, 2019, https://www.jsonline.com/story/sports/nfl/packers/2019/04/26/seven-other-times-packers-made-contentious-nfl-draft-pick/3587371002/
8. "Defensive end Bruce Clark," UPI, July 23, 1982, https://www.upi.com/Archives/1982/07/23/Defensive-end-Bruce-Clark-got-tired-of-losing-in/5755396244800/
9. "1979 NFL Opposition & Defensive Statistics," Pro Football Reference, https://www.pro-football-reference.com/years/1979/opp.htm
10. "Packers stay at home," Packers.com, August 14, 2016, https://www.packers.com/news/packers-stay-at-home-to-play-the-raiders-17489837
11. "Green Bay Station—weather," August 30, 1980, Weather Underground, https://www.wunderground.com/history/daily/us/wi/green-bay/KGRB/date/1980-8-30; "Severe weather awareness—heat waves," National Weather Service, Milwaukee/Sullivan, Wisconsin Office, https://www.weather.gov/mkx/heatwaves
12. Don Langenkamp, "Pre-game beer," *Green Bay Press-Gazette*, August 31, 1980, 1 https://greenbaypressgazette.newspapers.com/image/188853353/
13. "1980 NFL Punting," Pro Football Reference, https://www.pro-football-reference.com/years/1980/punting.htm
14. Christl, 542
15. Cliff Christl, "Broncos crush Packers," *Green Bay Press-Gazette*, August 31, 1980, 21 https://greenbaypressgazette.newspapers.com/image/188854397; Christl, *Greatest Story*, 582
16. "Fred von Appen quits," *Green Bay Press-Gazette*, September 4, 1980, 27, https://greenbaypressgazette.newspapers.com/image/188820816/
17. "Point parade," *Green Bay Press-Gazette*, September 8, 1980, 21, https://greenbaypressgazette.newspapers.com/image/188832454/; Cliff Christl, "Packers heal," *Green Bay Press-Gazette*, September 8, 1980, 21
18. Christl, *Greatest Story*, 588
19. Cliff Christl, "Packer board makes," *Green Bay Press-Gazette*, December 28, 1980, 31, https://greenbaypressgazette.newspapers.com/image/188824376/
20. Bob Harlan, interview with author, May 14, 2025
21. "1980s: The fight for free agency," NFLPA.com, https://nflpa.com/about/history/1980s-fight-free-agency

22. "History: 1981 NFL Draft," ProFootballHoF.com, January 1, 2005, https://www.profootballhof.com/news/2005/01/news-1981-national-football-league-draft/
23. Don Langenkamp, "Hey, being a fan," *Green Bay Press-Gazette*, 1, https://greenbaypressgazette.newspapers.com/image/193068720/
24. Documentary: *Legacy, "Down but not out"*; Box Score: Green Bay at Dallas, January 16, 1983, Pro Football Reference, https://www.pro-football-reference.com/boxscores/198301160dal.htm
25. David Vergun, "US remembers service members," US Department of Defense, Defense.gov, October 24, 2023, https://www.defense.gov/News/News-Stories/Article/article/3566652/us-remembers-service-members-killed-in-beirut-bombings-40-years-ago/; Andrew Glass, "United States invades Grenada," *Politico*, October 25, 2017, https://library.cqpress.com/cqalmanac/document.php?id=cqal83-1198476
26. Rob Reischel, "Game to remember," *Forbes*, December 7, 2019, https://www.forbes.com/sites/robreischel/2019/12/07/game-to-remember-green-bay-packers-48-washington-redskins-47/
27. *Legacy, "Down but not out"*
28. Box Score: Commanders at Packers, Pro Football Reference, October 17, 1983, https://www.pro-football-reference.com/boxscores/198310170gnb.htm
29. Chuck Salituro, "Packers get a victory," *Milwaukee Journal Sentinel*, October 18, 1983, https://archive.jsonline.com/sports/packers/223053621.html/
30. "1983 Week 7 MNF," November 6, 2011, by MJSIII, YouTube, 2:30:21 https://www.youtube.com/watch?v=voF2WaznTBc
31. Jim Hayes, "Bears mauled," *Green Bay Press-Gazette*, December 19, 1983, 26, https://greenbaypressgazette.newspapers.com/image/189914218/
32. Cliff Christl, "Packers fire Starr," *Green Bay Press-Gazette*, December 19, 1983, 1, https://greenbaypressgazette.newspapers.com/image/189913241/
33. Ibid.
34. *Legacy, "Down but not out"*
35. Cliff Christl, "Madden says Packer job," *Green Bay Press-Gazette*, December 20, 1983, 1, https://greenbaypressgazette.newspapers.com/image/189914656/
36. "Gregg's coaching record," *Green Bay Press-Gazette*, December 25, 1983, 46, https://greenbaypressgazette.newspapers.com/image/189924300/; "Forrest Gregg," Packers.com, https://www.packers.com/history/hof/forrest-gregg
37. Bob McGinn, "Bengals unanimous," *Green Bay Press-Gazette*, December 25, 1983, 46, https://greenbaypressgazette.newspapers.com/image/189924300/
38. Christl, *Greatest Story*, 625
39. NFL Draft: 1984, ESPN.com, https://www.espn.com/nfl/draft/rounds/_/season/1984; "Alphonso Carreker," Pro Football Reference, https://www.pro-football-reference.com/players/C/CarrAl20.htm
40. *Legacy, "Down but not out"*

41. Christl, 625
42. Cliff Christl, "Dick Corrick: John Madden topped," Packers.com, August 4, 2016, https://www.packers.com/news/dick-corrick-john-madden topped -packers-list-of-coaching-candidates-in—17420815
43. "Forrest Gregg," Pro Football Reference, https://www.pro-football-reference .com/coaches/GregFo0.htm
44. Paul Coffman, interview with author, January 23, 2025
45. "Bears beat Patriots," History.com, May 28, 2025, https://www.history.com /this-day-in-history/january-26/bears-beat-patriots-in-super-bowl-xx
46. "1986 Bears," Pro Football Reference, https://www.pro-football-reference.com /teams/chi/1986.htm
47. "Historic moments," ChicagoBears.com, https://www.chicagobears.com/photos /historic-moments-perry-s-first-td-run-17907966#140478ee-58eb-4a18-95fb -81871d3c568d
48. Jim Egle, "Bush whackers," *Green Bay Press-Gazette*, November 24, 1986, 19, https://greenbaypressgazette.newspapers.com/image/190369305/
49. Michael Janofsky, "Martin of Packers," *New York Times*, November 26, 1986, https://www.nytimes.com/1986/11/26/sports/martin-of-packers-suspended .html; Bob McGinn, "Martin incident," *Green Bay Press-Gazette*, November 25, 1986, 18, https://greenbaypressgazette.newspapers.com/image/190370678/
50. Bob McGinn, "Martin incident," *Green Bay Press-Gazette*, November 25, 1986, 18, https://greenbaypressgazette.newspapers.com/image/190370678/
51. Tom Murphy, Tony Walter and Dave Tianen, "City besmirched," *Green Bay Press-Gazette*, December 19, 1986, 1, https://greenbaypressgazette.newspapers .com/image/194106776/
52. Brian White, "Lofton suspended," *Green Bay Press-Gazette*, December 18, 1986, 2, https://greenbaypressgazette.newspapers.com/image/194103231/
53. Scott Hildebrand, "Packers' Cade," *Green Bay Press-Gazette*, November 14, 1985, 1, https://greenbaypressgazette.newspapers.com/image/189609481/; Vic Watia, "Green Bay Packers defensive back," *UPI*, May 23, 1987, https://www .upi.com/Archives/1987/05/23/Green-Bay-Packers-defensive-back-Tommories -Mossy-Cade-Saturday/7926548740800/
54. Vic Watia, "James Lofton, the all-time leading," UPI, December 18, 1986, https://www.upi.com/Archives/1986/12/18/James-Lofton-the-all-time-leading -pass-receiver-for-the/6764535266000/
55. AP, "Cade is given," *Washington Post*, July 29, 1987, https://www.washington post.com/archive/sports/1987/07/29/cade-is-given-twoyear-sentence/bf218c54 -1470-46e3-869d-4bf2c6f6943b/
56. Frank Deford, "Troubled times," *Sports Illustrated*, May 25, 1987, https://vault .si.com/vault/1987/05/25/troubled-times-in-title-town
57. "Timeline," Packers.com, https://www.packers.com/history/timeline
58. Ron Wolf, interview with author, May 20, 2025

59. David Marran, "Packers tabbed Tom Braatz," Kenosha.com, January 31, 2022, https://www.kenosha.com/2022/01/31/packers-tabbed-tom-braatz-as-vice-president-of-football-operations-in-1988/
60. Wolf did not recall if he was involved in the Lofton acquisition as player personnel director for the Raiders. Wolf interview.
61. Tony Walter and Keith Goldschmidt, "Coaches' appearance," *Green Bay Press-Gazette*, May 22, 1987, 9, https://greenbaypressgazette.newspapers.com/image/189954638/
62. Brian White, "Lofton cheered," *Green Bay Press-Gazette*, September 14, 1987, 21, https://greenbaypressgazette.newspapers.com/image/189969713/
63. "The irreplaceable players of the 1987 strike," NFLPA.com, https://nflpa.com/posts/the-irreplaceable-players-of-the-1987-strike; Emily Kaplan, "That '70s strike," SI.com, July 31, 2014, https://www.si.com/nfl/2014/07/31/1974-nfl-players-strike-hall-of-fame-game-canton
64. Bob McGinn, "Gregg now front-runner," *Green Bay Press-Gazette*, January 13, 1988, 1, https://www.newspapers.com/image/191695393/; Jim Egle, "Gregg didn't inform," *Green Bay Press-Gazette*, January 14, 1988, 4, https://greenbaypressgazette.newspapers.com/image/191696658/
65. Scott Hildebrand, "NFL delays," *Green Bay Press-Gazette*, May 26, 1987, 2, https://greenbaypressgazette.newspapers.com/image/189963247/
66. Dave Wilson, "'Oh, s—, here come all the billionaires,'" ESPN.com, December 17, 2024, https://www.espn.com/college-football/story/_/id/41136586/smu-football-acc-death-penalty-return-2024
67. "Perles decides," *Washington Post*, January 28, 1988, https://www.washingtonpost.com/archive/sports/1988/01/29/perles-decides-not-to-accept-packers-offer/ad6625b4-86b2-45c1-9a66-d3aaa1f86659/
68. "1987 NFL Standings & Team Stats," Pro Football Reference, https://www.pro-football-reference.com/years/1987/index.htm#all_team_stats; "1983 NFL Standings & Team Stats," Pro Football Reference, https://www.pro-football-reference.com/years/1983/index.htm#all_team_stats
69. Andrew Gribble, "1986 Browns tribute," Browns.com, October 26, 2016, https://www.clevelandbrowns.com/news/1986-browns-tribute-bernie-kosar-s-breakout-season-ignites-offense-17962316
70. "1988 NFL standings," Pro Football Reference, https://www.pro-football-reference.com/years/1988/index.htm
71. "Sterling Sharpe," Profootballhof.com, https://www.profootballhof.com/players/sterling-sharpe/
72. Matt Miller, "NFL Draft: Power ranking," Bleacher Report, April 10, 2011, https://bleacherreport.com/articles/660600-power-ranking-the-10-biggest-flops-at-running-back-since-1980; Bill Huber, "All-busts team," SI.com, April 12, 2025, https://www.si.com/nfl/packers/all-busts-team-greatest-packers-nfl-draft-busts-of-all-time; "NFL training camp," UPI, August 4, 1987, https://www.upi.com/Archives/1987/08/04/NFL-Training-Camp-Roundup/2371555048000/

73. Bob McGinn, "Packers seem," *Green Bay Press-Gazette*, April 23, 1989, 39, https://greenbaypressgazette.newspapers.com/image/189622749/
74. Don Langenkamp, "A larger-than-life mystique," *Green Bay Press-Gazette*, April 23, 1989, 39, https://greenbaypressgazette.newspapers.com/image/189622749/
75. Bob McGinn, "Packers seem," *Green Bay Press-Gazette*, April 23, 1989, 39, https://greenbaypressgazette.newspapers.com/image/189622749/
76. *Legacy, "Down but not out"*
77. Christl, *Greatest Story*, 660
78. Tom Mulhern, "Day of redemption," *Green Bay Press-Gazette*, September 18, 1989, 1, https://greenbaypressgazette.newspapers.com/image/185974658
79. "History of instant replay," NFL.com, https://operations.nfl.com/officiating/instant-replay/history-of-instant-replay/
80. "Bears Packers replay game," March 17, 2015, by Ironworker Jeff, YouTube, 7:22, https://www.youtube.com/watch?v=Bf21NB4bdRw
81. Pete Dougherty, "Instant replay game," *Green Bay Press-Gazette*, November 7, 2014, C1, https://greenbaypressgazette.newspapers.com/image/108829769/
82. Jim Hayes, "Bears replace," *Green Bay Press-Gazette*, November 6, 1989, 19, https://greenbaypressgazette.newspapers.com/image/188850220/
83. Mike Vandermause, "Instant replay ruling," *Milwaukee Sentinel*, November 6, 1989, https://archive.jsonline.com/sports/packers/183086841.html
84. "1990," profootballhof.com, https://www.profootballhof.com/football-history/football-history/1980-to-1999/1990/
85. "Don Majkowski," Pro Football Reference, https://www.pro-football-reference.com/players/M/MajkDo00.htm
86. Bob McGinn, "Mandarich to debut," *Green Bay Press-Gazette*, September 19, 1989, 13, https://greenbaypressgazette.newspapers.com/image/185975992/; "Tony Mandarich," Pro Football Reference, https://www.pro-football-reference.com/players/M/MandTo20.htm
87. Tony Walter, "Q and A: Mandarich separates," *Green Bay Press-Gazette*, September 17, 1989, 13, https://greenbaypressgazette.newspapers.com/image/185962219/

Chapter 9. Coronation

1. Bob McGinn, "No debate," *Green Bay Press-Gazette*, June 6, 1989, 16, https://greenbaypressgazette.newspapers.com/image/190774626/; Christl, 662–663
2. Bob Harlan, interview with author, May 14, 2025
3. Bob McGinn, "Tom Olejniczak added," *Milwaukee Journal Sentinel*, October 25, 2013, https://archive.jsonline.com/sports/packers/tom-olejniczak-added-to-packers-executive-committee-b99128194z1-229342461.html; Tom Olejniczak, interview with author, Green Bay, Wisconsin, October 2, 2024
4. Christl, 671–2
5. McGinn, 19

6. Ibid., 16
7. "Green Bay Packers," Pro Football Reference, https://www.pro-football-reference.com/teams/gnb/index.htm
8. Harlan interview
9. Kevin Isaacson, "Firing," *Green Bay Press-Gazette*, November 21, 1991, 22, https://greenbaypressgazette.newspapers.com/image/190729587
10. Kevin Isaacson and Tony Walter, "Packers pick," *Green Bay Press-Gazette*, November 27, 1991, 2, https://greenbaypressgazette.newspapers.com/image/190802597/
11. Harlan interview
12. When asked if he would have taken the job in 1987 under the same terms Harlan would offer Wolf in 1991, Wolf told the author unequivocally, "Yes." Wolf interview
13. Isaacson, et al.
14. Pearlman, 121
15. Wolf interview
16. *Legacy, "Return to Glory"*
17. Harlan interview
18. Tony Walter, "Packers suffer," *Green Bay Press-Gazette*, December 23, 1991, 1, https://greenbaypressgazette.newspapers.com/image/190573005/
19. Christl, 675
20. Walter, 1
21. Kevin Isaacson, "Packers' hunt," *Green Bay Press-Gazette*, December 23, 1991, 1, https://greenbaypressgazette.newspapers.com/image/190573005/
22. Wolf interview
23. "If not Parcells," *Green Bay Press-Gazette*, December 23, 1991, 1, https://greenbaypressgazette.newspapers.com/image/190573087/
24. "Packers hire Holmgren," UPI, January 11, 1992, https://www.upi.com/Archives/1992/01/11/Packers-hire-Holmgren-as-head-coach/5078695106000/
25. For a detailed rendering of Holmgren's coaching tree and that of its seedlings see: "Andy Reid—biography," Chiefs.com, https://www.chiefs.com/team/coaches-roster/andy-reid; "Jon Gruden biography," Raiders.com, January 6, 2018, https://www.raiders.com/news/jon-gruden-biography-20210171; "Steve Mariucci—coaching tree," Pro Football History, https://pro-football-history.com/coach/248/steve-mariucci-bio; "Packers name Sherman coach," ESPN.com, January 19 [Source doesn't include year] https://www.espn.com/nfl/news/2000/0117/296493.html; Adam Kilgore, "Branching out," *Washington Post*, October 12, 2018, http://washingtonpost.com/graphics/2018/sports/nfl-coaching-trees-connecting-every-active-coach/; "Mike Holmgren's sphere of influence," ESPN.com, June 10, 2013, https://www.espn.com/nfl/story/_/page/coachingtreeholmgren130610/greatest-nfl-coaches-mike-holmgren-coaching-legacy-influence

26. Christl, 684; Rosie's shuttered in 2018 after being open for 36 years.
27. "Terrell Buckley," cfbhall.com, https://www.cfbhall.com/inductees/terrell-buckley-2019/
28. Michael Bauman, *Ron Wolf and the Green Bay Packers* (Sports Publishing, 2019), 60
29. Chase Goodbread, "No margin," NFL.com, December 21, 2021, https://www.nfl.com/news/sidelines/the-high-wire-life-of-an-nfl-cornerback
30. Jeff Pearlman, *Gunslinger* (HMH, 2016), 41
31. Pearlman, 44–45
32. "Brett Favre: bio," ESPN.com, August 3, 2010, https://www.espn.com/nfl/news/story?id=5433631
33. Jason Munz, "Favre's legacy," *Clarion-Ledger*, July 31, 2016, https://www.hattiesburgamerican.com/story/sports/college/southern-miss/blitz/2016/07/31/munz-favres-legend-began-southern-miss-87/87759460/
34. Glanville has consistently stated he opposed the Favre draft. Recently, former general manager Ken Herock disputed early accounts that he was the impetus for the trade. Tom Silverstein, "13 years after," Packersnews.com, September 24, 2005, https://www.packersnews.com/story/sports/nfl/packers/2018/08/06/ron-wolf-recalls-how-he-pulled-off-trade-brett-favre/886426002/; Rob Demovsky, "The great Favre gamble," ESPN.com, August 4, 2016, https://www.espn.com/espn/feature/story/_/id/17211520/how-brett-favre-landed-green-bay-packers-made-happen
35. I.J. Rosenberg, "Jerry Glanville, Brett Favre," *The Atlanta Journal-Constitution*, November 19, 2015, https://www.ajc.com/sports/football/jerry-glanville-brett-favre-didn-see-eye-eye-things/hUV5zgmzMlqpiLU1fAcCIP/; Toni Monkovic, "Brett Favre, the Jets," *New York Times*, December 1, 2006, https://archive.nytimes.com/fifthdown.blogs.nytimes.com/2006/12/01/brett-favre-the-jets-and-browning-nagle/; Gregg Rosenthal, "Glanville's eye-opening," NBCSports.com, March 18, 2010, https://www.nbcsports.com/nfl/profootballtalk/rumor-mill/news/glanvilles-eye-opening-explanation-of-trading-favre
36. "Brett Favre—stats," ESPN.com, https://www.espn.com/nfl/player/stats/_/id/112/brett-favre
37. Wolf interview
38. Ibid.
39. Box Score: Green Bay at Tampa, September 13, 1992, Pro Football Reference, https://www.pro-football-reference.com/boxscores/199209130tam.htm
40. "1992 Week 2—Green Bay Packers at Tampa Bay Buccaneers," September 9, 2023, by Jamie Johnson, YouTube, 2:51:38, https://www.youtube.com/watch?v=WwK1I8RGYsA&t=9463s&ab_channel=JamieJohnson
41. "All matchups, Detroit Lions vs. Green Bay Packers," Pro Football Reference, https://www.pro-football-reference.com/boxscores/game_query.cgi?tm1

=det&tm2=gnb&yr=all; "Matt Millen—BTN Analyst," Fox Sports, https://www.foxsports.com/presspass/bios/on-air/matt-millen/

42. "Transcript: Steve Mariucci and Sterling Sharpe," Packers.com, September 17, 2007, https://www.packers.com/news/transcript-steve-mariucci-sterling-sharpe-interviewed-about-brett-favre--2442530; "Brett Favre," Pro Football Reference, https://www.pro-football-reference.com/players/F/FavrBr00.htm; "Sterling Sharpe," Pro Football Reference, https://www.pro-football-reference.com/players/S/SharSt00.htm; "Green Bay Packers player stats, 1996," ESPN.com, https://www.espn.com/nfl/team/stats/_/name/gb/season/1996/table/receiving/sort/receivingTouchdowns/dir/desc; "With Favre," *Los Angeles Times*, November 4, 1996, https://www.latimes.com/archives/la-xpm-1996-11-04-sp-61128-story.html (firewall); Martin Hendricks, "Favre-to-Freeman," *Milwaukee Journal Sentinel*, October 18, 2014, https://archive.jsonline.com/sports/packers/favre-to-freeman-was-most-productive-combination-for-packers-b99376595z1-280730532.html;
43. Box Score: Cincinnati at Green Bay, September 20, 1992, Pro Football Reference, https://www.pro-football-reference.com/boxscores/199209200gnb.htm; Matt David, "Remembering Favre's coming out party," Bleacher Report, August 3, 2010, https://bleacherreport.com/articles/429200-nfl-history-brett-favres-coming-out-party
44. "Kittrick Taylor," Pro Football Reference, https://www.pro-football-reference.com/players/T/TaylKi00.htm
45. "Chris Jacke," Packers.com, https://www.packers.com/history/hof/chris-jacke
46. "Bengals Packers 1992," May 18, 2017, by MrPacker 95, YouTube, 2:13:49 https://www.youtube.com/watch?v=PKNcdCHLkkI; Chris Havel, "Packers show," *Green Bay Press-Gazette*, September 21, 1992, 15, https://greenbaypress gazette.newspapers.com/image/190677348/

Chapter 10. Return to Titletown

1. "1956: The beginning," NFLPA.com, https://nflpa.com/about/history/1956-the-beginning
2. *Powell v. NFL*, 888 F.2d 559 (8th Cir. 1989) https://law.justia.com/cases/federal/appellate-courts/F2/888/559/203522/; "1980s: Fight for free agency," NFLPA.com, https://nflpa.com/about/history/1980s-fight-free-agency
3. *McNeil v. National Football League*, 790 F. Supp. 871 (D. Minn. 1992) https://law.justia.com/cases/federal/district-courts/FSupp/790/871/1879935/; Deubert, C., Wong, G. M, & Howe, J. (2012). All Four Quarters: A Retrospective and Analysis of the 2011 Collective Bargaining Process and Agreement in the National Football League. *UCLA Entertainment Law Review*, 19(1). http://dx.doi.org/10.5070/LR8191027149 Retrieved from https://escholarship.org/uc/item/0d4518tp P. 30

4. Deubert, et al., 10–11; "1980s: Fight for free agency"
5. Kris Schwartz, "Reverend Head-Slap Reggie," ESPN Classic, https://www.espn.com/classic/biography/s/White_Reggie.html; Josh Greer, "From Knoxville to Memphis," SI.com, April 24, 2025, https://www.si.com/college/tennessee/football/from-knoxville-to-memphis-why-reggie-white-chose-the-usfl-over-the-nfl-in-1984-01jsmw0ta5xk; Frank Thorsberg, "Memphis Showboats," UPI, January 19, 1984, https://www.upi.com/Archives/1984/01/19/Memphis-Showboats-get-Reggie-White-for-4-million/8712443336400/; "Reggie White," UTsports.com, August 15, 2003 https://utsports.com/news/2003/8/15/Reggie_White.aspx; Ken Lay, "Derek Barnett," Vols Wire, December 18, 2023, https://volswire.usatoday.com/story/sports/college/volunteers/football/2023/12/18/derek-barnett-records-sack-in-return-to-tennessee/79013660007/
6. "Reggie White; contract details," Spotrac.com, https://www.spotrac.com/nfl/player/_/id/75759/reggie-white
7. "Reggie White," ProFootballHoF.com, https://www.profootballhof.com/players/reggie-white/
8. Documentary: *"The Minister of Defense," 30 for 30,* ESPN, 2023
9. Greg Garber, "The $3.76 antitrust lawsuit," ESPN.com, March 5, [year omitted], http://espn.com/nfl/columns/lawsuit/1518733.html; Jeff Pearlman, *Football for a Buck* (Mariner, 2018)
10. "1990s: Growth of the union," NFLPA.com, https://nflpa.com/about/history/1990s-growth-of-the-union; "The history of free agency," NFL.com, https://operations.nfl.com/inside-football-ops/nfl-operations/2025-nfl-free-agency/the-history-of-nfl-free-agency/
11. *The Minister of Defense*
12. "60 Heroes: Minister of Defense for Free Agency," NFLPA.com, https://nflpa.com/posts/60-heroes-minister-of-defense-for-free-agency
13. Ibid.
14. Wolf interview
15. *The Minister of Defense*; Chris Havel, "White-letter," *Green Bay Press-Gazette,* April 7, 1993, 19, https://greenbaypressgazette.newspapers.com/image/189927299/
16. "Green Bay Packers Rosters, Stats, Schedule, Team Draftees—1992, 1993, 1996," Pro Football Reference, https://www.pro-football-reference.com/
17. Beech, 305
18. "1992 Week 11," January 29, 2022, by Jamie Johnson, YouTube, 2:07:21, https://www.youtube.com/watch?v=4JQ95P2uFTg; Documentary: *The Minister of Defense, ESPN 30 for 30,* 2023
19. Cliff Christl, *Greatest Story,* 690
20. "1992 NFL Standings & Team Stats," Pro Football Reference, http://pro-football-reference.com/years/1992/index.htm#all_team_conversions

21. "Team stats—1992," Packers.com, https://www.packers.com/team/stats/1992/reg; Player stats—passing—1992, *NFL.com*, https://www.nfl.com/stats/player-stats/category/passing/1992/post/all/passingyards/desc
22. Justin Skiba, "Packers' free agency," *Door County Pulse*, March 3, 2017, https://doorcountypulse.com/packers-free-agency-look-back/
23. "Green Bay Packers playoff history," Pro Football Reference, https://www.pro-football-reference.com/teams/gnb/playoffs.htm; Cliff Christl, "Packers own best," Packers.com, January 2, 2025, https://www.packers.com/news/packers-own-best-nfl-record-for-past-33-seasons
24. Beech, 307; "1993—Player stats—passing," NFL.com, https://www.nfl.com/stats/player-stats/category/passing/1993/REG/all/passingcompletionpercentage/DESC
25. "Green Bay at Detroit," May 10, 2018, by OberSports, YouTube, 9:55 https://www.youtube.com/watch?v=nxmtM-xNabI&ab_channel=OberSports; JR Radcliffe, "31 years ago," *Milwaukee Journal Sentinel*, February 7, 2025, https://www.jsonline.com/story/sports/nfl/packers/2025/02/07/31-years-ago-sterling-sharpe-helped-ignite-packers-return-to-glory/77582561007/
26. Kevin Isaacson, "Packers look ahead," *Green Bay Press-Gazette*, January 17, 1994, 15, https://greenbaypressgazette.newspapers.com/image/190561542
27. Christl, 693, 696
28. Emily Kaplan, "The way of the Wolf," SI.com, December 7, 2016, https://www.si.com/nfl/2016/12/07/nfl-draft-2017-ron-wolf-green-bay-packers-draft-philosophy-quarterbacks-reggie-mckenzie-john-dorsey; Tom Silverstein, "Packers GM," *Milwaukee Journal Sentinel*, February 24, 2015, https://archive.jsonline.com/sports/packers/packers-gm-ted-thompson-usually-passes-on-drafting-quarterbacks-b99450983z1-293967381.html. Wolf invited undrafted free agent and future Super Bowl MVP Kurt Warner to the 1994 training camp but released him before the season began. Cliff Christl, "Five biggest," Packers.com, July 31, 2014, https://www.packers.com/news/five-biggest-rookie-mistakes-by-packers-13351175
29. Christl, *Greatest Story,* 696
30. Documentary: *Legacy*, *"Return to Glory"*
31. Christl, 698
32. *Legacy*, *"Return to Glory"*
33. Christl, 698
34. Bauman, xiii
35. Christl, 698
36. Glenn Swain, *Packers vs. Bears*, (Charles, 1996) 373
37. Chris Havel, "Packers: bring," *Green Bay Press-Gazette*, November 2, 1994, 16, https://greenbaypressgazette.newspapers.com/image/190324026/
38. "1994-10-31 MNF Halftime," April 5, 2019, by Classic Sports, YouTube, 11:37, https://www.youtube.com/watch?v=sZiJFr8YbhA&ab_channel=ClassicSports;

Bernie Lincicome, "Bears 'thrown back,'" *Green Bay Press-Gazette*, November 1, 1994, 14; Swain, 374; Box Score: Packers at Bears, October 31, 1994, Pro Football Reference, https://www.pro-football-reference.com/boxscores/199410310chi.htm

39. Cliff Christl, "How Milwaukee became," Packers.com, June 22, 2023, https://www.packers.com/news/part-i-how-milwaukee-became-the-packers-second-home
40. Tyler Maas, "Looking back," *Milwaukee Record*, January 6, 202, https://milwaukeerecord.com/sports/looking-back-at-the-long-storied-history-of-packers-games-in-milwaukee/
41. *Legacy, "Return to Glory"*
42. Christl, *Greatest Story*, 705–8; "Green Bay vs. Atlanta," August 28, 2018, by OberSports, YouTube, 13:06 https://www.youtube.com/watch?v=5TY6Du1npyQ&ab_channel=OberSports
43. JR Radcliffe, "Sterling Sharpe, a Hall of Fame finalist," *Milwaukee Journal Sentinel*, December 15, 2024, https://www.jsonline.com/story/sports/nfl/packers/2024/12/05/sterling-sharpe-a-fascinating-figure-in-green-bay-packers-history/76775259007/; "Sterling Sharpe," Moldovassr, YouTube, June 3, 2012, https://www.youtube.com/watch?v=dC0YdP3lW_M; "Packers at Buccaneers," December 24, 1994, https://www.pro-football-reference.com/boxscores/199412240tam.htm; Pete Dougherty, "Sharpe will miss," *Green Bay Press-Gazette*, December 28, 1994, 1, https://greenbaypressgazette.newspapers.com/image/190781880/
44. "Box Score: Lions at Packers," December 31, 1994, ESPN.com, https://www.espn.com/nfl/boxscore/_/gameId/141231009
45. JR Radcliffe, "Packers pick invites," *Milwaukee Journal Sentinel*, April 27, 2018, https://www.jsonline.com/story/sports/nfl/packers/2018/04/27/packers-first-round-pick-alexander-invites-parallel-terrell-buckley-bad-thing-good-thing/558369002/
46. Frank Litsky, "Packers come up," *New York Times*, January 9, 1995, https://www.nytimes.com/1995/01/09/sports/pro-football-packers-come-up-small-on-big-plays.html
47. Jim Hayes, "Speed spurs," *Green Bay Press-Gazette*, January 8, 1995, 25, https://greenbaypressgazette.newspapers.com/image/190378990/
48. Bob McGinn, "Terrell Buckley still," *Milwaukee Journal Sentinel*, April 8, 1995, https://archive.jsonline.com/sports/packers/202039891.html
49. "1995 Steelers at Packers," October 5, 2019, by SW561, YouTube, 3:49, https://www.youtube.com/watch?v=zFhdyjGq_1I&ab_channel=SW561
50. Box score: Packers vs. Atlanta, December 30, 1995, ESPN.com, https://www.espn.com/nfl/game/_/gameId/151231009/falcons-packers
51. "1995 MVP awards voting," Pro Football Reference, https://www.pro-football-reference.com/awards/awards_1995.htm#voting_apmvp; Mike Spofford,

"Packers QB," Packers.com, February 10, 2022, https://www.packers.com/news/packers-qb-aaron-rodgers-wins-fourth-nfl-mvp-award

52. "1/6/1996 Green Bay Packers," October 10, 2019, by SW561, YouTube, 4:33 https://www.youtube.com/watch?v=SyAfcsjWnMc; Box score: Packers at 49ers, January 6, 1996, Pro Football Reference, https://www.pro-football-reference.com/boxscores/199601060sfo.htm
53. Tony Walter, "'It was destiny,'" *Green Bay Press-Gazette*, January 7, 1996, 1, https://greenbaypressgazette.newspapers.com/image/190775408/
54. Pete Dougherty, "Old nemesis awaits," *Green Bay Press-Gazette*, January 8, 1996, 19, https://greenbaypressgazette.newspapers.com/image/190825040; "1995 NFL receiving," Pro Football Reference, https://www.pro-football-reference.com/years/1995/receiving.htm; "1995 NFL standings and team stats," Pro football reference, https://www.pro-football-reference.com/years/1995/index.htm#all_rushing
55. "1/14/96 Green Bay Packers at Dallas Cowboys," October 12, 2019, by SW561, YouTube, 4:45, https://www.youtube.com/watch?v=dAnOFImr4no; Box score: Packers at Cowboys, January 14, 1996, Pro Football Reference, https://www.pro-football-reference.com/boxscores/199601140dal.htm
56. Pete Dougherty, "Dream dies," *Green Bay Press-Gazette*, January 15, 1996, https://greenbaypressgazette.newspapers.com/image/190874307/
57. Peter King, "Back to the future," *Sports Illustrated*, September 2, 1996, https://vault.si.com/vault/1996/09/02/back-to-the-future-in-a-rematch-of-the-first-super-bowl-between-the-chiefs-and-the-packers-four-worthy-men-will-realize-their-dreams
58. AP, "Favre named," *The Spokesman-Review*, January 2, 1996, https://www.spokesman.com/stories/1996/jan/02/favre-named-nfl-mvp-packers-qb-a-runaway-choice/
59. "Brett Favre's dangerous game," October 21, 2016, by NFL Films, YouTube, 6:23 https://www.youtube.com/watch?app=desktop&v=mEB_GER27Ww&ab_channel=NFLFilms
60. Pearlman, *Gunslinger*, 148
61. *Minister of Defense*
62. "SPORTS PEOPLE," *New York Times*, June 29, 1996, https://www.nytimes.com/1996/06/29/sports/sports-people-football-packers-favre-leaves-clinic.html
63. Will Brinson, "Favre reveals," *CBS Sports*, May 21, 2018, https://www.cbssports.com/nfl/news/brett-favre-reveals-he-went-to-rehab-many-more-times-than-packers-fans-believed/
64. "The mud bowl," *Green Bay Press-Gazette*, January 13, 1997, 87, https://greenbaypressgazette.newspapers.com/image/190466412/
65. John Morton, "Favre, reserves," *Green Bay Press-Gazette*, October 15, 1996, 15, https://greenbaypressgazette.newspapers.com/image/190927599/

66. Box Score: 49ers at Packers, *Green Bay Press-Gazette*, October 14, 1996, https://greenbaypressgazette.newspapers.com/image/190927510/
67. "Lambeau Field noise," *Green Bay Press-Gazette*, October 15, 1996, 2, https://greenbaypressgazette.newspapers.com/image/190926793/
68. McQuade Arnold, "1996 Packers, 49ers," TotalPackers.com, February 21, 2017, totalpackers.com/2009/11/1996-packers-49ers-riot-game-changed-everything/; Judd Gehl, interview with author, June 2, 2025
69. Christl, *Greatest Story*, 731
70. John Morton, "Bring 'em on," *Green Bay Press-Gazette*, January 5, 1997, 1, https://greenbaypressgazette.newspapers.com/image/190444793
71. "1/12/97 Panthers and Packers," January 12, 2020, by SW561, YouTube, 4:46, https://www.youtube.com/watch?v=IYOvPNccjTw; Box score: 1996–97 NFC championship, January 12, 1997, Pro Football Reference, https://www.pro-football-reference.com/boxscores/199701120gnb.htm; Bauman, 230
72. Box Score: New England vs. Green Bay, January 26, 1997, Pro Football Reference, https://www.pro-football-reference.com/boxscores/199701260gnb.htm
73. Christl, *Greatest Story*, 731; *Legacy, "Return to Glory"*
74. Don Langenkamp, "'An extreme honor,'" *Green Bay Press-Gazette*, January 28, 1997, 1, https://greenbaypressgazette.newspapers.com/image/190476516/

Chapter 11. Makeover

1. Michael Silver, "10 fearless predictions," *Sports Illustrated*, July 16, 1997, https://vault.si.com/vault/1997/07/16/10-fearless-predictions
2. Bob Matthews, "Magazines predict," *Green Bay Press-Gazette*, August 31, 1997, 34 https://greenbaypressgazette.newspapers.com/image/190825229/
3. Thomas Content, "Holmgren," *Green Bay Press-Gazette*, Augusts 21, 1997, 1, https://greenbaypressgazette.newspapers.com/image/190715415/
4. Tim Graham, "Bronco win," *Las Vegas Sun*, January 26, 1998, https://lasvegassun.com/news/1998/jan/26/bronco-win-has-sports-books-paying/
5. "Super Bowl history," Pro Football Reference, https://www.pro-football-reference.com/super-bowl/
6. Bill Pennington, "One more time," *New York Times*, January 21, 1998, C-1, https://www.nytimes.com/1998/01/21/sports/super-bowl-xxxii-one-more-time-with-feeling-elway-s-brilliant-career-with.html
7. News Release: "Super Bowl LIX makes TV," *Nielsen.com*, February 2025, https://www.nielsen.com/news-center/2025/super-bowl-lix-makes-tv-history-with-over-127-million-viewers/
8. Olivia Waxman and Merrill Fabry, "From an anonymous tip," TIME, May 4, 2018, https://time.com/5120561/bill-clinton-monica-lewinsky-timeline/

9. Broncos v. Packers, Super Bowl XXXII, Official stat book, NFL, January 25, 1998 https://www.nflgsis.com/1997/Post/04/18024/Gamebook.pdf; News Release: "Super Bowl LIX makes TV"; "1997 stats and standings"; Box score: Super Bowl XXXII, January 25, 1998, Pro Football Reference, https://www.pro-football-reference.com/boxscores/199801250den.htm; Super Bowl XXXII, November 15, 2016 by NFL, YouTube, 2:36:04, https://www.youtube.com/watch?v=JUe968JR8UM
10. Tom Perry, "'We had a good year,'" *Green Bay Press-Gazette*, January 26, 1998, 1, https://greenbaypressgazette.newspapers.com/image/190814032/
11. Steven Bruss, "'Dead silence,'" *Green Bay Press-Gazette*, January 26, 1998, 8, https://greenbaypressgazette.newspapers.com/image/190815802/
12. Joe Heller, Cartoon, *Green Bay Press-Gazette*, January 26, 1998, 8, https://greenbaypressgazette.newspapers.com/image/190815802/
13. A jury found the NFL in violation of anti-trust federal law but couldn't decide on the fine, so they slapped Pete Rozelle's league with a symbolic $1 penalty before letting the latter continue business as usual. See, Pearlman, *Football for a Buck* (Mariner, 2018).
14. Andrew Zimbalist and Roger G. Noll, "Sports, Jobs and Taxes," Brookings.edu, June 1, 1997, https://www.brookings.edu/articles/sports-jobs-taxes-are-new-stadiums-worth-the-cost/; Zimbalist and Noll, *Sports Jobs and Taxes*, (Brookings, 1997); Thomas Harrigan, "Every ballpark," MLB.com, September 28, 2025, https://www.mlb.com/news/mlb-parks-from-oldest-to-newest; Keith Jenkins, "Oldest to newest," ESPN.com, October 28, 2024
15. Christl, 737
16. "1990s: Growth of a union," NFLPA.com, https://nflpa.com/about/history/1990s-growth-of-the-union
17. Christl, 734–7
18. Tom Murphy, "18,707," *Green Bay Press-Gazette*, July 9, 1998, https://greenbaypressgazette.newspapers.com/image/190375292/
19. Christl, 740–1
20. Wisconsin State Legislature. Memo to legislators regarding Green Bay Packers. Undated. https://legis.wisconsin.gov/lab/media/mdukfm1z/green-bay-packers.pdf
21. Kevin Reichard, "NFL stadiums," Footballstadiumdigest.com, September 15, 2017, https://footballstadiumdigest.com/2017/09/nfl-stadiums-listed-oldest-to-newest/
22. Jim Kneiszel, "Packers again," *Green Bay Press-Gazette*, June 7, 1998, 2, https://greenbaypressgazette.newspapers.com/image/190734124/
23. Kneiszel, "Bonuses to Packers," *Green Bay Press-Gazette*, June 7, 1998, 2, https://greenbaypressgazette.newspapers.com/image/190734124/
24. Kneiszel, "Packers again," *Green Bay Press-Gazette*, June 7, 1998, 2, https://greenbaypressgazette.newspapers.com/image/190734124/

25. "Transcript—Mariucci and Sharpe," Packers.com, September 17, 2017, https://www.packers.com/news/transcript-steve-mariucci-sterling-sharpe-interviewed-about-brett-favre—2442530
26. Pete Dougherty, "They're down," *Green Bay Press-Gazette*, January 4, 1999, 27, https://greenbaypressgazette.newspapers.com/image/190439237/
27. Pete Doughtery, "Who follows?" *Green Bay Press-Gazette*, January 9, 1999, 15, https://greenbaypressgazette.newspapers.com/image/190445286/
28. Greg Meinholz, "The Packers multiverse," PackersTalk.com, April 10, 2023, https://packerstalk.com/2023/04/10/the-packers-multiverse-ep-ii-mike-holmgren-becomes-coach-gm/; Ed Albrent, interview with the author, July 18, 2025
29. News services, "Holmgren says," ESPN.com, December 31 [year omitted], https://www.espn.com/nfl/news/2002/1231/1485140.html
30. Pete Dougherty, "There's no doubt," *Green Bay Press-Gazette*, January 12, 1999, https://greenbaypressgazette.newspapers.com/image/190456686/
31. Christl, 754–56
32. Greg Bishop, "A scout at heart," *New York Times*, January 19, 2008, https://www.nytimes.com/2008/01/19/sports/football/19packers.html
33. Bauman, 97
34. "Hit the Rhodes!" CBSNews.com, January 3, 2000, https://www.cbsnews.com/news/hit-the-rhodes-pack-fire-ray/; Christl, *Greatest Story*, 761
35. "Hit the Rhodes!"
36. Christl, 767
37. "Harlan comments," *Green Bay Press-Gazette*, February 2, 1999, 2, https://greenbaypressgazette.newspapers.com/image/190669321/
38. Scott Hildebrand, "Capitol insider," *Green Bay Press-Gazette*, February 2, 1999, 2, https://greenbaypressgazette.newspapers.com/image/190669321/
39. And efforts also proved frustrating. At the time, the state was issuing $700 million in sales tax rebates per 1999 Wisconsin Act 10 (November 10, 1999). It was reported that 11 percent or about 240,000 checks had been uncashed a month after they were cut. That translated into approximately $70 million, just shy of the projected $75 million price tag for stadium improvements. AP, "Questions arise," *Green Bay Press-Gazette*, February 4, 2000, https://greenbaypressgazette.newspapers.com/image/187793811/; Wisconsin State Legislature. Memo to legislators regarding Green Bay Packers. Undated. https://legis.wisconsin.gov/lab/media/mdukfm1z/green-bay-packers.pdf
40. Paul Jadin, interview with author, Ashwaubenon, Wisconsin, May 29, 2025
41. "TV deals," AP, January 14, 1998, https://www.deseret.com/1998/1/14/19357699/tv-deal-puts-nbc-on-the-bench-sends-nfl-to-bank/; Bill Carter, "New TV contracts," *New York Times*, March 10, 1990, https://www.nytimes.com/1990/03/10/business/new-tv-contracts-for-nfl-s-games-total-3.6-billion.html

42. Thomas Content, "Packers execs," *Green Bay Press-Gazette*, June 1, 2000, 13, https://greenbaypressgazette.newspapers.com/image/188816337/
43. Content, "Local support," *Green Bay Press-Gazette*, May 3, 2000, 3, https://greenbaypressgazette.newspapers.com/image/188817340/
44. Bob Harlan, interview with author, May 14, 2025
45. Richard Parins, "Packers fans need," People's Forum, *Green Bay Press-Gazette*, September 2, 2000, https://greenbaypressgazette.newspapers.com/image/191261102/
46. Ron Wolf, interview with author, May 20, 2025
47. Scott Hildebrand, "Lambeau Field bill," *Green Bay Press-Gazette*, May 3, 2000, 3, https://greenbaypressgazette.newspapers.com/image/188817340/
48. 1999 Wisconsin Act 167, May 26, 2000, https://docs.legis.wisconsin.gov/1999/related/acts/167;
49. Thomas Content, "Lambeau bill," *Green Bay Press-Gazette*, May 14, 2000, 1, 4, https://greenbaypressgazette.newspapers.com/image/188888314/; Richard Ryman, "It was controversial," *Green Bay Press-Gazette*, October 15, 2020, https://www.greenbaypressgazette.com/story/news/2020/10/15/lambeau-field-sales-tax-still-pays-dividends-20-years-later-green-bay-packers/5817065002/; Substantial renovation and improvement of the existing stadium was the only option entertained by the team—never a new stadium.
50. Thomas Content, "Local support," *Green Bay Press-Gazette*, May 3, 2000, https://greenbaypressgazette.newspapers.com/image/188817340/
51. Bill Nusbaum, "To our readers," *Green Bay Press-Gazette*, January 23, 2000, 1, https://greenbaypressgazette.newspapers.com/image/185986115/
52. Jadin interview; Steven Bruss, "Green Bay mayor," *Green Bay Press-Gazette*, August 10, 2000, 11, https://greenbaypressgazette.newspapers.com/image/191373402/
53. Nathan Phelps, "Fan runs 'yes,'" *Green Bay Press-Gazette*, September 2, 2000, 9, https://greenbaypressgazette.newspapers.com/image/191261104/
54. Harlan interview
55. Thomas Content, "Yes to Lambeau," *Green Bay Press-Gazette*, September 13, 2000, 1, https://greenbaypressgazette.newspapers.com/image/191263093/
56. Harlan interview
57. "Wolf retires," UPI, February 1, 2001, https://www.upi.com/Archives/2001/02/01/Wolf-retires-from-Packers/1119981003600/
58. Cliff Christl, "Vince Lombardi," Packers.com, https://www.packers.com/history/hof/vince-lombardi
59. Cliff Christl, "Ron Wolf," Packers.com, https://www.packers.com/history/hof/ron-wolf
60. Nathan Phelps, "Group hug," *Green Bay Press-Gazette*, May 20, 2001, 1, 13, https://greenbaypressgazette.newspapers.com/image/191317500/
61. Rob Demovsky, "Brett Favre's only," ESPN.com, August 7, 2016, https://www.espn.com/blog/green-bay-packers/post/_/id/31866/brett-favres-only-regret-only-seven-seasons-with-mike-holmgren

62. "1999 NFL passing," Pro Football Reference, https://www.pro-football-reference.com/years/1999/passing.htm
63. Gregg did not hold the title "general manager" but he carried similar duties.
64. Marc Sessler, "Bob Harlan regrets," NFL.com, July 4, 2012, https://www.nfl.com/news/bob-harlan-regrets-making-mike-sherman-packers-gm-09000d5d82a54207
65. Christl, 800; Todd McMahon, "Mike Sherman's 'emotional,'" *Green Bay Press-Gazette*, March 12, 2015, https://www.greenbaypressgazette.com/story/life/faith/2015/03/12/mike-shermans-emotional-return-green-bay/70222862/
66. Eric Slater, "An army of critics," *Los Angeles Times*, January 5, 2003, https://www.latimes.com/archives/la-xpm-2003-jan-05-na-soldier5-story.html; "Packers waive CB Joey Thomas," Packers.com, November 1, 2005, https://www.packers.com/news/packers-waive-cb-joey-thomas-2460354
67. "Statues of Lambeau," Packers.com, https://www.packers.com/news/statues-of-lambeau-lombardi-unveiled-2476023
68. "Lambeau Field," Packers.com, September 6, 2003, https://www.packers.com/news/lambeau-field-fun-facts-2476152
69. Christl, 791
70. Zach Kruse, "Packers corporate," Packerswire.com, July 17, 2024, https://packerswire.usatoday.com/story/sports/nfl/packers/2024/07/17/packers corporate-reserve-fund-rises-above-500-million/74443452007/
71. Richard Ryman, "Packers' Lambeau," *Green Bay Press-Gazette*, April 13, 2025, A4, https://greenbaypressgazette.newspapers.com/image/1190640175/; NEWS RELEASE: Lambeau Field renovations, Miron.com, https://miron-construction.com/project/lambeau-field-north-south-end-zone-stadium-improvements/;
72. Christl, *Greatest Story*, 698
73. Ibid. 794–5; BJ Sander, Joey Thomas, Ahmad Carroll, Pro Football Reference, various sites; "Raiders take gamble," ESPN.com, June 28, 2006.
74. Christl, 793

Chapter 12. Redemption

1. Sam Seale, interview with Larry McCarren, "The Unsung," Packers.com, https://www.packers.com/video/the-unsung-sam-seale-2023
2. Christl, "Sam Seale nailed reports," Packers.com, February 29, 2024, https://www.packers.com/news/sam-seale-nailed-reports-on-aaron-rodgers-clay-matthews-davante-adams-kenny-clark
3. California Community Colleges, "Aaron Rodgers," https://www.cccco.edu/About-Us/Notable-Alumni/Aaron-Rodgers
4. Jake Curtis, "The Cal 100," SI.com, August 6, 2023, https://www.si.com/college/cal/news/aaron-rodgers-no-2

5. Christl, 803–6
6. Dan Aulbach, "Aaron Rodgers sheds life," Today.com, December 18, 2024, https://www.today.com/popculture/aaron-rodgers-family-feud-rcna184115; Lindsey Eidell, "Aaron Rodgers' family," People.com, December 17, 2024, https://people.com/all-about-aaron-rodgers-family-ups-downs-8415009
7. Jason Wilde, "From experience," The Athletic, May 9, 2020, https://www.nytimes.com/athletic/1803786/2020/05/09/from-experience-brett-favre-has-advice-for-aaron-rodgers-and-jordan-love/
8. Wire service, "Brett Favre foresaw," ESPN.com, October 5, 2011, https://www.espn.com/nfl/story/_/id/7061578/brett-favre-asks-why-aaron-rodgers-super-bowl-title-ring-green-bay-packers-took-long
9. Documentary: *Untold: The Fall of Favre*, Netflix, 2025, https://www.netflix.com/title/81748451
10. "2005 NFL Passing," Pro Football Reference, https://www.pro-football-reference.com/years/2005/passing.htm
11. "NFL game winning drives," Pro Football Reference, https://www.pro-football-reference.com/leaders/gwd_career.htm
12. Doug Rush, "Eli Manning," Bleacher Report, May 31, 2018, https://bleacherreport.com/articles/1379911-eli-manning-where-giants-qb-ranks-among-best-4th-quarter-qbs-in-nfl-history; Scott Kacsmar, "Brett Favre," Bleacher Report, May 31, 2018, https://bleacherreport.com/articles/1266026-brett-favre-why-the-gunslinger-was-not-a-clutch-quarterback
13. AJ Daulerio, "Brett Favre's cellphone," Deadspin.com, October 7, 2010, https://deadspin.com/brett-favres-cellphone-seduction-of-jenn-sterger-upda-5658206/; JR Radcliffe, "A timeline," *Milwaukee Journal Sentinel*, September 24, 2024, https://www.jsonline.com/story/sports/nfl/packers/2022/09/21/timeline-brett-favre-involvement-mississippi-fraud-case-green-bay-packers/10379028002/; Jemele Hill, "Brett Favre allegations," ESPN.com, October 12, 2010, https://www.espn.com/espn/commentary/news/story?page=hill/101012
14. Pete Dougherty, "Time's up," *Green Bay Press-Gazette*, January 3, 2006, A-1, https://greenbaypressgazette.newspapers.com/image/192127920/; Dougherty, "'It's time,'" *Green Bay Press-Gazette*, January 3, 2006, C-1, https://greenbaypressgazette.newspapers.com/image/192127976/
15. Chris Havel, "Brother not sure," *Green Bay Press-Gazette*, January 1, 2006, 29, https://greenbaypressgazette.newspapers.com/image/192126618/
16. Pete Dougherty, "Packers' victory," *Green Bay Press-Gazette*, January 2, 2006, https://greenbaypressgazette.newspapers.com/image/192127858/
17. Ken Belson, "Ted Thompson," *New York Times*, July 29, 2021, https://www.nytimes.com/2021/01/23/sports/football/ted-thompson-packers-dead.html
18. Cliff Christl, "Ted Thompson," Packers.com, https://www.packers.com/history/hof/ted-thompson

19. Mary Whitfill Roeloffs, "8 coaches," Forbes.com, January 14, 2024, https://www.forbes.com/sites/maryroeloffs/2024/01/11/eight-coaches-have-left-nfl-teams-this-season-the-highest-turnover-since-record-tying-2021/
20. Pete Dougherty, "Payton in," *Green Bay Press-Gazette*, January 6, 2006, 13, https://greenbaypressgazette.newspapers.com/image/192128938/; Dougherty, "Packers to hire," *Green Bay Press-Gazette*, January 12, 2006, 1, https://greenbaypressgazette.newspapers.com/image/192131752/; Dylan B. Tomlinson, "Favre's agent," *Green Bay Press-Gazette*, January 7, 2006, 15, https://greenbaypressgazette.newspapers.com/image/192129282/
21. Pete Dougherty, "'A football guy,'" *Green Bay Press-Gazette*, 1, https://greenbaypressgazette.newspapers.com/image/192132054/
22. Brad Zimanek, "Favre's just riding," *Green Bay Press-Gazette*, November 19, 2007, 37, https://greenbaypressgazette.newspapers.com/image/361130627/
23. "Sights set," *Green Bay Press-Gazette*, January 13, 2006, 1, https://greenbaypressgazette.newspapers.com/image/192132010/
24. Dougherty, "'A football guy'"
25. "Packers pleased," Packers.com, April 25, 2006, https://www.packers.com/news/packers-pleased-that-favre-is-returning-2451536; Eric Goska, "Favre's TD," *Green Bay Press-Gazette*, April 27, 2006, https://greenbaypressgazette.newspapers.com/image/192311951/
26. Andrew Robeson, "Brett Favre: A timeline," Bleacher Report, August 6, 2010, https://bleacherreport.com/articles/430992-brett-favre-a-timeline-of-the-goodand-the-bad
27. Alan Shipnuck, "Brett Favre," *Sports Illustrated*, December 10, 2007, https://vault.si.com/vault/2007/12/10/brett-favre-sportsman-of-the-year; "Thompson named," Packers.com, March 24, 2008, https://www.packers.com/news/thompson-named-george-young-nfl-executive-of-the-year-2423797
28. Zimanek, "Favre's just riding"
29. Mike Woods, "Investment in Rodgers," *Green Bay Press Gazette*, November 22, 2007, 53, https://greenbaypressgazette.newspapers.com/image/361133842/
30. Cliff Christl, "Bob Harlan," Packers.com, https://www.packers.com/history/hof/bob-harlan
31. Rob Demovsky, "Bob Harlan's election," ESPN.com, June 5, 2015, https://www.espn.com/blog/green-bay-packers/post/_/id/20935/bob-harlans-election-26-years-ago-today-changed-packers-for-the-better; Cliff Christl, "Packers own," Packers.com, January 2, 2025, https://www.packers.com/news/packers-own-best-nfl-record-for-past-33-seasons
32. "Mark Murphy—chairman emeritus," Packers.com, https://www.packers.com/team/front-office-roster/mark-murphy
33. Dougherty, "On to the next," *Green Bay Press-Gazette*, July 20, 2007, C6, https://greenbaypressgazette.newspapers.com/image/361119891/

34. Dougherty, "'Fireworks,'" *Green Bay Press-Gazette*, December 2, 2007, C1, https://greenbaypressgazette.newspapers.com/image/361128338/
35. Richard Ryman, "Packers board," *Green Bay Press-Gazette*, December 4, 2007, 1, https://greenbaypressgazette.newspapers.com/image/361136347/
36. Dougherty, "'Fireworks'"
37. John Painter, "Where are they?" GoColgateRaiders.com, September 14, 2012, https://colgateathletics.com/news/2012/9/14/FB_0914122222
38. Richard Ryman, "Packers rake," *Green Bay Press-Gazette*, June 24, 2007, 1, https://greenbaypressgazette.newspapers.com/image/361107733/
39. Admin. "2008 NFC championship," PredictEm.com, June 21, 2013, https://www.predictem.com/nfl/2008-nfc-championship-game-new-york-giants-vs-green-bay-packers-preview-and-pick/
40. "Giants upset Favre," October 7, 2016, by NFL, YouTube, 2:15:13, https://www.youtube.com/watch?v=5aOffogdd4Y
41. "Brett Favre's FIRST," February 11, 2019, by NFL Throwback, YouTube, 1:07:06 https://www.youtube.com/watch?v=ILdHqEzE3TY
42. Cliff Christl, "Brett Favre," Packers.com, https://www.packers.com/history/hof/brett-favre
43. Christl, "Brett Favre," https://www.packers.com/history/hof/brett-favre; Hutson played fewer seasons and games than Favre. Christl, "Don Hutson," Packers.com, https://www.packers.com/history/hof/don-hutson
44. "'Mentally tired,'" ESPN.com, March 4, 2008, https://www.espn.com/nfl/news/story?id=3276034
45. Box Score: Packers at Cowboys, November 29, 2007, ESPN.com, https://www.espn.com/nfl/game/_/gameId/271129006/packers-cowboys; Christl, *Greatest Story* 824–5
46. "Favre timeline," *Green Bay Press-Gazette*, July 12, 2008, 16, https://greenbaypressgazette.newspapers.com/image/361258590/
47. Andy McCue, "Branch Rickey," Sabr.org, https://sabr.org/bioproj/person/branch-rickey/
48. Christl, *Greatest Story*, 827
49. Tom Silverstein, "Packers trade," PackersNews.com, August 6, 2018, https://www.packersnews.com/story/sports/nfl/packers/2018/08/06/aug-6-2008-packers-trade-brett-favre-jets/839638002/; Christl, 828–830
50. Ibid., 829–30
51. Ed Werder and Chris Mortensen, "Favre tells Jets," ESPN.com, February 11, 2009, https://www.espn.com/nfl/news/story?id=3898942
52. Kelsey Givens, "Brett Favre: timeline," Bleacher Report, August 17, 2010, https://bleacherreport.com/articles/438280-brett-favre-timeline-of-favres-retirements-in-the-nfl
53. "Report: Favre," AP, June 8, 2009, 11, https://greenbaypressgazette.newspapers.com/image/361441300/

54. Dougherty, "Favre family," *Press-Gazette*, June 9, 2009, 13, https://greenbay pressgazette.newspapers.com/image/361441372/
55. "Favre signs," ESPN.com, August 18, 2009, https://www.espn.com/nfl/news /story?id=4406963
56. Liz Hochstedler, "Packer fans look," *Chippewa Herald*, October 4, 2009, https://chippewa.com/news/packer-fans-look-forward-to-game-against-favre -vikings/article_d80930f2-067a-539d-ab63-fd696b78b2a1.html
57. Ron Wolf, interview with author, May 20, 2025
58. Tom Pelissero, "Drama revisited," *Press-Gazette*, November 1, 2009, 29, https:// greenbaypressgazette.newspapers.com/image/361063742/
59. Kevin Seifert, "Visual proof," ESPN.com, February 2, 2010, https://www .espn.com/blog/nfcnorth/post/_/id/9690/visual-proof-of-favres-injuries
60. Brendan Sugrue, "Bears and Brett," *USA Today*, December 17, 2020, https:// bearswire.usatoday.com/story/sports/nfl/bears/2020/12/17/chicago-bears -throwback-thursday-minnesota-vikings-brett-favre-2010/75983267007/; Kareem Copeland, "Brett Favre: Final play," NFL.com, April 13, 2013, https://www.nfl.com/news/brett-favre-final-play-was-first-time-i-was-knocked -out-0ap1000000159622; Dave Campbell, "Favre knocked out," MPR/ AP, December 20, 2010, https://www.mprnews.org/story/2010/12/20/bears -vikings
61. "2008 passing," Pro Football Reference, https://www.pro-football-reference .com/years/2008/passing.htm
62. "2010 NFL standings," NFL.com, https://www.nfl.com/standings/division /2010/reg; "2010 NFL passing," Pro Football Reference, https://www.pro -football-reference.com/years/2010/passing.htm
63. Rob Reischel, "Johnny Jolly," *Milwaukee Journal Sentinel*, August 6, 2013, https://archive.jsonline.com/sports/packers/johnny-jolly-grateful-for-second -chance-b99967049z1-218614681.html
64. "2010 Green Bay Packers schedule," ESPN.com, https://www.espn.com /nfl/team/schedule/_/name/gb/season/2010; "Ankle, leg injuries," NFLcom, September 14, 2010, https://www.nfl.com/news/ankle-leg-injuries-will-force -packers-grant-to-miss-season-09000d5d81a87f7f (Grant); "Packers prepare," NFL.com, October 7, 2010, https://www.nfl.com/news/ankle-leg-injuries -will-force-packers-grant-to-miss-season-09000d5d81a87f7f (Barnett); Kevin Seifert, "Jermichael Finley," ESPN.com, October 13, 2010, https://www .espn.com/blog/nfcnorth/post/_/id/17885/jermicael-finley-indicates-hes-done -for-year (Finley); JR Radcliffe, "Packers' 2010 road," *Milwaukee Journal Sentinel*, September 22, 2020, https://www.jsonline.com/story/sports/nfl /packers/2020/09/22/green-bay-packers-revisiting-2010-super-bowl-run -week-2/3475988001/
65. "Andy Reid," Chiefs.com, https://www.chiefs.com/team/coaches-roster/andy -reid

66. "2010 NFL," Pro Football Reference, https://www.espn.com/blog/nfcnorth/post/_/id/17885/jermicael-finley-indicates-hes-done-for-year; Pete Dougherty, "Packers hold down," *Press-Gazette*, January 10, 2011, 25, https://greenbaypressgazette.newspapers.com/image/361103676/; Box Score: Packers at Eagles, *Press-Gazette*, January 10, 2011, 28, https://greenbaypressgazette.newspapers.com/image/361103686/
67. "Green Bay Packers @ Philadelphia Eagles," October 14, 2024, by Just Sim, Baby, YouTube, 2:06:20 https://www.youtube.com/watch?v=5HZ254hyhLM
68. Zach Kruse, "5 observations," Bleacher Report, January 15, 2011, https://bleacherreport.com/articles/574182-packers-vs-falcons-5-observations-from-green-bays-annihilation-of-atlanta; AP, "Packers roll," Packers.com, January 15, 2011, https://www.packers.com/news/ap-game-summary-packers-roll-over-falcons-48-21-3247539
69. Mike Tierney, "With Rodgers," *New York Times*, January 16, 2011, https://www.nytimes.com/2011/01/16/sports/football/16falcons.html; Box score: Packers vs. Atlanta, Pro Football Reference, January 15, 2011, https://www.pro-football-reference.com/boxscores/201101150atl.htm
70. Bill Huber, "Five greatest games," SI.com, January 5, 2025, https://www.si.com/nfl/packers/five-greatest-games-in-packers-bears-history
71. Dougherty, "Packers ride," *Press-Gazette*, January 24, 2011, 29, https://greenbaypressgazette.newspapers.com/image/361094810/; Box score: Packers at Bears, Pro Football Reference, January 23, 2011, https://www.pro-football-reference.com/boxscores/201101230chi.htm#pbp_94.000
72. Judy Batista, "Packers put," *New York Times*, February 6, 2011, https://www.nytimes.com/2011/02/07/sports/football/07super-bowl-packers-steelers.html
73. "Super Bowl XLV," July 29, 2016, by NFL, YouTube, 2:28:01, https://www.youtube.com/watch?v=WdakQksuoBg; Box score: Packers vs. Steelers, February 6, 2011, https://www.pro-football-reference.com/boxscores/201102060pit.htm
74. Kevin Rogers, "Super Bowl betting," VegasInsider.com, https://www.vegasinsider.com/nfl/superbowl/history/
75. Kareem Copeland, "MVP Rodgers," *Green Bay Press-Gazette*, February 7, 2011, https://greenbaypressgazette.newspapers.com/image/361099235/
76. Mike Vandermause, "Packers stand," *Green Bay Press-Gazette*, February 7, 2011, 32, https://greenbaypressgazette.newspapers.com/image/361099235/

Chapter 13. Reckoning

1. "Two years since," *Cap Times*, February 2, 2013, https://captimes.com/news/local/govt-and-politics/two-years-since-scott-walker-dropped-the-bomb-and-state-economy-is-still-shattered-pr/article_d1653dd5-3119-57ec-ab8f-1360f4e4ea4b.html

2. Criag Gilbert, "Measuring the union vote," *Milwaukee Journal Sentinel*, February 18, 2011, https://archive.jsonline.com/newswatch/116488043.html
3. Melissa Schultz et al., "Capitol protests," UW–Madison Libraries, https://www.library.wisc.edu/archives/exhibits/campus-history-projects/capitol-protests-2011-oral-history-project/;
4. Legislators cannot be recalled unless they have served at least one year in their current term. Half of senators were eligible in 2011; the other in 2012. Governor Walker survived his own recall election the following year.
5. John Nichols, interview with author, July 10, 2025
6. Kristin Parisi, "Packers-49ers," *Spectrum News*, January 22, 2024, https://spectrumnews1.com/wi/milwaukee/news/2024/01/22/49ers-packers-game-sees-record-ratings
7. Brooke Gains, "NFL viewership," *Evoca.tv*, August 13, 2025, https://evoca.tv/nfl-3/viewership-statistics/
8. "NFL averages," ESPN.com, January 10, 2024, https://www.espn.com/nfl/story/_/id/39277615/nfl-averages-179m-viewers-2023-7-previous-year; Arif Islam, "Lions v Packers," Sportspro.com, December 10, 2024, https://www.sportspro.com/news/detroit-lions-green-bay-packers-amazon-tnf-streaming-ratings-record-december-2024/
9. Rob Demovsky, "Packers top," ESPN.com, December 31, 2014, https://www.espn.com/blog/green-bay-packers/post/_/id/16983/packers-top-nfl-in-capturing-local-market
10. Alexandra Hudson, "Bowling alone," *National Affairs*, Fall 2020, https://www.nationalaffairs.com/publications/detail/bowling-alone-at-twenty
11. "4,000 yard season," Profootballhof.com, 2021, https://www.profootballhof.com/football-history/4000-yard-seasons-by-team/; "Packers single-season—2024," https://www.pro-football-reference.com/teams/gnb/single-season-passing.htm; Rodgers would surpass his own record in 2020 with 48 TDs. Mark Krummel, "Green Bay Packers 2011," Bleacher Report, June 6, 2018, https://bleacherreport.com/articles/696874-green-bay-packers-2011-the-best-packers-team-ever; ESPN.com, "GBP player stats—2011," 2025, https://www.espn.com/nfl/team/stats/_/name/gb/season/2011/seasontype/2/table/
12. "Brett Favre vs. Aaron Rodgers," Stathead, https://stathead.com/football/vs/brett-favre-vs-aaron-rodgers
13. JR Radcliffe, "These are the biggest," *Milwaukee Journal Sentinel*, September 26, 2023, https://www.jsonline.com/story/sports/nfl/packers/2023/09/26/these-are-packers-biggest-fourth-quarter-comebacks-in-history/70962622007/; Radcliffe, "Brett Favre," *Milwaukee Journal Sentinel*, September 12, 2018, https://www.packersnews.com/story/sports/nfl/packers/2018/09/12/brett-favre-impressed-aaron-rodgers-says-qb-part-doc/1279866002/; Box Score: Chicago at Green Bay, Pro Football Reference, September 9, 2018, https://www.pro-football-reference.com/boxscores/201809090gnb.htm; Video: Aaron

Rodgers Top 10, NFL.com, https://www.nfl.com/videos/green-bay-packers-quarterback-aaron-rodgers-top-10-career-moments-257367

14. Bruce Vielmetti, "Aaron Rodgers picks," *Milwaukee Journal Sentinel*, September 11, 2018, https://www.jsonline.com/story/news/2018/09/11/aaron-rodgers-picks-legal-action-packers-social-justice-donation/1270714002/
15. Mike Spofford, et al., "Former Packers," Packers.com, January 21, 2021, https://www.packers.com/news/former-packers-gm-ted-thompson-dies-at-68
16. Cliff Christl, "Ted Thompson," Packers.com, https://www.packers.com/history/hof/ted-thompson
17. *Untold: The Fall of Favre*
18. Anthony Olivieri, "Brett Favre," ESPN.com, May 9, 2023, https://www.espn.com/nfl/story/_/id/37565299/brett-favre-mississippi-welfare-case-line-explained
19. Reg Chapman, et al., "Brett Favre reveals," CBS News, September 24, 2024, https://www.cbsnews.com/minnesota/news/brett-favre-parkinsons-disease/
20. "Brett Favre," TMZ, November 23, 2024, https://www.tmz.com/2024/11/23/brett-favre-talks-parkinsons-battle/
21. Box Score: Bears at Packers, November 27, 2015, ESPN.com, https://www.espn.com/nfl/game/_/gameId/400791510/bears-packers
22. NFL.com, "Brett Favre's jersey retirement," Facebook, April 2, 2020, https://www.facebook.com/watch/?v=3060429423977892; Box score: Packers at Bears, Pro Football Reference, October 31, 1994, https://www.pro-football-reference.com/boxscores/199410310chi.htm
23. "'I wrote the book,'" *Guardian UK*, September 25, 2024, http://theguardian.com/sport/2024/sep/25/i-wrote-the-book-on-head-trauma-favre-was-diagnosed-with-parkinsons-in-january; Rob Goldberg, "Brett Favre executive-producing," Bleacher Report, January 9, 2018, https://bleacherreport.com/articles/2753290-brett-favre-executive-producing-documentary-about-concussions-nfl-career
24. Andy Thompson, "Study on brain trauma," *Appleton Post Crescent*, July 30, 2017, https://www.postcrescent.com/story/news/2017/07/30/appleton-native-ann-mckee-spotlight-amid-research-nfl-players/516248001/; Doug Most, "BU finds CTE," *The Brink*, February 27, 2023, https://www.bu.edu/articles/2023/bu-finds-cte-in-nearly-92-percent-of-former-nfl-players-studied/
25. Dorothy Neufeld, "Ranked," *Visual Capitalist*, October 20, 2024, https://www.visualcapitalist.com/nfl-ticket-cost-inflation-over-the-last-decade/
26. Emily Mae Czachor, "How much," CBS News, February 9, 2025, https://www.cbsnews.com/news/how-much-super-bowl-tickets-2025/
27. Cork Gaines, "The 10 most," *Business Insider*, January 21, 2024, https://www.businessinsider.com/most-expensive-nfl-tickets-by-team-raiders-49ers-eagles-packers-2024-1

28. "Fan cost index of NFL teams," Statista, 2025, https://www.statista.com/statistics/202584/nfl-fan-cost-index/
29. Michael Ozanian, "Internal NFL ticket reports," CNBC, September 4, 2025, https://www.cnbc.com/2025/09/04/internal-nfl-ticket-report-reveals-49ers-at-top-titans-at-bottom.html
30. This figure is as of 2025. Chase Peterson-Withorn, "Forbes 400," *Forbes*, 2025, https://www.forbes.com/forbes-400/
31. "NFL's richest owners," *PFSN.com*, February 9, 2025, https://www.profootballnetwork.com/nfl-richest-owners-net-worth-ranked/
32. Mark Patricof, "The average NFL," *Fortune*, March 31, 2023, https://fortune.com/2023/03/31/nfl-owners-age-net-worth-teams-deals-franchises-sport-football-mark-patricof/
33. Jessica Golden, et al., "NFL owners," CNBC, August 27, 2024, https://www.cnbc.com/2024/08/27/nfl-private-equity-ownership-vote.html
34. "Team Histories: Giants," NFL.com, https://operations.nfl.com/learn-the-game/nfl-basics/team-histories/national-football-conference/east/new-york-giants/
35. Christina Gough, "NFL—average franchise value," Statista, June 24, 2025, https://www.statista.com/statistics/193435/average-franchise-value-in-the-nfl-since-2000/
36. Michael Ozanian, "Rising NFL valuations," CNBC, September 5, 2024, https://www.cnbc.com/2024/09/05/rising-nfl-valuations-massive-returns-for-owners.html
37. Reem Abdalazem, "The is the lowest," AS.com, February 9, 2025, https://en.as.com/nfl/this-is-the-lowest-paid-player-in-the-nfl-is-there-a-minimum-salary-in-american-football-n-2/
38. NFL.com, "Player contracts," 2020, 2025, https://www.nfl.com/photos/nfl-s-biggest-contracts-for-2020, https://www.nfl.com/photos/ranking-the-nfl-s-biggest-contracts-for-2025
39. "2000s: A landmark CBA," NFLPA.com, https://nflpa.com/about/history/2000s-a-landmark-cba
40. Kurt Badenhausen, "The NFL's biggest mismatch," Forbes.com, Mar 15, 2020, https://www.forbes.com/sites/kurtbadenhausen/2020/03/16/the-nfls-biggest-mismatch-owners-vs-players-in-cba-negotiations/
41. "Mark Murphy, chairman emeritus," Packers.com, https://www.packers.com/team/front-office-roster/mark-murphy; Richard Sandomir, "Ed Garvey," *New York Times*, February 22, 2017, https://www.nytimes.com/2017/02/22/sports/football/obituary-ed-garvey-nfl-players-union.html
42. Christl, 840 (Chart: Eric Goska, Pro Football Reference); Cliff Christl, "Packers own best," Packers.com, January 2, 2025, https://www.packers.com/news/packers-own-best-nfl-record-for-past-33-seasons#:~:text=Total-,1.,5t.
43. Jacob Robinson, "Chaos around," The Athletic, July 14, 2025, https://www.nytimes.com/athletic/6493415/2025/07/14/nfl-collusion-nflpa-lamar-jackson

-ruling-second-round-pick-holdout/; Joel Corry, "Agent's take," CBS Sports, May 15, 2024, https://www.cbssports.com/nfl/news/agents-take-four-meaningful-concessions-players-should-seek-from-nfl-before-accepting-18-game-regular-season/; JC Tretter, "Setting a new standard," NFLPA.com, April 12, 2022, https://nflpa.com/posts/setting-a-new-standard-for-guaranteed-contracts

44. Lori Nickel, "Young coach," *Journal Sentinel*, January 28, 2019, https://www.jsonline.com/story/sports/2019/01/28/green-bays-matt-lafleur-cant-point-many-past-examples-young-coach-leading-mvp-like-rodgers-great-suc/2698905002/; "GBP coaches," Pro Football Reference, https://www.pro-football-reference.com/teams/gnb/coaches.htm (As of 10/21/25)
45. Richard Ryman, "Mark Murphy selected," *Press-Gazette*, November 18, 2024, https://www.greenbaypressgazette.com/story/sports/nfl/packers/2024/11/18/mark-murphy-selected-for-induction-into-green-bay-packers-hall-of-fame/76403144007/; "Mark Murphy," Packers.com, https://www.packers.com/team/front-office-roster/mark-murphy
46. JR Radcliffe, "Caleb Williams," *Journal Sentinel*, November 8, 2024, https://www.jsonline.com/story/sports/nfl/packers/2024/11/08/caleb-williams-is-37th-bears-starting-qb-since-packers-get-brett-favre/76073318007/ (As of November 2024)
47. Ryan Wood, "NFL's highest paid," Packersnews.com, July 26, 2024, https://www.packersnews.com/story/sports/nfl/packers/2024/07/26/see-where-jordan-love-ranks-among-the-nfls-highest-paid-quarterbacks/74460631007/
48. Jeff Eisenberg, "A decade in the making," YahooSports.com, November 4, 2021, https://sports.yahoo.com/a-decade-in-the-making-jordan-loves-time-has-come-193727940.html
49. Stan Becton, "Jordan Love," NCAA.com, January 11, 2025, https://www.ncaa.com/news/football/article/2025-01-11/jordan-love-college-football-career-stats-highlights-records
50. "Brian Gutekunst," Packers.com, https://www.packers.com/team/front-office-roster/brian-gutekunst; "NFL draft," ESPN.com, 2020, https://www.espn.com/nfl/draft/rounds/_/season/2020
51. Nick Shook, "Ranking all 59," NFL.com, February 13, 2025, https://www.nfl.com/news/ranking-all-59-nfl-starting-quarterbacks-from-2024-lamar-jackson-or-josh-allen-at-no-1
52. "Luxury boxes," Biztimes.com, April 16, 2018, https://biztimes.com/luxury-boxes/; "Quick facts: Green Bay, Wisconsin," Census.gov, https://www.census.gov/quickfacts/fact/table/greenbaycitywisconsin/TAW120222
53. Jonathan Krause, "Wisconsin dominates," WHBY.com, October 19, 2021, https://www.whby.com/2021/10/19/wisconsin-dominates-list-of-drunkest-counties-in-the-us/

54. NFL.com, "Top 10 jerseys," 2025, https://www.nfl.com/photos/top-10-team-jerseys-0ap3000000908391#cdd0bc15-7a19-4adc-a48d-59b3f9147db4
55. Whitwell, Slater, Crafton, Kay, and Taylor, "The Glazers," The Athletic, May 10, 2025, https://www.nytimes.com/athletic/6260871/2025/05/11/the-glazers-the-real-story-of-their-manchester-united-takeover-20-years-on/
56. Wesley Stephenson, "How the Glazer family cost," BBC, June 6, 2025, https://www.bbc.com/sport/football/articles/cd9lwdegxvxo
57. Andrew Preston, *Total Defense* (Harvard, 2025), 173

Acknowledgments

1. "Lee Remmel," Packers.com, https://www.packers.com/history/hof/lee-remmel
2. *Legacy, "Last Hurrah"*
3. "Lavvie Dilweg," Packers.com, https://www.packers.com/history/hof/lavvie-dilweg

Index